Better a Shrew than a Sheep

Better a Shrew than a Sheep

Women, Drama, and the Culture of Jest in Early Modern England

PAMELA ALLEN BROWN

CORNELL UNIVERSITY PRESS

ITHACA AND LONDON

A modified version of chapter 5 first appeared in *English Literary Renaissance*, vol. 29 (1999) 201–24 as "Laughing at the Cony: A Female Rogue and the 'Verdict of the Smock.'"

First published 2003 by Cornell University Press
First printing, Cornell Paperbacks, 2003

Printed in the United States of America

Library of Congress Cataloging-in-Publication Data

Brown, Pamela Allen.
  Better a shrew than a sheep : women, drama, and the culture of jest in early modern England / Pamela Allen Brown.
    p. cm.
Includes bibliographical references and index.
  ISBN 0-8014-4024-6 (cloth : alk. paper) — ISBN 0-8014-8836-2 (pbk. : alk. paper)
    1. English drama—Early modern and Elizabethan, 1500–1600—History and criticism.   2. Women and literature—England—History—16th century.
3. Women and literature—England—History—17th century.   4. English drama—17th century—History and criticism.   5. English drama (Comedy)—History and criticism.   6. English wit and humor—History and criticism.   7. Jestbooks, English—History.   8. Comic, The, in literature.
9. Sex role in literature.   10. Women in literature.   I. Title.
  PR658.W6 B76 2002
  822'.309352042—dc21   2002011310

Contents

Illustrations

Acknowledgments

This book almost didn't make it. At a crucial stage the manuscript was stolen and miraculously restored, making it dearer to me than it would have been had I had an easier time of it. A Brooklyn couple named Charles and Mindy Libin found my files dumped in front of their building a few blocks away from mine and decided that my work wasn't garbage. Using clues in the pile, they tracked me down by doing the kind of dogged archival research that might put many scholars to shame. I owe so much to two people whose sense of neighborhood makes me marvel.

To jest is to perform. I am grateful to my "good gossips" Melinda Gough, Susan O'Malley, Renate Bridenthal, and Joy Wiltenburg, who were my co-actors in attempts to stage the early modern neighborhood and alehouse at conferences ranging from Attending to Women to the Berkshire Conference on the History of Women. "O such a rogue should be hang'd!" was our theme song.

My deepest thanks go to everyone who read the manuscript, especially Jean Howard, Anne Prescott, David Shields, Ian Moulton, Joy Wiltenburg, and Elaine Combs-Schilling. Their praise was heady; their "buts" were crucial. David sent music and poems along with his criticism, unmatchable matching gifts. With mock severity, Ian did not let me evade that crucial question, "So what?" Joy helped tighten my arguments with the aid of her historian's keen eye, while Elaine offered her

creative exuberance. Anne's heady blend of *sapientia* and *sprezzatura*
gave me confidence—if she liked it, I stood a chance. Frances Dolan and
Barbara Hodgdon, readers for Cornell University Press, provided won-
derfully astute comments that made the final months of revision unex-
pectedly enjoyable. Other generous souls read chapters and offered their
thoughts, including Laura Gowing, Tom Cartelli, Lena Orlin, Bernard
Capp, Bob Hasenfratz, Renee Tursi, Jean Gallagher, Susan O'Malley,
and Lauren Kozol. Along the way, Liz Hart, Gail Paster, Peter Parolin,
and Lynda Boose inspired and encouraged me. At the final stage, Teresa
Feroli stepped in like a good neighbor to help discipline an unruly conclusion, while David Kunzle kindly loaned me his photograph of *The
Amazing Woman*. For their loving support I thank my sisters, Barbara
Calhoun and Paula Seebode; my brothers, J. Stanley Brown and Ethan
Brown; my mother, Carmele Brown; and my grandparents, the late Ros-
alia Giardinieri Spadafora and Frank Spadafora, whose hard work in the
needle trades helped fund my first year of graduate school. My father,
Gerald Brown, first taught me that jokes are important, mainly by re-
peating a few so many times. My writing group provided much-needed
comfort and joy; *baci e grazie a* Bianca Calabresi, Julie Crawford, Nancy
Selleck, Rachel Poulsen, Sasha Roberts, and Cristine Varholy.

Several important funding sources allowed me to pursue this project:
a Whiting dissertation fellowship; a W. M. Keck fellowship and a Mayer
fellowship at the Huntington Library; and a New Faculty Grant from
the University of Connecticut, which enabled me to complete research
at the British Library. I would also like to thank Sven Beckert, who
kindly arranged for me to gain access to the Harvard libraries. At the
Huntington I benefited from Paul Zall's willingness to share his deep
knowledge of jests and I learned how to decipher manuscripts under
Tony Thompson's patient tutelage. There I also had the good fortune to
meet Susan O'Malley, who also had had a manuscript stolen once. She
became a wonderful friend whose political commitment and feminist
wit make her an abiding influence on this book.

No one ever ends these things on a crass note, so let me be the first.
Jean Howard deserves more than a Turkish kilim and a Peking duck for
all her work on this project. Brilliant, conscientious, and demanding,
she made me take myself more seriously and think more critically.
Maybe some night she will open this book, read a bit, and laugh, de-
lighting in the realization that she is its prime mover and ideal reader.

Like many people she has taught and touched, I owe my career to her. Jonathan Soffer talked me out of quitting grad school when he hardly knew me. He was with me five years later when the manuscript was stolen, and was instantly ready to help me start over. When I needed his labor he gave it freely; when I soured on the book he praised it unduly. His kind heart, wide-ranging mind, and adventurous spirit are mingled in these pages. For these reasons I have incurred an enormous debt to both Jean and Jonathan, one that will be harder to repay than my student loans.

Better a Shrew than a Sheep

Introduction
Sauce for the Gander

Women and men lived in very much the same cultural
world, hearing and using the same set of stories, jokes, and
songs. But that culture included nevertheless some stories
that made sense primarily to men, and some, harder to
trace, that made more sense to women.

Laura Gowing

In early modern parlance a shrew was a garrulous, domineering, and
intractable wife. Shrew bad, patient wife good: everyone knew that. So
it is curious to come across a proverb that gives the shrew precedence
over the submissive wife: *better a shrew than a sheep.*[1] Unauthored and
unoriginal, the maxim presents uncommon wisdom as common and
displays contrarian wit. Under what circumstances and for whom, exactly, is a shrew better than a sheep?

The answer won't be found in proscriptive works haranguing wives
about their proper subjection, or in plays and sermons applauding the
sheeplike patience of a Griselda. After all, depending on a speaker's delivery, the proverb may even mock the patient wife: sheep are famously
gormless, too passive to protest being shorn or butchered. Not surprisingly, the proverb often surfaces in popular texts about conjugal con-

---

1 Tilley, *A Dictionary of Proverbs*, S412, S415, S414. The word "shrew" was sometimes used to derogate men, but in general use it referred to women. On the interplay
between the common and uncommon in proverbs, see Crane, *Framing Authority*,
50–52. To Anthony Fletcher *better a shrew* implies that "the English liked strong
women," but this suggestion is overshadowed by men's "obsession with the dangers
ascribed to womankind" in popular literature (*Gender, Sex*, 4). He does not consider
the saying's possible meanings for women.

flict. In ballads women use it to criticize wives who let their husbands go whoring; in plays women use it to scoff at the idea of becoming doormats. Outnumbered by misogynist tags geared to men, the proverb offers a tantalizing glimpse of an oppositional stance. One variant would sound best in a woman's mouth: *better be a shrew than a sheep*.[2] In its anonymous availability, the proverb is not a simulation of a woman's voice, but a cue for any woman's taking.

This book addresses the genre of which this proverb is a part—the jesting literature—to imagine how the culture of jest shaped women's experience of the social dramas of everyday life and the dramas they saw on stage. The choice of jest may seem perverse. Women were so often skewered by "old fond paradoxes to make fools laugh i' th' alehouse" that jest has been read as generically antifeminist, a discourse closed to women.[3] By piecing together many kinds of popular and documentary sources, however, I have found that early modern women were not always objects of ancient saws; silent, humiliated butts of jokes; or passive auditors of men's jests—their typical positions in jesting situations even today.[4] Although women were in theory phlegmatic, consigned by their cold and moist humours to a natural slow-wittedness, popular texts tell a different story, harping on their annoying cleverness (*a woman's answer is never to seek*) and their superior resourcefulness (*a woman's wit at a dead lift is better than a man's*). In many jesting texts women are bawdy storytellers, instigators of practices, witty answerers, and keen satirists. The spirit of artful ridicule also marks the work of

2 Tilley, *Dictionary*, S412. Another variation is geared toward men: *Better marry a shrew than a sheep*. A gossip sings, "a shrew's better far than a sheepe," in "Well Met Neighbour" from *The Roxburghe Ballads*, 3:98–103. At the end of *The Taming of a Shrew* Emelia bridles at her sister's lecture and answers her husband's curt, "I say thou art a shrew" with "Thats better than a sheepe" (*The Taming of a Shrew*, ed. Farmer, sig. G2). In Samuel Rowlands's *A whole crew of kind Gossips*, a wife who vows to take on her stingy husband exclaims, "A Shroe is ten times better than a sheepe" (sig. A4).

3 The quotation is from Desdemona's putdown of Iago in *Othello* (2.1.138–39; unless otherwise noted, all Shakespeare citations are from *The Riverside Shakespeare*). On the gender exclusivity of jest, see Jones, "Counterattacks," in which she remarks that Joseph Swetnam's *Arraignment* (1615), uses "contemporary jokes that illustrate the everyday hatred attributed by misogyny to all sexual relations. Such anecdotes suggest that he was assembling a jestbook, which as a genre could break rules of realism and propriety. This was not a discourse open to women" (48).

4 McGehee calls jesting an aggressive act, leading girls and women to avoid it in mixed-gender groups ("The Role of Laughter," 225). Women writers have long used comic aggression and witty anger in their work, although their humor has often been misread or ignored, argues Barreca, *Last Laughs*, 6.

women writers, despite the widely held assumption that literary satire is an unrelievedly masculinist mode.[5] My main concern is not with women writers, however, or with paragons of wit such as Elizabeth I but with the ordinary women who filled playhouses and who were sometimes represented onstage. By crediting non-elite women with a measure of wit and agency and the power to wound or reward with their responses, jests suggest how they responded to plays that were seeking their laughter and judgment.[6]

My term *the jesting literature* is deliberately broad, encompassing any verbal, gestural, or dramatic form that could be used to spur laughter or ridicule. Casting a horn into a neighbor's yard is a kind of jest; so is *Utopia*. Popular jest genres overlap and interpenetrate. They include texts meant to be read (and most often read aloud), such as jest books, novella collections, and rogue tales; short narratives and sayings meant to be heard, such as riddles, mock proclamations, and proverbs; images meant to be seen and deciphered, such as woodcuts and emblems; texts intended for amateur and professional performance, such as ballads, jigs, mocking rhymes, and plays; and rites woven into the social fabric, such as horn fairs, Hocktide binding, skimmingtons, and other forms of shaming. Within this heterodox field women's jesting constitutes a pre-

5 Satire is deemed a masculine genre in Streip, "Just a *Cérèbrale*," 117, and Richlin, *The Garden of Priapus*, xxvi. Nonetheless, early modern women often employ the satiric mode, as in the anticlerical writing of Margery Kempe and Anne Askew, the barbed novellas of Marguerite de Navarre, the polemics of Rachel Speght, poems by Isabella Whitney and Katherine Phillips, the satire-laden romance of Lady Mary Wroth, and the plays and prose of Margaret Cavendish. Even Mary Sidney may have tried her hand: Penny McCarthy maintains that Sidney may have published unsigned satiric sonnets taking Harvey's side against Nashe ("Milksop Muses."). On the Duchess of Newcastle's satiric personae, see Suzuki, "Margaret Cavendish and the Female Satirist." I wish to thank Professor Mihoko Suzuki for showing me her essay before publication.

6 *Ordinary* and *non-elite* refer to women who were not gentle by birth or marriage. Contemporary accounts divided society into a bottom rank of artisans, day laborers, and retailers; a second composed of rural smallholders; a third of citizens and burgesses; and a fourth of gentry and nobles. The non-elite also encompassed vagrants, whores, and hucksters. More than 95 percent of England's population was non-elite. Details are from Gurr, *Playgoing*, 50–80; on non-elite women playgoers, see 57–64. Also see Jordan, "Renaissance Women," 90–106, and Mendelson and Crawford, *Women in Early Modern England*, 5–6, 55–56, 145–48.

On the social mix within audiences see Gurr, *Playgoing*, 49–69, and Harbage, *Shakespeare's Audiences*, 53–91. Cook maintains that playgoing "was much above the reach of the poorer sort" (*Privileged Playgoers*, 271). Butler rebuts Cook, arguing that many of the poorer sort did attend plays regularly (*Theatre and Crisis*, esp. app. 2).

viously unnoticed vector of critique and social power, which may at times threaten and even disrupt reigning ideologies enforcing female subjection. In certain stories, plays, and songs, women's mockery helps limit the violence of wife-beating husbands and the assaults of lechers. In tales about the abjectly patient wife, women scorn the idea of taking such a "tame fool" for a model. While women are savaged by misogynist jesting in some of my sources, in others they solve impossible riddles, outsmart the gullible, and deflate the arrogant.

Thinking through the ways and means of female jesting offers scholars of drama some important new tools. First, listening for women's laughter forges an interpretive grid for resituating drama in relation to their desires and experiences. Women went to the theater to hear plays that sometimes show signs of being tailored to appeal to their taste and their judging wit, both of which were honed in an oral and print culture filled with jest and satire. Second, it illuminates moments in drama whose humor depended on an audience's familiarity with various forms of jest, game, and festivity that are now obscure to us. Third, seeing jest as a discourse open to women refocuses scenes in which female characters succeed by getting the laugh. As actors and playwrights knew, being able to prompt and harness laughter was a vital theatrical skill. In the wider society, in which print, performance, and writing permeated and reinforced the spoken word, the art of the "quick answer" was so prized that rhetoricians appended jests to their manuals and gave pointers on delivery.[7] In the theaters the ability to arouse laughter could define a player's career or ensure a play's success, and the audiences that granted that power contained significant numbers of women.[8]

Acknowledging that real women took part in the culture of jesting

7 See Fox, *Oral and Literate*, 4–6; Smith, *Acoustic World*, 12. Rhetoricians follow the lead of Cicero, Quintilian, and Castiglione in offering tips on verbal and physical jesting, with examples that stress aggressive ripostes. Thomas Wilson demonstrates "snudgyng wittily rebuked," "words overthwart aunswered," and "an aunswer from evyll to worse" (*Arte of Rhetoricke*, 28). George Puttenham offers lessons in taunts, flouts, and "the Fleering frumpe" in *The Arte of English Poesie*, 188–91. On the "immense power of speech" in the period and on women's acknowledged rhetorical prowess, see Mendelson and Crawford, *Women in Early Modern England*, 215.

8 On women theatergoers see Gurr, *Playgoing*, esp. 6–9, 19–20, 28–30, 61–64; Howard, *Stage and Social Struggle*, 73–92; and Harbage, *Shakespeare's Audience*, 74–79. Scholars who maintain that women's presence influenced playwrights include Levin, "Women in the Renaissance Theatre Audience;" Orgel, "Nobody's Perfect," esp. 8; and Woodbridge, *Women and the English Renaissance*, 250–52.

points to their cultural competence in unlooked-for arenas.[9] They could use a jest or ballad to answer attacks on women or to launch their own criticisms of men. Some women may have been "chaste, silent and obedient"; but others left traces of their audible, visible, irreverent performances in records and representations of everyday social spaces: the threshold, the neighborhood, the alehouse. This is not to imply that such jests were intentionally feminist or that they were as common as jests in which men best or deride women. The streams of female wit are far narrower than the torrents of antifeminist jest.[10] Jokes and saws about women's faults were mainstays of antifeminist writers in the controversy over women. Discussing Edmund Gosynhyll's defense of women, *Mulierum Pean*, Linda Woodbridge speculates that he uses no jests against the opposition because there was "simply no body of antimasculinist jests on which he could draw." He does address his work to a female friend, however, and "posits a world where men jest with the 'femyny'"—a world in which women may "counterattack in the spirit of fun."[11]

That posited world is no phantom. In the pages of the jesting literature women do counterattack—but not always in the spirit of good clean fun. Stories in which wives seek "wild justice" against unruly husbands, for example, form a sharp contrast to the many japes about unruly wives. In this type of jest male drunkenness figures large. A man reels home from the alehouse, beats his wife, then falls to the floor in a stupor. When his wife tries to carry him to bed, he roars, "It is my house and I will lie where I list." The next night, he gets drunk again, stumbles in and falls in the fire. When the servant tries to move him, the wife stops her: "'Tis his house, let him lie where he lists." Echoing

---

9 Davis calls for recognition of the cultural competence of non-elites in "Some Themes," 308, 313. Also see Chartier, "Culture As Appropriation," 241.

10 For a sampling, see Utley, *Crooked Rib*, and Rogers, *Troublesome Helpmate*. On the conventions of antifeminist satire, see Nussbaum, *Brink of All We Hate*. In 1670 John Ray remarked that of all nations England had the greatest number of "proverbial invectives against women" (*Collection of English Proverbs*, 54). On gender stereotypes in proverbs, see Mendelson and Crawford, *Women in Early Modern England*, 60–65.

11 Woodbridge, *Women and the English Renaissance*, 31–32. A similar contradiction arises in Robson's *Courte of Civill Courtesie*, which warns readers it is unseemly to make women targets of laughter because they are "unworthy opponents" yet adds some women may be "jested with, if their wit be such as they delight in the like, and can in good sporte enterchaunge in the same manner" (in Holcomb, *Mirth Making*, 119–120).

her husband in a parody of obedience, this jesting woman improvises on
the script handed to her. If, as Judith Butler has shown, gender binaries
are naturalized through reiteration, they can be interrogated through
deliberate reappropriation and performance.[12]

In a jest directed at a father rather than a husband, a four-year-old girl
unmasks the awesome patriarch who was to be feared as "a little God in
the family."[13]

> As a pretty Jest happened lately at a Supper amongst some Gentlemen
> and women, where one of the gentlemen tooke a Cup in his hand, and
> said to a little girl of 4. Yeares of age: *wife I will drinke to you* : the
> Child answered him, saying, *I will be none of your Wife: Why,* said he?
> *Because you were drunke yesterday,* said she : and with that they all
> laught heartily. But the man replyd, and said to the Child, *Sweetheart,*
> *you shall be my wife for all that ; for I will bee drunke no more* : To
> whom she answered, *So my Father said the other day, when he was*
> *sicke, but since hee is well againe, hee hath forgot his Promise, and is*
> *worse now than ever he was.*[14]

Sharply critical female wit is too often discounted as male-authored
satire against women's unchaste tongues or as the symptom of a mo-
mentary and futile reversal of gender roles. Common wisdom has it
that a woman who gains verbal mastery is always marked as a shrew or
a scold. If she leaps "on top" during a holiday such as Hocktide, when
women tied men up to extract parish funds[15], her monstrous regiment
lasts only a moment, until ordinary time demotes her. Such a view is
far too limiting. Festivity never fully contained the appealing vigor of
this anarchic humor, nor did earnest beshrewing and stern lectures entirely nullify it. Natalie Zemon Davis famously argued that ordinary
women could draw on stories and images of "women on top" to fanta-

---

12 Butler, "Performance Acts," 275. The jest is from an anonymous manuscript in
the Huntington Library (ca. 1635), HM 1338, f. 71v. Another version occurs as jest 8
in *Tarlton's Jests* (see Zall, *A Hundred Merry Tales*). Like this jest, many anti-husband jests expose the flaws of drunken, gross, and wastrel men, generally elaborated
by disgusted women, as in *The Parliament of Women,* sig. B3. For a view that con-
strues such humor as anti-husband but not antimasculinist, see Curlee, "One Said."

13 The phrase "little god in the family" is from Whately's marriage sermon, *A
Bride Bush* (first pub. 1616).

14 *The womens sharpe revenge,* sigs. K2v–K3.

15 On hocking by women, and the survival of Hocktide rites into the seventeenth
century despite reformers' attacks, see Hutton, *Rise and Fall,* 120, 229; and Brand,
Observations, 104, 105.

size about vengeance or great deeds, to reconsider the givens of female inferiority, and to gird them for confrontations at home and in public. Such effects reverberate far beyond holidays and do not end with the laugh line of a jest: "Rather than expending itself primarily during the privileged duration of the joke, the story, the comedy, or the carnival, topsy-turvy play had much spillover into everyday 'serious' life, and the effects there were sometimes disturbing and even novel. . . . this inversion could prompt new ways of thinking about the system and reacting to it."[16]

Studying jesting women spurred me to explore new ways of thinking that lie within the japes and saws of everyday life. I have relied on the work of Davis and other historians and literary scholars, including Laura Gowing, Margaret Ferguson, Ann Rosalind Jones, Jean Howard, Frances Dolan, Linda Woodbridge, and Margaret Ezell, who have sought to discover how women may have taken part in revising, negotiating, or resisting ideological paradigms rather than assuming that women were tragic victims, passive ciphers, or cultural sponges.[17] Their insights in related fields have given me the tools I use to question reigning assumptions about women's lives—the assumption that a woman's bawdy wit or outspoken eloquence was always equated with whorishness, that a woman had no weapons against defamation, that non-elite women were excluded from most forms of popular culture, and that jesting culture was monolithically antifeminist. While it is crucial for historians and literary scholars to study the increasing enclosure of women within the household, the rise of witchcraft prosecutions, and

---

16 Davis, "Women on Top," 143.

17 Laura Gowing documents how women used the church courts to define honesty, narrate experience, and affect processes of social control in *Domestic Dangers* and "Women, Status and the Popular Culture of Dishonour." Ann Rosalind Jones argues that women poets resisted being "interpellated into a tragic female speechlessness" in *Currency of Eros*, 2. Discussing the fears aroused by women's playgoing, Jean E. Howard asks whether women "might have been empowered, and not simply victimized, by their novel position within the theater" (*Stage and Social Struggle*, 78). In her study of violence by women, Frances E. Dolan reads their stories as "cultural scripts" that force women's "subjectivity into visibility," some showing active resistance, some indicating "a range of less visible, less violent resistances and self-assertions" (*Dangerous Familiars*, 5–6). Woodbridge argues that women acted on culture in many ways, for example by walking out of theaters staging misogynist plots and protesting both law and Christian doctrine when told they had no rights to their clothing (*Women in the English Renaissance*, 130, 252). Margaret J.M. Ezell demonstrates that elite women had far more agency and authority than once assumed (*Patriarch's Wife*).

the horrifying controls placed on women's tongues, from cuckstool to scold's bridle, it is also important to consider narratives of women's speech and actions that do not transgress norms severely enough to provoke reproof.[18] Jesting women do not get hauled off to court or the cuckstool for shutting someone's mouth with their wit, which these brief narratives often represent as devastatingly effective.[19]

When read in concert with other kinds of evidence about women, jesting texts can help scholars measure the fissures between the theory and practice of subordination. Because jesting literature was accessible to women, drew on their skills, and courted their pleasure, even the homely retort *better a shrew than a sheep* may have functioned as one of the "oppositional practices of everyday life," a means for ordinary people to contest social practices that ordain them as subordinates.[20] Such contestations do more than volley dead clichés: they force into view the rupture between gendered worldviews. This rupture invites an answer. A misogynist saw—"four things take great beating: a featherbed, a stockfish, milstone, a woman"—would not render hearers mute. Its aggression might draw a sharp rebuttal, such as the adaptably antimasculinist *sawce for the goose, is good for a gander.*[21] Playwrights mined this rift for comic material. When Benedick piles up insults against marriage in *Much Ado about Nothing,* he draws on a familiar topos of misogyny in which a confirmed bachelor paints any contact with women as debasing and effeminizing. When Beatrice vows to die a maid, she draws on a countertradition of antimasculinist suitor mockery that finds fault with *all* men, young or old, beardless or hairy, would-be wits or downright dullards. When she longs to eat Claudio's

18 Important works about curbs on women's speech include Lynda E. Boose, "Scolding Brides," and David Underdown, "Taming of the Scold."

19 I do not argue that jesting never brought real women into conflict with kin, neighbors, or the law, only that fictional jesting women are rarely punished. Women often used jests in the language of insult and ridicule (Gowing, "Women, Status," 227; Fox, "Ballads, Libels," 52, 59). Types that landed women in court include the mocking rhyme and satiric jig; for an example, see the beginning of chapter 3.

20 Michel de Certeau's "Oppositional Practices" is cited and discussed in Shershow, "New Life," 27–28, which criticizes Certeau for reifying social hierarchy through the distinction of popular and elite.

21 Like *better a shrew than a sheep,* this adage seems especially fitted for female rhetorical uses. In *A Collection of English Proverbs* (1670), John Ray identifies it as a "woman's proverb" (quoted in Mendelson and Crawford, *Women in Early Modern England,* 217). For a persuasive argument that proverbs can "provide a vivid insight into the structure of mental categories," see Fox, *Oral and Literate Culture,* 113 and ch. 2.

heart in the marketplace, she uses the language of scathing female satire against slanderers.[22] Her arsenal is no less ancient than Benedick's,
but it is far less visible because it has been so rarely named as female
satire with roots in social practice.

Of the many types of jests that seem to appeal for women's laughter, I
have selected those with potential as resources for female resistance and
productive fantasy. My chapters examine stage plays in relation to antimasculinist cuckoldry jokes and rituals, performances and shaming tactics used to combat slander and sexual assaults against women, jests
and ballads against wife beaters, and mocks leveled at credulous gulls
and the foolishly patient Griselda. I do not claim that any given jest or
scene reliably produced laughter or that it circulated only among
women. Successful jests are by nature mobile, unauthorized, and pro-
tean, traveling from street to stage to court with stunning ease, even
jumping across oceans.[23] Any generalization about them as cultural
texts must consider their viral adaptability and theatrical riskiness. I do
argue that the mark of gender in history suggests who might be laughing
at certain jokes, who might be yawning, and who, perhaps, is groaning.

The appeal for women's laughter manifests itself in specific ways.
The following markers do not appear en masse in any one jest, but the
presence of one or more characterizes nearly all the comic narratives
discussed in this book:

- A woman is the laugh getter through her words or actions
- The fiction mentions an internal audience that includes women
  who approve the actions of the laugh getter
- A male, often a husband, father, cleric, or unwanted suitor, is the
  butt of laughter brought down on him through the agency of a
  woman or women

22 It is possible that Beatrice's cannibalistic rage is part of a lost tradition of female insult. Ralph Houlbrooke cites a Star Chamber case of three sisters who, while
taunting an elderly man who had come to arrange the unwanted leasing of their land,
threaten to kill and eat him ("Women's Social Life," 180).

23 A famous example: Elizabeth is credited with a quick answer at the expense of
a courtier who farted in her presence. He went abroad for years, shamed to the quick.
When he finally returned, Elizabeth greeted him with "that Smell was long since out
of her nostrils, but she shou'd not forget the sound." I believed she was the sole author until I heard the joke in Istanbul—but this time with Mehmet the Conqueror
making the crack, well before Elizabeth's day. The Turkish academic who told me
was indignant that the English had tried to steal this example of the great man's wit
(quotation from Huntington Library manuscript HM 1338, c. 1635, f. 68r).

- A woman solves a riddle a man cannot solve or succeeds at a seemingly impossible task
- A woman who has carried out a clever trick or jest is not subjected to internal criticism or a dour concluding moral

In some jests women insult other women: "Two women scolding, the one call'd the other Whore; who answered her again, 'tis true, and thou would bee one too, but that thou art so ugly, that no man will have to go with ye."[24] These are fairly rare, however. When women get the laugh it is usually directed against men, and in modes ranging from playful tit-for-tat to brutal satire.

Laughter and jest are ignored by most early modern historians to their detriment, argues Keith Thomas, who sees great value in trying to place some forms of laughter in historical perspective:

> The historical study of laughter brings us right up against the fundamental values of past societies. For when we laugh we betray our innermost assumptions. Moreover, laughter has a social dimension. Jokes are a pointer to joking situations, areas of structural ambiguity in society itself; and their subject-matter can be a revealing guide to past tensions and anxieties.[25]

Besides casting light on early modern social practices, jest books contain a genuine thread of critique. By continually deriding those in power, calling the law an ass, nobles greedy, and clergymen lechers, they had "an insidious effect." While the laughter sought was mostly conservative in effect, "there was also a current of radical, critical laughter which, instead of reinforcing accepted norms, sought to give the world a nudge in a new direction."[26] The necessary subjugation of slow-witted woman to quick-witted man was among the norms nudged. Radical laughter can have homely causes:

> A Citizen that was more tender of himself than his Wife, did use to make her first to bed in the winter time and lie in his place to warm it, and when he came, to remove to her own, and for this cause did always

24 Chamberlain, *A New Booke of Mistakes*, 134.
25 Thomas, "Place of Laughter," 77.
26 Ibid., 76, 81.

call her, His warming pan; which she not very well relishing, went one night (according to her custom) to warm his bed, and when he was ready to come, she (Sir reverence) shit in his place. He suddenly leaping into it, and finding himself in a stinking pickle, Wife, quoth he, I am beshit : No husband, sayes shee, it is but a Coal dropt out of your warming Pan.[27]

A grotesque realism erupts here, one that isn't quite inversionary in the festive, Bakhtinian sense nor totally demonizing in the sense of being exclusionary. This narrative bears the marks of what Peter Stallybrass and Allon White call "hybridization, a second and more complex form of the grotesque, which produces new combinations and strange instabilities in a given semiotic system. It therefore generates the possibility of shifting the very terms of the system itself, by erasing and interrogating the relationships which constitute it."[28] Demonization, inversion, and hybridization are mixed in this jest as they are in other scatological tales featuring women as actors. The wife is not exactly celebrated, but she is not demonized; nor is her husband. Both will apparently continue to share the same bed every night. Her inversionary tactic does not seem intended to provoke festive laughter but to change her husband's tiresome ways. Grotesque yet pragmatic, her trick certainly does destabilize the semiotic system that encodes her body as a warming pan.

This kind of jest is a staple of my study: set in everyday time and place, focusing on an affront and rebuttal, often in the form of a woman's deed or trick. When a woman told or heard such a story, it may have functioned as part of what James C. Scott calls "the hidden transcript of resistance," a theory developed through studying the day-to-day strategies of slaves, serfs, and untouchables surviving under harshly repressive regimes. These groups engage in low-level campaigns of resistance through sotto voce grumbling, disguise, parody, behind-the-back mimickry, jesting, and inversion ritual—performances and interactions that give pleasure to the dominated and rehearse resistance when open rebellion is impossible. This transcript does not always stay hidden but can be glimpsed in many forms of popular culture, however

27 *A Choice banquet*, jest 139.
28 Stallybrass and White, *Politics and Poetics*, 58.

thoroughly they are satirized, sanitized, or mediated by elite scribes.[29] Tales and jests told by and appealing to the harshly subjugated class known as women may have circulated in just this way, surfacing occasionally in the works of women writers, more often in the anonymous or male-authored texts of popular literature. Early modern women were not slaves or serfs; the degree and quality of their subordination and agency depended on their social and marital status, age, religion, occupation, and ethnicity. They did live in a world that granted them no legal existence when married and gave husbands the legal right to beat them; and unlike male children and servants, women and girls were subject to lifelong, divinely ordained subjection due to their supposedly natural propensity for evil and thus had much need of narratives to arm and sustain them.[30]

The most powerful institution enforcing female subordination was the church. Despite (or because of) the flood of sermons and pamphlets instructing them about their lowliness, jesting women display a bracing lack of reverence for their spiritual guides. Although scholars of popular satire usually point out that clerics are traditional targets, they fail to mention how often *women* do the satirizing.[31] In some jests women combat antifeminist preaching by citing scripture to devastating effect, in the manner of Margery Kempe or Anne Askew:

29 Scott, *Domination*, 191. He calls the transcript "a condition of practical resistance rather than a substitute for it" (191). Some material of violent revenge and ridicule is "smuggled" into popular culture and is reproduced, often unintentionally, in printed works. The smuggling occurs because non-elite culture by definition embodies some subordinate values, contains dissonant ripostes to a demeaning official culture, and encourages protective polyvalence and disguise (157). Also see Scott, "What Is Resistance?" in *Weapons of the Weak*, 289–304.

30 See Jordan, "Renaissance Women," and Crawford and Mendelson, *Women in Early Modern England*, chs. 1–3 and 6. One must not treat women's oppression as absolute, of course. Some women had considerable control over their own property; some were apprenticed to guilds; others even attempted to vote in Parliamentary elections (ibid., 328–29, 347–48, 396–97; Erickson, *Women and Property*). Phyllis Rackin usefully summarizes the evidence for women's partial autonomy in "Misogyny Is Everywhere," 50–52. Women's legal nonbeing did not prevent them from using courts to press complaints against masters, husbands, and creditors, as Stretton shows in an important new study, *Women Waging Law*.

31 In the preface to her anthology of early modern jests, Bowen does not address women's jokes about, and tricks on, priests as anticlerical satire. She does point out that women are laugh getters in some jests despite being traditional satiric butts (*One Hundred Renaissance Jokes*, xviii).

That witty wench returned to a Dunce in a Cassock a shrewd an answer
(though she ever reflected more religiously upon her conjugal honour;)
Who telling this Maid, that Women were at best but Necessary Evils,
and that they were never needfull to any but in time of necessity:
wheareas the Lord stood in need of such as him. "Truly, quoth she, I
highly honour your place, yet did I never read that the Lord had need of
anything but an Asse."[32]

Other tales show women taking on boring sermonizers. In a jest set in
church during service, a friar grows annoyed at "a wife little disposed to
contemplation" who ignores him.

[She] talked with a gossip of hers of other feminine tales, so loud that
the friar heard and was somewhat perturbed therewith. To whom therefore openly the friar spoke and said: "Thou woman, there in the tawny
gown—hold thy peace and leave thy babbling. Thou troublest the word
of God." This woman suddenly abashed because the friar spake to her
so openly that all the people beheld, answered shortly and said: "I
beshrew thee hard, that babbleth the more of us two." At which saying
the people did laugh because they felt but little fruit in his sermon.[33]

The moment is hardly revolutionary, but it does show a woman who
uses language to get an audience firmly on her side. Seizing her opportunity, she turns a moment of shame onto her detractor by saying what
everyone else has been thinking. Such retorts were not an impossibility:
laughter and joking were quite common in church, along with spitting,

32 Brathwait, *Ar't Asleep Husband?* 303. She refers to an incident preceding
Christ's entrance to Jerusalem: Jesus tells his disciples to take an ass from a village,
and if anyone stops them they should answer "the Lord hath need" (Matthew 21:
2–3). Other jokes target priestly greed: "A poor olde woman being sicke and weake,
bequeathed after her death to the Priest her Henne, because shee had nothing more:
now the Priest came and tooke her away yet living; (Quoth shee,) nowe I peerceyve,
that our priest is worse than the Divell, because I have oftentimes bid the devill take
her, and the Foxe take her, yet still I had her, but the Priest not" (Scott, *Philosophers
Banquet, newly furnished*, 243).

33 Zall, *A Hundred Merry Tales*, 118. Situating women's anticlerical satire in the
context of Reformation movements and later radical sectarianism demands a closer
study than I can give it here. While she does not explore women's anticlerical jests,
Linda Woodbridge makes the persuasive argument that jokes about sinful priests,
monks, and nuns played an important role in the Reformation, helping to purge hearers of sympathy toward both charitable orders and the poor (*Vagrancy*, 80–108).

knitting, playing cards, and dozing.[34] Sometimes those who listened made it plain that they "felt but little fruit" in sermons directed squarely at them. When William Gouge preached, against custom, that a wife had no right to own any property, even her own clothing, he aroused a fierce public outcry. "Many that can patiently hear their duties declared in general terms, cannot endure to heare those generals exemplified in their particular branches," he complained.[35]

Impatience is a vital quality: it can train a mind to be critical. The unwillingness of some women to hear their duties "exemplified" by sages such as Gouge marks female satire in both the popular literature and the *querelle des femmes*, where "feminist wit penetrated to the core of male pretension in the irrefutable arguments and commonsensical adages that supported men's power over women," as Joan Kelly once wrote.[36] She was speaking of the learned women who took part in the querelle, such as Christine de Pizan. Yet some women who were never authors in the usual sense of the word nor engaged in philosophical debates about women's worth also used the tool of critical wit to gain a measure of control over experience. Jesting helped shape their mental worlds, including their responses to the public plays that recruited their laughter, identification, and judgment.

In trying to understand women's part in the culture of jest, I have kept David Aers's words in mind: "Any reading that hopes to have relevance to a particular text must include an attempt to relocate it in the web of discourses and social practices within which it was made and which determines its horizons."[37] The early modern neighborhood emerged as an illuminating social context for retracing the horizons and actions of non-elite women, including jesting practices. Neighborhoods functioned as schools for manners and behavior, unofficial courts of local judgment, and stages on which neighbors created the performances that built repu-

---

34 Behavior reported in complaints against churchgoers include "practical joking" along with "fighting, spitting, letting off guns, vomiting, urinating, farting, knitting, sewing, trading, playing cards, and singing" (Reay, *Popular Culture in Seventeenth Century England*, 92). Women did not always attend church with downcast eyes and folded hands, and one contemporary print shows women ignoring the man in the pulpit (see fig. 3, scene at top center).

35 From the "Epistle dedicatory" to *Of Domesticall Duties*, quoted in Woodbridge, *Women and the English Renaissance*, 129.

36 Kelly, "Early Feminist Theory," 19.

37 Aers, *Community, Gender and Individual Identity*, 3.

tation and identity. In both the jesting literature and stage comedie women rarely sit on their hands: there are simply too many cues for sympathy, laughter, and scorn. They rush to take sides, a habit bred within closely watched neighborhoods, where women held sway over matters of sexual honesty and reputation, and the laughter of ridicule functioned as a "crude form of moral censorship."[38] In chapter 1 I show that women's laughter served as vector of the collective judgment vital to the creation of dramatic and social meaning. In some plays mockery and jest by male and female neighbors are methods of social control, supplementing the flawed judicial processes by which communities tried to regulate behavior.[39] In my chosen example, *The Merry Wives of Windsor*, a pair of neighbors expertly uses the arts of disguise, wit, timing, and counterplotting to combat threats to their reputations in a closely watched village. The Windsor wives' strategies include summoning the censure of neighbors to control a violently jealous husband and deploying theatrical tricks and charivari to confound a sexual aggressor. At the heart of their hilarity is their need to deflect shaming away from female targets and toward male ones, directing the crushing ridicule of neighbors and spectators at the losers.

Freud's notorious *What do women want?* is close kin to the generalizing question of misogynist writers, *what is woman?* I would like to displace these with a more specific query: *where were women?* In chapter 2, I follow them to a vitally important site for women's jesting and community life: the alehouse. Until now, early modern drinking places have been treated as male-dominated milieus that were off limits and off-putting to "respectable" women. Peter Clark's *The English Alehouse* celebrates it as a nearly all-male "neighborhood theatre" where men could "discover another dimension" of their lives.[40] In fact, tens of thousands of women ran alehouses or worked in them, married couples drank together there, maidservants and young women gathered there, and lovers met and even held weddings there. Alehouses could also be used as the place where women neighbors met to settle local disputes. As owners, customers, consumers, and as critics, women were deeply engaged in alehouse culture; there they heard and bought ballads, told jokes, danced

---

38 Thomas, *Religion*, 77.
39 Alison Findlay makes a similar argument in her stimulating *Feminist Perspective*, 133.
40 Reay, *Popular Culture in Seventeenth Century England*, 11; Clark, *English Alehouse*, 131–32.

jigs, hauled husbands home, and heard news of their neighbors and the wider world. Popular representations of jesting alewives and tippling gossips, including Noah's Wife, Mother Bunch, and Long Meg, situate women as skilled players in the "neighborhood theatre" that linked the dramas of everyday life to the dramas of the stage.

Scholars have found the early modern obsession with cuckoldry especially mystifying, but they have seldom read horn humor as a social practice in which women participated. Chapter 3 discerns a strong current of female laughter against cuckolded and horn-mad husbands, arguing that women had special reasons for enjoying the vast sea of cuckoldry jests that fill popular culture and plays. Far from being counters traded between men, women in many cuckoldry narratives act as subjects and directors, with husbands and lovers as objects. Further, some narratives show women trading and judging horn tales. It is likely that the gender of audiences affected reception, a situation that ballad writers and playwrights took into account. Accordingly, I explore how the presence of female audiences, performers, and tale tellers offers a valuable key to unlocking the cuckoldry paradigm in popular stage and print works.

Neighbors acted as witnesses and allies in plays and jesting texts, as they did on the streets and yards of the neighborhood. Men's brutality toward their wives was the business of the neighborhood, not a private matter; and abused wives usually turned to women neighbors first for help. Chapter 4 examines modes of resistance to male violence against women, arguing that female gossip, mockery, and shaming humor could limit abuse within tight-knit communities. Jesting women vehemently contested the ideal of female submission to male blows; taken together, their arguments constitute a counterhegemonic discourse that may have made a great deal more sense to women than sermons and marriage manuals did. Even when couched in farce, game, and jest, some jests communicate that while beatings and slander might be suffered one on one, some protection and even retribution could spring from collective action.

Women's pleasure in judging and shaming dupes is the main focus of chapter 5, which analyzes two 1595 pamphlets: one a coney-catching book featuring a rogue who cheats two sets of gulls, the second a pamphlet in which one of her victims undergoes a mock trial by the women of her neighborhood. After exploring points of contact between the rogue plot and Chaucer's "Tale of Sir Thopas," Spenser's *Faerie Queene*,

Shakespeare's *A Midsummer Night's Dream*, and Jonson's *The Alchemist*, all of which involve a fairy queen, female judgment, women on top, and male humiliation, I propose that the pamphlets constitute a print skimmington against the coneys. While the trial pamphlet satirizes the women's "Quest of Enquirie," it also pays backhanded tribute to the women's skepticism and common sense.

A jesting woman is not always a shrew, but she is never a sheep. She would scoff at the idea of laying her hand beneath her husband's foot as Kate—"a second Grissel"—does in *The Taming of the Shrew*. Griselda was the most celebrated example of wifely patience in the early modern period, but she was also a bitter irritant to at least some women told to emulate her. Chapter 6 tracks clashes between jesting women and the "persuasive fiction" of the patient wife, whom Renaissance writers knew from Chaucer's "Clerk's Tale" and Petrarch's Latin exemplum, which drew a Christian moral from his reworking of the final tale of Boccaccio's *Decameron*. Griselda's myth mutates in tandem with the widespread changes that new forms of capitalism wrought on marriage, kin, and community during an age in which married women lost status within the household yet were increasingly enclosed within it. The history of women who repudiated this shining model of wifely submission, even as it was being forced down their throats, is faint yet legible in ballads, jests, and proverbs and in plays, including Phillip's interlude *The Comodye of Pacient and Meeke Grissill*; Preston's *Cambyses*; Shakespeare's *The Winter's Tale* and *The Taming of the Shrew*; Elizabeth Cary's *Tragedy of Mariam*; and Dekker, Chettle, and Haughton's *The Pleasant Comodie of Patient Grissill*.

Some jests and ballads discussed here have long been known to scholars; but they have rarely been read as artifacts suggesting women's agency, much less as possible cues for contestation, negotiation, or resistance. Determining intersections between the jest tradition, the lives of early modern women, and popular culture has therefore been crucial.[41] Defining early modern popular culture inspires heated debate

---

41 I draw extensively and gratefully on the work of scholars who study non-elite women and early popular culture, especially Wiltenburg, *Disorderly Women*; Amussen, "Gendering of Popular Culture"; Capp, "Separate Domains?" and "Double Standard Revisited"; Davis, *Society*; Dolan, *Dangerous Familiars*; Gowing, *Domestic Dangers*; Houlbrooke, "Women's Social Life"; Woodbridge, *Women and the English Renaissance*; Thomas, "The Double Standard" and *Religion and the Decline of Magic*; and Mendelson and Crawford, *Women in Early Modern England*.

among historians, who struggle to arrive at a conceptual framework
that fits an age before the Industrial Revolution and mass media. Some
scholars see the culture of the people as entirely separate from that of
educational and political elites; others see popular culture as forms
shared by elites and non-elites; still others treat the popular as whatever
is most often consumed.[42] In this book, "popular culture" signifies any
text or performance that became familiar in part because it was either
cheap, or free to be heard, seen, or performed oneself. Developed from
Roger Chartier's model of cultural appropriation, my definition emphasizes performance situation rather than authorship, giving new prominence to the arenas in which women experienced jesting, in both the
everyday dramas of the neighborhood and the spectacles of the stage. I
establish that certain jest motifs were familiar by showing that they circulated through multiple trajectories of speech, drama, writing, ritual,
and print.[43] Jest topoi were strongly stereotyped, repeated countless
times in a variety of forums and media: chapter 3, for example, tracks
the motif of "women laughing at cuckolds" in jest books, ballads, chapbooks, festive rituals, and plays.

Although my subject is women and jesting culture, I do not want to
replicate what Stuart Hall calls "those self-enclosed approaches . . .
[that] analyse popular cultural forms as if they contained within themselves, from their moment of origin, some fixed and unchanging meaning of value."[44] The meaning of a jest is never fully encompassed by its
content or the teller's intentions, just as no single theory can encom-
pass the meanings of laughter. Thinking about how women might have
worked within and against the generally hostile culture of jesting mili-

42 Scribner, "Is a History of Popular Culture Possible?" On early popular culture,
the central work (although outdated in regard to women) is still Burke, *Popular Culture*. For England, key works are Reay, *Popular Cultures in England, 1550–1750* and
Popular Culture in Seventeenth Century England; Harris, *Popular Culture;* Spufford,
Small Books; Watt, *Cheap Print;* Dugaw, *Warrior Women;* Yeo and Yeo, *Popular Culture and Class Conflict;* Thompson, *Customs in Common;* Malcolmson, *Popular
Recreations.* Important studies about Europe include Muchembled, *Popular Culture
and Elite Culture in France;* Scribner, *For the Sake of Simple Folk;* and Davis, *Society
and Culture.*

43 Chartier stresses the ways in which "the same goods, the same ideas, and the
same actions" pass through many "trajectories" of print, speech, act, and writing.
The model avoids "identifying various cultural levels merely on the basis of a description of the objects, beliefs, or acts presumed to have been proper to each group"
(*Cultural Uses of Print,* 6).

44 "Notes on Deconstructing 'the Popular,'" quoted in Shershow, *Puppets,* 165, n.
81; also see Shershow's essay on "the problem of the popular" ("New Life").

tates against such blinkered views, as does thinking about the fluid yet connected arenas of theater and neighborhood. To maneuver within the culture of jest women had to know it intimately, so establishing its availability and familiarity is key to my argument. This book deals largely with stories or performances that were free to all or cost at most a penny or two and were readily available through oral repetition from memory or from shared reading aloud.[45] Women were privy to jesting through many channels: everyday talk, ballads, proverbs, jest books, plays, rituals, and festivity.

My approach to "the popular" intends to broaden the interpretive space needed to register women's engagement in quotidian culture. The foundational work in the field, Peter Burke's *Popular Culture in Early Modern Europe* (first published in 1978, revised in 1994, and widely cited), treats non-elite women as culturally inarticulate and mostly unknowable. In his formulation, the learned elite may participate fully in both the "big tradition" of literary culture and the popular "little tradition" of oral culture and festivity; but the non-elites have access only to the little tradition.[46] Some historians still follow Burke's dictum that poorer women played no active role in most forms of popular culture despite being key to transmission; like Burke, they state that women's illiteracy was an important bar to full involvement.[47] In an influential

45 Access to reading aloud would have been more important for women than for men, as Jonathan Barry points out in "Literature and Literacy," 82. Also see Chartier, "Leisure."

46 Burke, *Popular Culture*, 23–28.

47 According to Burke, "women's culture" is hard to assess because it was "a culture of the inarticulate" (ibid., 49). Women were excluded from guilds and often from fraternities. "The world of the tavern was not for them either. The occupational variations . . . can have meant little" (49). Stressing the lack of evidence, he maintains that "if anything is clear in this murky area, it is that women's culture was more conservative than that of their men" and that women's lower literacy "added to the list of cultural items that women did not share" (50). Women were "guardians of the oral tradition" (50) who were involved in the transmission of popular culture (91) yet remain unknowable because of their inarticulateness and illiteracy.

Burke did not alter these passages on women in his 1994 revised edition. His influence has been pervasive, with the result that women's active participation in popular culture has been largely ignored until recently. Reay's widely cited *Popular Culture in Seventeenth Century England*, for example, repeats many of Burke's assertions, although it does offer essays by Martin Ingram and Bernard Capp touching on women's roles in skimmingtons, noncompliance with sexual norms, and consumption of popular literature. In contrast, Reay's 1998 book *Popular Cultures in England, 1550–1750* opens with an excellent chapter titled "Sexualities" and includes valuable discussions of women in festive drama and ritual, riots, and the culture of witchcraft.

essay collection, Barry Reay echoes Burke in stating that "women were excluded from many points of contact for popular culture," which he identifies as guilds (although some women joined through apprenticeships or held positions through marriage), the tavern and alehouse (women were "probably" not comfortable going there alone), and the bearbait and cockfight (women were mere spectators).[48] *Ergo* women were marginal players in both the elite and the popular, invited to neither the big nor the little feast.

The split between a historian's reading and a literary scholar's could hardly be wider. To the latter, the term popular culture connotes practices and places that not only include women—especially poorer women—but feature them as chief actors. Within the neighborhood that formed the basic social arena, the storyteller was more likely to be a gammer than an author, the most talented flyter the fishwife, the buyer of ballads the serving maid, and the local chroniclers the gossips. Even the most celebrated local jester could be an alewife like Mother Bunch or a roaring girl like Moll Frith. As for the gendering of festivity, most of the pastimes, dances, games, and rites marking major holidays were traditionally (and to reformers, notoriously) enjoyed by girls and women, not just men and youths. Pudency seems to have been less an impediment than has been assumed: despite all the admonitions against naughty songs, tales, and plays, some women sought them out. Bawdy satires on inept wooing were legion. In one ballad a rural maid laughingly warns a fond suitor not to make a sticky mess in his futile passion over her, taunting him with the refrain "Good sir, you'll wrong your breeches."[49] Ian Moulton has found bawdy jests and erotic satires scattered liberally through women's commonplace books and manuscripts; a gentlewoman named Margaret Belasys, for example, saw fit to include Thomas Nashe's *A Choyce of Valentines*—a male lover's lament over being bested by a dildo—along with other jests in her commonplace book.[50] A seventeenth-century manuscript records scores of jests told at a great manor in Norwich. Gentlewomen fire off puns on pricks and yards, and an aged aunt tells a tale about "a simple Ideott"

48 Reay, *Popular Culture in Seventeenth Century England*, 10–11. Also Burke, *Popular Culture*, 49.
49 *Pepys Ballads*, 1:41.
50 Moulton, *Before Pornography*, 57–64. Among passages of poetry by Donne and others, the Belasys manuscript contains satires and jokes about Puritan women and men, witless suitors, a farting parliamentarian, and the Duke of Buckingham (62).

who bets a cheese that another man cannot "wimble" his way through the fool's wife's back.[51] At theaters trading in lubricious jokes and word-play, "there were certainly women in the audience, and bawdy jests are appreciated by both genders."[52]

Did widespread illiteracy among women block their access to popular culture? Many scholars still rely on the controversial work of David Cressy, who used data on the ability to sign one's name to estimate that female literacy remained low throughout the period, rising from just 5 percent to 10 percent of all women between 1550 and 1650, while men exceeded that figure by 20 percent or more.[53] Margaret Spufford and Keith Thomas have shown that Cressy's stress on women's ability to sign documents virtually erases evidence about their reading ability, which was far more widespread; many girls were taught to read but not to write. In a recent study Eve Sanders concludes that reading skills actually "appear to have been distributed fairly equally between men and women."[54] Girls in non-elite families often acquired those skills from mothers and grandmothers or from women who ran dame schools. One jest credits such a teacher for saving her grandson's neck: "A fellow having his booke at the Sessions, was burned in the hand, and was commanded to say, God save the King : the King, said hee, God save my Grandam, that taught me to read, I am sure I had bin hanged else."[55]

In other words, some non-elite women could decipher popular texts; but far more gained access through the spoken word. Jests and ballads were experienced mainly through the ear, and jest books were commonly read aloud, often to groups of listeners. A new trove of jests did not remain private for long. If a jest book entered a village in someone's pocket, sooner or later "every man, woman and child" would hear

---

51 Le Strange, *Merry Passages*, 43, no. 114; 77, no. 248. This manuscript, a cross between a journal and a jest book, contains more than six hundred jests, with more than one hundred transcribed from the lips of his mother, his wife, his sister, and other female kin and friends. The joke about the "Ideott" is ascribed to "Aunt Cat-line" (Dorothy Catline, his aunt by marriage).

52 Bly, *Queer Virgins*, 4.

53 Cressy, *Literacy*, 177. Judged by the criteria of signing ability, literacy rose sharply for London women only at the end of the seventeenth century (147, tables on 120–21).

54 Sanders, *Gender*, 167. Margaret Ferguson argues that finer distinctions are needed among types of literacies in her forthcoming book, *Dido's Daughters*.

55 Spufford, *Small Books*, xvii–xviii, 34–37, and "First Steps"; and Thomas, "Meaning of Literacy." The scaffold jest is from John Taylor, *All the Works*, item 100.

everything in it, either by reading aloud or by word of mouth.[56] When sung aloud, ballads were accessible to virtually anyone with a grasp of the language.[57] Broadsides decorated with woodcuts made a frank visual appeal to consumers, making at least part of the message available to all. Some jest books cued readers typographically, combining italic type in the body of a text with black letter in the key laugh lines, possibly providing a performance cue for those telling the jest and stressing the most important lines in the mode of print most familiar to non-elite readers (see fig. 1). Such visual and graphic signals arguably made printed jests and ballads more accessible to female readers and listeners with low or partial literacy.[58]

Cost was an obstacle to owning some jesting texts, but most people could spare a halfpenny or a penny for a ballad now and then. New chapbooks cost from three to four pence, rising to shillings and pounds for longer comic works, placing them out of the reach of many. But jests also appeared in "street literature"—cheaper pamphlets and broadsides offering "songs, jokes, news and stories," all of which "reached a far wider audience than more sedate volumes. . . . Many who were unable or unwilling to buy or read the texts heard them sung or spoken in taverns, fairs and streets." Sellers offered up jesting patter along with songs and comic ballads often began with "direct exhortations to buy, addressed to both sexes and to all social levels: good Christians, young men, maidens, wives, fathers. . . . the obvious intent is to cast the net as widely as possible."[59]

Like the ballad culture it drew on and fed, theater was a prime locus for the dissemination of jests. While city women had their choice of theaters offering japes and jigs, women in remote villages could watch the occasional jest-filled play staged by traveling troupes, see a jig at a local alehouse, or seek out ballads, playbooks, and romances from traveling chapmen. Playwrights certainly associated such diversions with women's tastes. Francis Beaumont skewers the female consumer of popular literature in his portrait of the Citizen Wife in *Knight of the*

---

56 Paul Zall, personal communication. Copies often fell to pieces under this intensive use; Zall maintains that "more people read jestbooks than read the works of Chaucer, Spenser, and Milton combined" (*A Nest of Ninnies*, ix). For a partial listing of jest books published between 1510 and 1609, see Woodbridge, *Vagrancy*, 285–93.

57 Watt, *Cheap Print*, 13.

58 Thomas, "Meaning of Literacy," 99–100.

59 Quotations and information on costs from Wiltenburg, *Disorderly Women*, 29–30; also see Watt, *Cheap Print*, 11–12, 260–62.

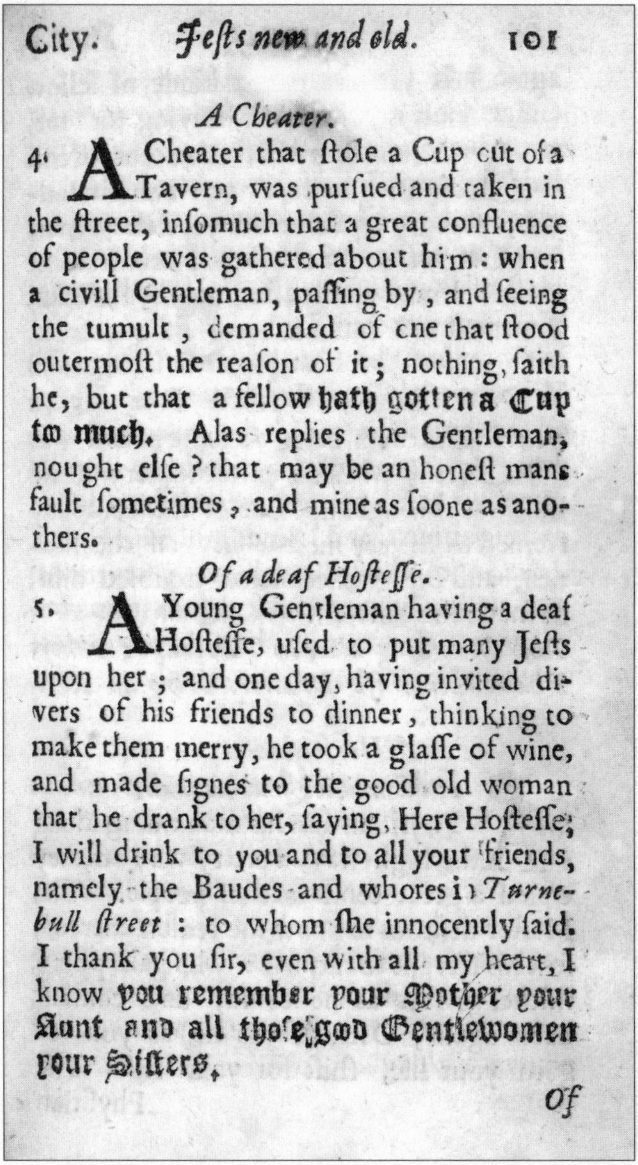

A Cheater.

4. **A** Cheater that ſtole a Cup cut of a Tavern, was purſued and taken in the ſtreet, inſomuch that a great confluence of people was gathered about him : when a civill Gentleman, paſſing by, and ſeeing the tumult, demanded of cne that ſtood outermoſt the reaſon of it; nothing, ſaith he, but that a fellow hath gotten a Cup too much. Alas replies the Gentleman, nought elſe ? that may be an honeſt mans fault ſometimes, and mine as ſoone as anothers.

Of a deaf Hoſteſſe.

5. **A** Young Gentleman having a deaf Hoſteſſe, uſed to put many Jeſts upon her ; and one day, having invited divers of his friends to dinner, thinking to make them merry, he took a glaſſe of wine, and made ſignes to the good old woman that he drank to her, ſaying, Here Hoſteſſe; I will drink to you and to all your friends, namely the Baudes and whores i) *Turnebull ſtreet* : to whom ſhe innocently ſaid. I thank you ſir, even with all my heart, I know you remember your Mother your Aunt and all thoſe good Gentlewomen your Siſters,

Of

Fig. 1. From *A Banquet of Jests New and Old* (1657). Reproduced by permission of The Huntington Library, San Marino, California.

Burning Pestle, and Jonson and others sneered at women for favoring
the likes of Robert Greene, John Taylor, and George Wither. One writer
belittles Taylor's maidservant readers for poring over his writings in
their "kitchen cobweb-nooks," while Thomas Overbury's character of a
chambermaid has her devouring the works of Greene.[60] While hard evidence about what non-elite women read is scanty, better evidence exists that some elite women read and enjoyed the jesting literature.
Dame Alice L'Estrange was a connoisseur of jests, which her son collected and transcribed; a Staffordshire gentlewoman, Frances Wolfreston, bought jest books and romances for her large book collection.
Queen Elizabeth herself called for *The Hundred Merry Tales* to be read
to her as she lay dying.[61]

The broadside ballad plays a special role in this book because it was
so deeply marked by female participation. With 3 to 4 million copies
circulating in England at the end of the sixteenth century, ballads were
"the cheapest, most accessible, and most widely available form of print
operating on the boundaries "between the oral and the written, between
commercial transaction and free circulation; it was delivered to its audiences initially in public places such as marketplaces, alehouses, and
playhouse entrances, and was thus equally available to men and to
women."[62] The lovelorn milkmaid weeping into her pail was stereo-

---

60 Jonson caricatures Wither as a favorite of maidservants and fishwives in *Time
Vindicated to Himself and to His Honors* (1623), quoted in Riggs, *Ben Jonson,* 275.
On Taylor's appeal to non-elite women, see Capp, *World of John Taylor,* 69–72; quo-
tation on 72. On Overbury see Clark, *Elizabethan Pamphleteers,* 21. Lori Newcomb
persuasively attacks the stereotype of the servant-girl as Greene's typical reader
(*Reading the Romance,* 89–91). On the ways in which writers associated female readership with vulgar commodification and notions about "the popular," permanently
feminizing and degrading the romance, see ibid., chapter 2, esp. 94–95, and
McLuskie, *Dekker and Heywood,* 106. On women collecting playbooks, see Hackel,
"Rowme," and Roberts, "Women Reading Shakespeare," 1–6. I thank Sasha Roberts
for showing me her essay before publication.

61 Le Strange, *Merry Passages,* contains scores of jests told by the compiler's
mother, Dame Alice (see note 51). The anecdote about Elizabeth is from Woodbridge,
Vagrancy, 292. On Wolfreston, see Morgan, "Frances Wolfreston." This avid book
collector owned plays and romances by Shakespeare, Greene, Pettie, and many others; her stock of jesting literature included Armin's *Foole upon Foole* (1605),
Bachelars Banquet (1603), *Boccace's Tales* (1657, 1655), *Booke of Merrie Riddles*
(1617), *Maps of Merrie Conceits* (1656), *Merry Devill of Edmonton* (1617), *Mirth in
Abundance* (1659), *Pleasant Conceits of Old Hobson* (1640), *A Pleasant History of
the Life and Death of Will Summers* (1637), *The Penniles Parliament of Threed-Bare
Poets* (1608), and twelve books by John Taylor the Water Poet. See Morgan's appendix,
211–19.

62 Clark, "Economics"; Watt, *Cheap Print,* 11,42. I thank Sandra Clark for gener-
ously allowing me to read and quote her essay.

typed as a ballad consumer; but there is extensive literary and anecdotal evidence of widespread circulation in all ranks, including servants, marketwomen, middling goodwives, gentlewomen, and prostitutes.[63] Although most printed ballads are either anonymous or male-authored, we should not assume women did not write any, given that many ballads were composed orally and never written down or published, many accompanied women's work, and many were traditionally sung only by women. Furthermore, some women who could not write did create mocking rhymes and songs, composing them and then having someone else transcribe them.[64]

The ballad market responded to women's lively interest by anticipating the concerns of the female buyer and casting many songs in women's voices. "To a much greater extent than in the 'great tradition,'" writes Bruce Smith, "popular ballads invited singers and listeners to occupy a female subject position."[65] According to Joy Wiltenburg, many ballads "attribute to women a high degree of self-consciousness, a weighing of their life's pattern against other possible patterns instead of a stolid acceptance of their lot."[66] In ballad after ballad, singers debate the ways and means of living under the codes of gender. Songs are often cast as pairs of ballads—one in the voice of a woman, the other in the voice of a man; or both voices traded stanzas in one song. As Natascha Wurzbach has shown, the balladmonger had to pay attention to the gender mix in his come-on, quickly identifying target listeners yet often attempting at the close to placate those who were offended.[67] The intrinsic dialogism of the ballad form gestures outward, to an active group of auditors who are arguing, judging, and interjecting, rather than to isolated and sedentary readers. Constantly cued to participate, this audience bears a striking resemblance to both the contemporary theater au-

---

63 Wiltenburg, *Disorderly Women*, 27–31, 38–9; Wurzbach, *Rise*, 17, 71, 72, 190–93, app. 1.3; and Rollins, "Black-Letter," 267, 280, 305, 307. In *The Return from Parnassus* (1599), the milkmaid motif appears in a speech that mockingly acknowledges the powers of ballad writers and the desires of their customers in what seems a parody of the final lines of Sidney's *Apology for Poetry*. When a ballad writer complains about getting no respect, a youth tells him "no doubt but that countries will miss you when you are gone. . . . The maidens shall want sonnets at their pails, and the country striplings ditties to sing at the maid's windows; the cart-horses will go discontented for want of the wonted music, and the cows low for the want of their Lothario" (quoted in Rollins, "Black-Letter," 303).

64 Wiesner, *Women and Gender*, 186; Fox, *Oral and Literate*, 305, 306, 312.

65 Smith, *Acoustic World*, 200. He lists dozens of ballads written in the first-person female voice.

66 Wiltenburg, *Disorderly Women*, 50.

67 Wurzbach, *Rise*, 54, 74–80.

dience and the juries of neighbors who enforced locally determined codes of neighborly behavior and sexual propriety.

Women did not simply consume ballads and jests; they put them to use. A handful of women even gained fame and fortune from jesting and singing. A celebrated ballad singer named Alyce Boyce performed for Elizabeth; and Mary I, Mary Queen of Scots, and Elizabeth all employed female jesters, as did their counterparts in Spain, France, and Italy.[68] Probably the most common use for jests and ballads lay in providing narrative elements that shaped identity and experience. Laura Gowing has written brilliantly about the ways in which non-elite women fashioned narratives from their experiences and articulated them in the church courts. In forming their lives into stories for others to judge, women frequently used themes, phrases, and techniques derived from familiar jesting forms. The fact of a woman's low status did not prevent her from employing "insults, jokes and rumours and references to popular culture" to attack those much higher in station, as Gowing shows in her study of Star Chamber defamation suits.[69] Adam Fox has documented instances of women who wrote or dictated mocking rhymes, songs, and libels, showing that they were far from silent in the noisy arenas of popular satire; while James Stokes, a scholar working on the Records of Early English Drama project, has uncovered evidence of women's participation in jest-filled dramatics combining mockery and festive play.[70]

The strong resemblances between making fun and making theater suggest further connections between jest and drama. Like a stage play, jest is also "gest," created at the moment it is enacted, rendering the jest more an event than an utterance.[71] Like plays, jests are intended to be heard, not read; and both fail or succeed because of the somatic reac-

68 On Boyce, see Rollins, "Black-Letter," 319. Mary Queen of Scots employed Jenny Colquohoun as a fool and brought "La Jardinière" from France; Mary I had a fool named Jane; and Elizabeth's retinue included Thomasina, a jester dwarf (Otto, *Fools*, 67–68).

69 Gowing, "Women, Status," 227.

70 Fox, *Oral and Literate Culture*, 305, 306, 312. In his study of the Wells Shows of 1607, James Stokes reports that women took roles in a play satirizing a prominent Puritan, who opposed the shows and later sued the players for libel ("Women and Mimesis," 186–96). On the festivities and resulting lawsuit, also see Smith, *Acoustic World*, 133–34.

71 English, *Comic Transactions*, 5. Another theorist maintains that a joke's ultimate author is the audience, which laughs or does not, because it alone has the power to grant the teller the position of subject (Weber, "Divaricator," 25–26). Also see Smith's brilliantly suggestive chapter on gest/jest, "Games, Gambols, Gests, Jests, Jibes, Jigs," in *Acoustic World*, esp. 138, 166.

tions of an audience. In an age in which audiences made Tarlton and Kemp the most powerful players in their companies, clowning and jests were imported into plays from cheap print, festivity, and oral culture. In turn, plays provided material for jesting beyond the stage doors, in the familiar theaters of the table, yard, alehouse, and village green. Women were never excluded from the wider arenas of performance, playing a significant role in the jesting culture that surrounded and nurtured the public stage.

This book addresses jesting literature dating from the Tudor period up to the Restoration, ranging from decades in which religious and folk drama were vital and flourishing, to the beginnings of professional playing companies in London and the end of the great pageants, to the radical attacks on playing and festivity that preceded the Civil War. Jesting culture was more durable and slower to change than was the theater that drew on it. There were fewer discernible breaks in content, with jest books and ballads treating the same kinds of topics over the entire period. Street literature and oral culture continued to disseminate jests throughout all segments of society, and the social space of the table, yard, and street remained important and stable venues largely impervious to censorship and Puritan control. Change was not entirely absent: jest books showed a marked trend toward shorter jests by the mid-seventeenth century, and topical and political jests came to play a larger role. Social venues for jesting expanded with the important innovation of the admission-charging, clown-dominated, and jest-saturated arena of the public stage. Finally, the production of ballads and jest books soared, prompted in part by rising literacy and wealth among the middling sort. On the other hand, reformers' attacks on theaters; city and village alehouses; laughter in church; ballad-selling; and "papist" revels such as wakes, wassails, and May games decisively closed off many important sites for the transmission of communal forms of revelry and jesting. Attacks on irreligious lewdness played a role in the crackdown on sites and occasions of jesting; but they did not curtail the circulation of many comic songs, merry tales, and jests, some of which were still appearing in jest books and ballad collections almost unchanged in the nineteenth century.[72]

---

72 English jest books did not segregate jests "suitable for ladies" until the latter half of the seventeenth century; nonetheless, women of all classes continued to read and exchange bawdy tales, as Margaret Spufford has shown (*Small Books*, esp. 62–63, 79–80 n. 60; also see Le Strange, *Merry Passages*, for bawdy jests told by gentlewomen

Because interiority is not the point of jesting, I have avoided psychoanalytic readings of jests, attempting instead to historicize the social
meanings of jesting in the common places of women's lives. Many
studies of women and joking begin with Freud's *Jokes and Their Relation to the Unconscious* (1905), which depicts the primal scene of joking as always and essentially between three people: two men, with a
woman just out of earshot. The joke originates from sexual desire. The
joker wants to excite the woman, and the dirty joke is his tool. The
woman is bound to be disgusted by his gift, however; so he tells a man,
which stimulates both of them. This scenario pushes woman out of
earshot for reasons of prudery and repression (both hers and his); instead of being the excited hearer, she becomes an exciting threat, an
erotic noise rather than a voice. It is her ear that must not hear the
taboo subject, whose presence and absence are the preconditions for all
the joking.

The Freudian model is not very useful for examining Renaissance attitudes toward laughter and joking. Where Freud investigated the ways
in which jokes reveal the shapes and workings of repression, Renaissance physicians were primarily interested in laughter as a physical process like breathing or digestion, analyzing jesting and comedy as ancil-
lary topics. Laurent Joubert's *Treatise on Laughter* (1579) offers a better
roadmap for puzzling through early modern jests and "determining
their contemporary comic weight."[73] Reading Joubert summons up a
profoundly different somatic universe, one that does not see laughter as
Hobbes's brutal "sudden glory," which merely transmits the laugher's
attitude of cruel superiority.[74] Nor is it evidence of the mechanical operation of the spirit—"the absence of feeling," in Henri Bergson's
much-cited formula.[75] Joubert's humoral universe was markedly more

---

from the 1630s to the 1660s; many were also printed in jest books). In an essay on
Italian jesting practices, Peter Burke maintains that women were often "both jokers
and victims" in various forms of humor and practical jokes (*beffe*) from the fourteenth century to the late sixteenth century, when verbal humor came to be preferred
to *beffe* and writers began to censor themselves, citing women's "modesty." Burke
concludes, however, by giving examples of women's bawdy *beffe* targeting men in
modern times ("Frontiers of the Comic," 69–73). On attacks on traditional festivity
and the Stuart countercampaign, see Marcus, *Politics of Mirth.* On printed jests before and during the Civil War, see Brewer, "Prose Jest-Books," 105–7; on ballad censorship, see Smith, *Acoustic World,* 201. Also see Ingram, "Reform of Popular Culture?" in Reay, *Popular Culture in Seventeenth Century England.*

73 Gregory de Rocher, preface to Joubert, *Treatise,* 3.
74 Hobbes, *Leviathan,* 32.
75 Bergson, "Laughter," 63.

optimistic about the social meanings and medical efficacy of laughter and joking. In his encyclopedic work it is an awesome somatic force, sometimes mortally dangerous, sometimes beneficent, capable of breaking through paralysis and clearing fistulas: "For such joy moves the languishing and crushed heart, spreads the pleasure throughout the body, and makes it come to the aid of Nature . . . which strengthened by such help, combats the sickness with great vigor." Joubert gives examples of both men and women who could harness and direct this explosive power; and he reasons that women are more inclined to laughter than men because they "engender much good blood."[76]

The early modern attitude toward laughter and jesting is no longer in vogue. Freud's sour dicta continue to ramify in modern studies of joking. Some male commentators continue to segregate women from this comic zone or figure "woman" as either "the other" or "the castrator." As recently as 1970, a male critic opined that "women have no humor in themselves but are the cause of the extinction of it in others. . . . they are the undifferentiated mass from which the contradictions of the real and the ideal arose, and they are the unlaughing at which men laugh."[77] Partly because of the gynophobia that permeates such criticism and many forms of comedy, some feminists suspect that being funny is in itself masculinist and that a truly nonpatriarchal world would require a total revolution in female subjectivity, or even a new language. Classicist Amy Richlin maintains that "it is hard to see how an oppressed group . . . could transform anything without a whole new language. . . . While some discourses may be suited to transcending patriarchy, I doubt that humor is among them."[78] This claim is dangerously defeatist. First, it assumes that women possess no powers worth mentioning in the language they use every day. Second, by requiring women to form an elite that speaks only to itself, it asks them to do what no other subordinated group has ever done: to reject the social collaboration known as language along with its codes for survival.

Richlin's pessimism finds echoes in contemporary psychoanalytic criticism. Katherine Streip argues that women writers are "not narcis-

---

76 Joubert, *Treatise*, 62, 104, 128. On the ways his theory upsets hierarchies of gender and rank, see Paster, *Body Embarrassed*, 124.

77 Blyth, *Humor*, 15. This libel has a long ancestry, which includes Congreve's "But I must confess I have never made an Observation of what I apprehend to be true Humour in Women" (from Congreve's "Concerning Humor in Comedy," quoted in Barreca, *Last Laughs*, 3).

78 Richlin, *Garden of Priapus*, xxvi.

sistic enough" to be funny writers or successful satirists and that their attempts are usually full of *ressentiment* and "self-laceration."[79] Streip summons a closed world of internal psychic struggle from which women cannot escape. Such views present a cul de sac to anyone wishing to study early modern societies—or modern ones, for that matter. Anthropologists now realize that women's satire and mockery is widespread but insufficiently studied, partly because it has been dismissed as unimportant and partly because most observers have been men, who are excluded from many kinds of female conversation. Nonetheless, some field studies have documented satiric mockery by women in Polynesian and Kwakiutl tribes and among Western city office workers. Some Arab cultures have longstanding traditions of female satire, while ancient Ireland once boasted fearsome female satirists who awed rulers and rhymed rats to death.[80]

Some texts discussed in this book bear the names of male authors but circulated among women as well as men. Jest books are deeply unoriginal: their merry tales can often be traced to collections predating them by decades or even centuries. While some bear the name of a male author who claims that the contents are "all new, none heard before," no one makes good on his claim. It makes little sense, therefore, to base an interpretation of any given jest solely on the gender or the elite status of the "author" of a merry book or ballad.[81] It makes even less sense to

79 Streip, "Just a *Cérèbrale*," 117. For a far more convincing study, which perceives authorial satiric aggression as self-defense and a subversive act in novels by Austen, Gaskell, and Eliot, see Gillooly, *Smile of Discontent*.

80 See Apte, *Humour and Laughter*, 74–79; Randolph, "Female Satirists"; and Elliot, *Power of Satire*, 17. I want to thank the anonymous benefactor who left the Elliott book in my box at Columbia many years ago.

81 On the anonymity and longevity of jests and their frequent reincarnations in print, see Zall, *A Hundred Merry Tales*, 1–10. On the impact of classical and humanist *facetiae* on English jest, see Lipking, "Traditions." On the "omnipresent, though often ignored, orality of print" in the period, see Reay, *Popular Cultures in England*, 36–70. Garrett Sullivan and Linda Woodbridge see jest books and jests as the wholesale creation of a humanist elite, which eventually disowned them; the jokes trickled down through society and bear scant traces of oral tradition or non-elite contributions ("Popular culture in print," 273–78; also see Woodbridge's arguments in *Vagrancy*, 17–22). Their views beg the question of whether the great facetiae "authors," such as Poggio Bracciolini, were primarily collectors and embellishers of jokes they had heard; it fails to explain the similarities in jests told in separate continents many centuries apart (as folklorists have demonstrated) or the provenance of orally inflected mocking rhymes, jesting songs, Aesopian tales, comic proverbs, and riddles. The "hybridity of print, orality and literacy" in the period also militates against reading jests purely as written products of a scholarly elite (Reay, *Popular Cultures in Print*, 58). Most important, this analysis erases the crucial role of performance and audience in granting success to any jest and agency to the jester.

imagine that the performers or audiences of any jest are "all male." A truly vital feminist criticism must be inclusive, and it must consider women not only as authors and performers but as audiences. In the words of Kathleen McLuskie,

> It is not enough to reject all literature of the past as the product of "male" culture or "male" critical traditions. . . . It is clearly not enough simply to privilege works by women writers, many of which are far from feminist in consciousness or tendency. . . . The strengths of a feminist criticism lie in its rejection of pre-existing meaning created by assuming an audience is male, and the process of deconstruction that inevitably ensues.[82]

In sum, jests and comic proverbs, verses, ballads, and jigs were available to women at all social levels. All jests are cultural scripts that women could use as prompts for their own performances or that could spur their laughter when enacted by others. Any such script—female-authored, male-authored, pseudonymous, or anonymous—could be reauthored by the interpretive act of performance.[83] Whether they sang comic ballads, wrote mocking rhymes, read jests out loud, acted out a scandal in a jig, or repeated merry tales from memory, women could and did perform popular texts. And even the most misogynist jape, inflicted on the most unlettered girl, may have evoked a scornful mock.

Jests gave non-elite women dramatic cues and scripts, a range of positions from which to speak and act. Antimasculinist jests bait, shape, and sometimes best antifeminist jesting. Some jests signal means for the social control of male violence, while others mock the pernicious ideal of the patient wife. Some jests show women acting in concert as neighbors to shame transgressors. Jests do not always arouse laughter that seeks to uphold the status quo: the person whose ox is gored, who is silenced and huffs away with a flea in his ear, is often a figure of power and authority, such as a judge, a priest, or a father. Some jests are extremely cruel, condemning both men and women to utter humilia-

---

82 McLuskie, "Feminist Deconstruction," 39.

83 Elizabeth Reitz Mullenix argues that women often perform resistance by "rearticulating" a male-identified model ("Public Women/Public Acts," esp. 109, 114), and Jeanie Forte asserts that performance itself positions women as "speaking subject[s]" and places them "in dissonance with their representations" (quoted in ibid., 111–12). Valerie Wayne usefully calls for "reading strategies that resist reliance on an originary, gendered author" and argues that "anonymous and pseudonymous publication enabled alliances with and among women" ("Dearth of the Author," 222–23).

tion. Nevertheless, often the most aggressive, satiric, and shaming jests are the ones that promote social change.

Because jests and laughter are important dramatic elements in both everyday discourse and stage plays, attending to them can enrich the study of early modern drama. As judging spectators who could grant or withhold laughter, women wielded a small but palpable form of social power. Although they did not act on the professional stage, they were highly competent in using words, gestures, and songs to appeal for laughter and direct mockery at chosen targets. In the theater, they became part of a crowd that more closely resembled a vocal and self-aware jury than the silent and submissive audiences of today. Schooled in local processes of control, including the culture of jest and ridicule, women were likely to read the conflicts onstage through the lens of neighborhood, where they were called on to intervene and to tolerate intervention, to judge and be judged.

To track some of the links between jesting and judging, I look in the following chapters at social dramas in relation to theatrical ones, using the neighborhood-based *mentalité* of women spectators as the primary frame of analysis. How did conflicts touching on supposedly unshakable myths of gender—the intellectual superiority of men, the right of husbands to beat their wives, the evil misrule of the woman on top, the unassailable virtue of Patient Griselda—hold up under their gaze?

1 Near Neighbors, Women's Wars, and *Merry Wives*

In a jest from a Stuart commonplace book, a husband seizes his chance to have sex with a maidservant while his wife recovers from childbirth, surrounded by her gossips:

> A good Wife lay in; and her Husband could not hold, but whensoever the mayde came into the cellar to draw a Gossips cuppe, he must have a taste of Her; his wife had some Hint on it and presently turnes her away; Neighbours wondring at the suddainesse of it, enquire the cause, the wench reports it was only for drinking a draught of the Best; the neighbours intercede and mediate for her; hange her Queane, she lyes sayes the Good Wife, for I have turned the Barrell over and over and over, and Ile take my corporall oath, she has not left one Droppe in't.[1]

Consider the efficiency and extent of the social network implied here. The teller takes it for granted that the hearer knows a birth would bring neighbors into a house for the labor and the lying-in afterward, creating a festive and (to some annoyingly) female period of time.[2] Dur-

---

1 Le Strange, *Merry Passages*, 77–78. The manuscript was probably compiled between 1630 and 1655.
2 On gossips at childbed and churching, see Cressy, *Birth, Marriage and Death*, 84–87, 201–3. A husband complains about his wife's gossips in "The humor of a woman lying in childbed," in *Bachelors Banquet* (1603), an Englished version of *Les quinze joies de mariage*.

ing the month-long lying-in the wife was sexually off-limits to the husband, a practice that would have been familiar to the original hearers of the jest and one that provides a motive for the husband's lust.[3] In featuring furtive sex between female servant and master, the jest presents a well-worn comic scenario, which in real life harried and burdened families, parishes, and courts.

This brief fiction—crammed into one sentence like a crowded house—also assumes that the neighbors will quickly hear about a sudden firing, that the maid has allies among them who don't think drinking "a draught of the Best" is adequate cause, and that their intercession is ordinary and unremarkable. The jest casually parodies legal discourse, as the neighbors "enquire . . . intercede and mediate" on behalf of the servant.[4] But the jest suddenly reveals an alternative story. The wife's punning "corporall oath" temporarily silences the neighbors by exposing the limply depleted husband, who is given no chance to rebut. By giving her the last word, the jest applauds her rhetorical and deductive powers without faulting her for shrewish speech. Yet the history of this jest does not end here, in the space beyond the punchline. It survives in the present as part of a uniquely revealing commonplace book in which women are credited by name as the sources of many jests within its pages.[5]

The jest features an important motif in English comic culture: the undoing of the foolish, lecherous, or impotent husband and his exposure to the laughter of a group of women. When a male eavesdropper "reports" on secret female conversation about men in a jest fiction, the rhetoric of authenticity seems intended to arouse the prurient curiosity of the male reader.[6] In jest literature as a whole, however, such tales are outnumbered by stories showing women laughing together with no male spy on hand. When real women's participation in jesting culture is

---

3 Thomas, *Religion*, 42.
4 Female servants were intimately involved in neighborhood dynamics, with networks of alliances in nearby households. See Jones, "Maidservants."
5 Le Strange lists "Brother Spring" as his source for the "empty barrell" joke, but attributes about 15 percent of his 611 jests to female relatives, with his mother and aunts providing the greatest number (see index, *Merry Passages*).
6 In William Goddard's *A satyricall dialogue* (1616), "that truly woman-hater Diogynes" cross-dresses as a wife to spy on a whorish coven of gossips and shrews. In the preface to Samuel Rowlands's *Tis Merry When Gossips Meet* (1607) a bookseller promises a customer the double erotic charge of spying on the group of women in the book and then pocketing the book to "finger them in his breeches" at leisure. I am grateful to Susan O'Malley for calling my attention to this passage.

taken into account, it is difficult to dismiss all such stories as products of "the phantasmatic [male] fear of being excluded" or the misogynist stereotype that women, when alone, always gossip about men.[7] It is more likely that early modern women did sometimes satirize men, a common enough practice in many cultures today.[8] Records of defamation cases furnish evidence that women often talked to each other about men's flaws: insults uttered first in a female group might move from there to a man's hearing, while taunts against husbands who fathered bastards on their maidservants might circulate among female neighbors and result in men's defamation cases against their detractors.[9]

The "empty husband" jest is peculiarly mobile, traveling from household accusation to neighborhood inquiry and back, blurring the usual distinction between private and public. Rather than providing a keyhole glimpse into a private domestic drama, it portrays a community's response to a set of events within its jurisdiction. While boozy gossips' gatherings were satirized in texts long and short ("gossips and frogs, they drink and talk"), this tale has other aims in mind.[10] It is unquestioned that neighbors will form the first audience and jury for the competing narratives. As traveler Philip Julius reported in 1602, "In England every citizen is bound by oath to keep a sharp eye at his neighbor's house, as to whether the married people live in harmony."[11] Unlike the anonymous urban block or suburban subdivision of today, the neighborhood was newsroom, living room, court, theater and market, the

---

7 Linda Woodbridge finds it impossible to determine whether or not real women criticized and compared men (*Women and the English Renaissance*, 236–37), while Domna Stanton sees the genre as a byproduct of male paranoia: "the devaluation of female discourse, and the androcentric notion that women only talk about and compete for men, recuperate and assuage the phantasmatic fear of being excluded, or becoming targets of criticism by the second sex, and thus reversing roles in the sexgender system" ("Recuperating Women," 248).

8 All-female groups tend to discuss, among other things, "men's physical appearance, their social behavior, their idiosyncrasies, their sexuality, their status-seeking activities, and their religious rites. These characteristics are generally presented in an exaggerated and mocking fashion" (Apte, *Humor*, 76).

9 See Mendelson and Crawford, *Women in Early Modern England*, 253; and Capp, "Double Standard," 71. I would like to thank Bernard Capp for discussing his article with me.

10 Tilley, *Dictionary*, G381. Examples of satires on gossips include *The Gospelles of Dystaves* (c. 1510); Skelton's *The Tunnynge of Elynour Rummynge* (c. 1517); *Bachelor's Banquet* (1603); Rowlands's *Tis Merry* (1602, 1607, 1609) and *A Whole Crew of Kind Gossips* (1609); *Westward for Smelts* (1620); and *Gossips Greeting* (1620).

11 Philip Julius, quoted in Orlin, *Private Matters*, 7.

prime arena for transactions between the individual and the state and between neighbor and neighbor.

Fittingly enough, the jest implies a fairly transparent domestic space—a permeable household that is not a walled terminus but a node in a network of people and activities, economic and sexual. As Lena Orlin observes, "The basic distinction available for early moderns was not that of the public and the individual space but that of the public and the shared."[12] The close living quarters of masters, mistresses, servants, and children, with rooms full of shared beds and pallets, and the everyday reality of neighbors, relatives, and customers passing in and out, meant that little could be done in complete secret. (A jest points up a common result of this proximity: "Says a Lady to her maid, What! You are with Child? Yes, a little, forsooth: And who got it? My master, forsooth. Where? In the truckle bed forsooth: why did you not call out then, you whore? Why says she, would you have done so?"[13]) Among all sorts there were fewer deeds done alone and less that was unmentionable; more people in each other's sight and hearing at all times; and fuller rooms and greater access to all interior spaces, resulting in a higher degree of social surveillance, intercession, and mediation. Keeping neighbors out by installing locks and bars could actually draw suspicion, prompting people to ask, "What are they hiding?"[14]

Because so much jesting took place in the course of everyday sociability and because jesting links the drama of neighborhood with theater itself, this book attends closely to neighborhood reception and judgment. Using neighborhood as a hermeneutic frame also seems fittingly inclusive. Whether city dwellers or country folk, most Englishwomen and men lived within settlements rather than in isolated houses and thus had neighbors: people who lived near enough to mind each other's business, were included in local codes of collective judgment, and shared responsibility for enforcing neighborly behavior.[15] Some neigh-

12 Ibid., 185. My use of the term *transparency* is based on Orlin's discussion of a Montacute House frieze showing a skimmington (5–6).

13 Hickes, *Oxford Jests,* 156.

14 Archer, *Pursuit of Stability,* esp. 53–99; Gowing, *Domestic Dangers,* 71.

15 Boulton, *Neighbourhood,* 145. My decision to focus on the everyday social nexus rather than margins has kept this book to a manageable length, but regrettably it has excluded the vast popular culture of witchcraft and its jesting texts. An excellent recent study on this topic is Kirilka Stavreva, "Fighting Words: Witchspeak in Late Elizabethan Docu-Fiction."

bors might be related through blood or marriage, but most were not; and many people became bound more closely to neighbors than to kinfolk living elsewhere. (*A good neighbour is my nearest relation* went one proverb.)[16] Even in the gigantic city of London, which had a highly transient population, neighborhoods were extremely important sources of support and identity for residents, new or old.[17] Keith Wrightson goes so far as to argue that one's status as a neighbor was probably the preeminent index of one's standing in a community in the sixteenth and seventeenth centuries.[18] Achieving the status of householder was a key criterion of social standing in a neighborhood, and not all householders were male. In London, between 15 and 20 percent of all households were headed by unmarried women, most of them widows. Almost one out of five city households, therefore, were under the control of women who acted without direct male supervision in matters concerning themselves and the neighborhood.[19]

The early modern concept of *neighborhood* marked out a lived geography rather than a legally determined one; from birth to death, neighbors shaped and weighed one's identity, creating narratives that determined one's reputation. Obeying "the rule of neighborhood" meant showing one's readiness to render counsel, to contribute to local feasting, to help in times of sickness, and "to accept the neighbors as a reference group in matters of behavior and to promote harmonious relations among them."[20] Neighbors were expected to take an active interest in each other's households; and "if families were not orderly, neighbours were to impose order."[21]

16 Wrightson, *English Society*, 54–55.

17 Although migration meant that most Londoners did not live where they were born, most worked, raised families, and died within a very limited geographical area. Some historians, following the lead of Stone and Thomas, believe that anomie reigned in London, where residents had much less neighborhood involvement and face-to-face contact than in villages, partly because of high migration and servant mobility. Opposing this view, Boulton persuasively argues that turnover did not affect neighborhood stability any more than in small villages (*Neighbourhood*, 206–27, 246–47); and Archer maintains that city neighborhoods still provided a far greater sense of identity than did companies, wards, or parishes (*Pursuit*, 74–80).

18 Wrightson, *English Society*, 55.

19 Boulton, *Neighbourhood*, 127–32. Women may have been especially attuned to the theaters of street and stage in London's Southwark, where most of the theaters were found and where 16 percent of the households were headed by women. Statistic from Diana Henderson, quoted in Callaghan, *Feminist Companion*, 50.

20 Wrightson, *English Society*, 55.

21 Amussen, *Ordered Society*, 50.

Juries of the Threshold

For a woman, being a good neighbor meant having a stake in the local dramas and gendered transactions that made up every day. A thumbnail sketch of a good neighbor appears in *Westward for Smelts* (1620):

> She'd spend her quart
> With all her heart . . .
> Her time she'd passe
> In working good:
> If neighbours stood
> In needed of ought
> She sold or bought,
> They should it have,
> If they did crave.[22]

While women helped out neighbors of both sexes, women were especially dependent on the good will of other women. Female friends asked each other for loans and for counsel about finances, women helped each other choose among suitors, and a prospective bride's friends were acknowledged as parties who could broker or suspend an engagement.[23] While her word carried less weight than a man's in court, she could be called on to bear witness about neighbors or to participate in the legal process of compurgation, in which neighbors swore to an accused's good repute so that he or she could avoid prosecution or penalties; the accused had to have compurgators of the same gender and social standing.

Some neighborhood duties were far less benign. A woman might serve on a "jury of matrons" charged with searching women's bodies for marks of pregnancy, witchcraft, or illicit sexual activity.[24] Women as well as men could be instrumental in having offenders whipped or publicly shamed for adultery or for fathering a bastard; they could also press

---

22 "The Fishwife of Twiknam," in *Westward for Smelts*, sigs. D2r-v.

23 On loans, see Boulton, *Neighbourhood*, 87–88, 242. Women made bequests to neighbors and their children more often than did men, who usually limited bequests to wives, children, and other kin (242). Women's interlocking obligations came under increasing pressure in the period, with refusals figuring large in laments for the decline of hospitality and neighborhood and playing a role in witchcraft accusations. See Thomas, *Religion*, 662–64. On engagements, see Amussen, *Ordered Society*, 108.

24 Ingram, *Church Courts*, 51, Amussen, *Ordered Society*, 99. On juries of matrons, see Oldham, "On Pleading the Belly," Sharpe, "Women, Witchcraft," and Houlbrooke, "Women's Social Life," esp. 174–75.

suits and seek fines for defamation. Neighbors punished young men as well as maids, and husbands as well as wives using such measures.[25] If they chose, male and female neighbors could write and broadcast mocking rhymes and songs to harass an offender. These "might be just as damaging to victims as any physical assault, indeed perhaps much more so," because "the loss of reputation among their immediate neighbors still mattered greatly to most."[26]

Gossip was basic to this system of control—a form of oral culture that paradoxically gave women a measure of power as arbiters of behavior. One merry book describes a fabulous land in which no one stands in danger of scandal because men and women keep their mouths shut about the flaws of their spouses and neighbors:

> If a woman were married to a foole,
> let him walke to wind yarne, or picke nuts.
>
> If a man had a whore to his wife,
> to think on his own case, and so to conceale his sorrowe,
> or to bee rid of his mischiefe.
>
> If a woman be married to a Eunuche,
> to do something to save his shame from knowledge.[27]

Closely watched streets formed the breeding ground for much slander litigation. Thresholds were favorite locales for the trading of insults, especially "whore" and "cuckold," and in these places women kept a sharp eye out for other kinds of trangressions.[28] To clear their names or to charge others with slander, women often took their grievances to

25 Examples from court records include a brewer who was whipped along with his lover after his wife found them in bed and an angry wife who told her neighbors about her husband's whoring, leading to his prosecution in Bridewell. See Capp, "Double Standard Revisited," 73.

26 Fox, "Ballads, Libels," 77.

27 *Choice, Chance, and Change* (1606), sig. D1. With the two-part structure of its sentences, the text strongly resembles the courtly game of "news," in which gentlemen and women posed and answered satiric sententiae on set topics. Lady Frances Southwell, chief lady-in-waiting to Queen Anne, played it often, using the game as a model for "Certain Edicts from a Parliament in Eutopia," included in a 1615 edition of Overbury's *The Wife*. See the entry for Southwell in Blain et al., *Feminist Companion*, 1010.

28 Archer, *Pursuit*, 76. For an intriguing argument about the literary evidence of women appearing at windows and doorways, see Orlin, "Women on the Threshold."

local magistrates. Nowhere were they more quick to go to court than in
London. The number of women plaintiffs grew fivefold in the city between 1572 and 1640, making the principal ecclesiastical jurisdiction
resemble what Gowing calls a "woman's court."[29] Jest books make
sport of this common practice:

> One whose name was Gun called a woman w[hore]. She, being moved
> at it, had him before a justice of the peace about it. The justice reprov'd
> him for it, and deeply charged him not to call her so againe. As they
> were going home, the woman told him, Master Gun, you heard what
> the justice saide; I hope, being so deeply charg'd, you will henceforth
> give a better report.[30]

Like a badly loaded gun, a bad report was potentially explosive. Under
the strictures of the double standard it was vital for women to maintain
a "good report," so it is not surprising that women complained most
often about sexual insults while men complained about being called
knaves, blasphemers, or drunkards.[31] Men also sued to protect their
own sexual reputations, sometimes negotiating "composition" (often
cash settlements) with women who were threatening court action.[32]
Nonetheless, one word and one gender dominated the litigation: most
defamation cases were fought between women over the word
"whore."[33] The reasons are complex, but one inference is especially rel-
evant to the culture of jest. Women's opinions mattered to other women
because they were the chief judges of the female performances that

29 See Gowing, "Language," 28, and *Domestic Dangers*, ch. 2, esp. 33–34, 60. On
the litigiousness of the period see Sharpe, "People and the Law."

30 Chamberlain, *Conceits, Clinches, Flashes, and Whimzies* (1639), in Hazlitt,
Shakespeare Jest-Books, 3:46, jest 185. Another jest shows the detachability of the
epithet: "Two young fellows falling out, began to grow into very violent and bitter
tarmes: at length said the one to the other, well, for thy Mother, I know her to bee as
honest a woman, as any is in England, but for thine own part, thou art no better than
the sonne of a Whore" (*New Booke of Mistakes*, 93). Perhaps this "young fellow" did
not want to be taken to court by the mother in question.

31 See Thomas, "Double Standard"; and Amussen, *Ordered Society*, 101–3.

32 Capp, "Double Standard Revisited," 70–72. He takes issue with Gowing's assertion that men could not be defamed for sexual behavior (*Domestic Dangers*, 62),
showing that adulterous husbands, especially those who fathered a child on a servant, were subjected to neighbors' "opprobrium," including taunts of "whoremas-
ter," leading some men to sue to restore their sexual reputations.

33 From the table showing London cases from 1570 to 1640 in Gowing, *Domestic
Dangers*, 60.

made up "honesty," keenly observing each other's words and deeds.[34] Male judges ruled on the formal claim, but women were the local arbiters of competing narratives about chaste and unchaste behavior; they could also be witnesses for and against a woman if she were defamed. For a woman, then, maintaining an honorable reputation depended heavily on her theatrical and rhetorical skills—being able to act and speak so as to convince others of her honesty—but even more on her social skills in forming alliances with friends who would give her a good report on the street and swear to it in court. A woman who could tell a tale well and had a pleasing wit was probably more likely to attract allies than one with poor rhetorical skills.

Placing jesting on the stages of the neighborhood offers the sine qua non of drama: conflict. Early comedies often displayed the workings of participatory social drama—what a modern lawyer might call officious intermeddling. In Henry Porter's *The Two Angrie Women of Abingdon* (1599) Mistress Barnes explodes in jealous fury at Mistress Goursey, suspecting her of dallying with her husband. Master Barnes tries to shut up his wife before she can bewhore her neighbor in front of their children and servants: "What will the neighbring countrie vulgar say, / When as they heare that you fell out at dinner?" At his wit's end, he invokes a "law" that does not issue from Bible, sermon, or conduct book: "Me thought the rules of love and neighbourhood, / Did not direct your thoughts."[35]

While this warning has no immediate effect—Mistress Barnes threatens to scratch out Mistress Goursey's eyes—the play presents scene after scene of neighbors and kin attempting to influence the peace process to their benefit; and as a result, the two women eventually lay down their cudgels.

The idea of neighborly peacemaking was more than a comic convention. Neighbors of both genders were often called in to resolve a crisis before it escalated into a lawsuit or to cope with conflicts that the courts could not resolve.[36] Female neighbors could serve as arbiters in

---

34 Ibid., 123.

35 Porter, *Two Angrie women of Abington*, ll. 99–100, 512–13.

36 See Ingram, "Ridings," 33–34; Amussen, *Ordered Society*, 174–75; and Archer, *Pursuit*, 80. This familiarity undergirds the many legal parodies and mock courts of the period, some run by men (*Jacke of Dover His Quest of Inquirie*) and some by women (*A Quest of Enquirie, for women to know*, discussed in chapter 5).

disputes over slander, for example. In a late sixteenth-century case, one
Jane Mapples manages to reconcile two angry women from Snaith. The
warring neighbors, Katherine Hodgekinson and Emott Belton, meet
with a curate and "dyvers others" in an alehouse, where

> One of the company, Jane Mapples, "being then and there present said
> unto the said Katherine and Emott I would to God yow two were
> frend[es], for this is not the best meanes neighbours one to sue an
> other." The two women agreed to drop their legal battle, and the hostil-
> ities were ended after Hodgekinson drank a toast to Belton, telling her
> "that she loved no suites nor troubles and if her frend[es] were so con-
> tented . . . she could find in her harte that all were lovers and
> frend[es]."[37]

Not everyone shared in or benefited from community life, of course.
Peter Laslett's view that close-knit villages gave most people a vital
sense of belonging has been largely dismantled by scholars who documented the lives of vagrants and people in service far from families.[38]
Other historians have attacked the narrowness and prying endemic to
small communities. Laurence Stone called the early modern neighborhood full of "back-biting, malicious slander . . . and petty spying,"
while Keith Thomas excoriated "the tyranny of local opinion," calling
village life "harshly intolerant" and "hostile to privacy and eccentric-
ity, and relying not on the sanction of reason but of ridicule."[39]

A few historians manage to find *some* virtues in neighborhood. Keith
Wrightson argues that even in London, where there was a high degree of
social mixing within streets and buildings, "good neighborhood" was a
unique and extremely important leveler in a harshly vertical world
ruled by paternalism and deference:

> [F]inally and crucially, it was essentially a horizontal relationship, one
> which implied a mutuality between partners to the relationship, irre-

---

37 Sharpe, "Such Disagreement," 175–76.
38 Laslett, *World We Have Lost*, 21.
39 Stone, *Family*, 105–14, quotation on 98. On "tyranny," see Thomas, *Religion*,
628–29; for "intolerant," see Thomas, "Place of Laughter," 77. For studies taking
issue with Stone, Houlbrooke, and others for biases tending to value the western,
white, heterosexual, nuclear family, see Armstrong and Tennenhouse, *Imaginary Puritan*, 75, 234–35, nn. 15, 19, 23.

spective of distinctions of wealth or social standing. The reciprocity of neighborliness was a reciprocity in equal obligations, the exchange of comparable services between *effective*, if not actual equals.[40]

A neighbor's gender, as well as age, marital status, livelihood, and length of residence, could greatly modify this leveling effect. Nonetheless, as Wrightson points out, women of various ranks were "powerful actors" in the "moral community" composed of neighbors.[41] They acted partly through exchanging labor and goods; but in a deeper sense they acted powerfully by taking responsibility for the lives of their neighbors, as Jane Mapples did when she helped resolve the dispute between Katherine Hodgekinson and Emott Belton. Many forms of jesting culture, including drama, concern themselves with representing the concepts of neighborhood that bound social relationships and defined identity.

"Ye shall see women's war!"

Jesting women in drama are often keenly aware that being the object of any sexual overture places them on trial before a jury of neighbors and kin. This judging role was mirrored in the theater audience, where, Alison Findlay argues, playgoers often acted as a "censoring community."[42] In Nicholas Udall's *Ralph Roister Doister* (ca. 1557), Dame Custance is publicly "tried" before her betrothed Gawyn Goodluck and his servant on the charge of encouraging Ralph's suit. She produces evidence and witnesses to win her case. Part of her exculpatory evidence is that she has recruited her servants and a neighbor to wage a burlesque battle against Ralph and his crony Matthew Merrygreek, using brooms and shovels to rout them from her yard. Custance musters her allies with the stirring cry: "ye shall see women's war!"[43]

Alice Ford and Margaret Page wage an undercover women's war in *The Merry Wives of Windsor*. Set in motion by the wives' need to combat slander, sexual assault, and jealousy, *Merry Wives* seems designed

40 Wrightson, *English Society*, 51.
41 Wrightson, "Politics of the Parish," 20–21.
42 Findlay, *Feminist Perspective*, 133.
43 Udall, *Ralph Roister Doister*, 4.6.35.

to appeal to female audiences, whether or not it was brought into being by the desires of a powerful female spectator who wanted to see Falstaff in love. The play goes out of its way to demonstrate the value of good alliances and performance skills for women who were faced with sexual aggressors and unwanted seducers, pests who harassed married women almost as often as they did maids and widows. To an unusual degree *Merry Wives* trades on the paradox that a supreme commodity, female chastity, is not empirically demonstrable and that truth is generally a consensual affair, a matter of narrative credibility and rhetorical prowess. To cope in the court of neighborhood, women had to possess the vital ability to construct credible narratives and act on them.[44]

From first to last, the play draws on forms of jesting clearly marked with female participation and laughter: the merry tale and ballad mocking the obnoxious suitor; the novella, farce, and jig against the absurdly jealous husband; and the festive rituals of Hocktide and Horn Fair. The play boisterously invites spectators to ridicule Falstaff and Ford, suggesting that it sought laughter from all, but especially from women. Female spectators had ample reason to side with the wives because they themselves were constantly examined for unchaste behavior by kin and neighbors, bearing the burden of the double standard and risking public shame for even small deviations. *Merry Wives* may have been less appealing to certain male spectators, warning them to reform lest they bewray their credit with their neighbors, as Falstaff and Master Ford do so decisively.

Windsor is not a place that should make wives especially merry. The town is crawling with fortune-hunting suitors, easily bribed servants, an impotent justice of the peace who can't even get a poacher punished, a parson whose words of peacemaking are ignored, and a pack of parasites moving in to rob and seduce. Rosemary Kegl demonstrates that the play's opening scene mocks the "elaborate legal machinery" of the Elizabethans as "ludicrously ineffective," in part because it encumbered officials, such as justices of the peace, with competing state and local allegiances.[45] Justice Shallow's mounting confusion, anger, and insults throw the conflict with Falstaff into the jurisdiction of the church, which also fails to contain it. Although Parson Evans appoints himself,

---

44 Gowing brilliantly examines "narratives of litigation" and the skills women showed in constructing them (*Domestic Dangers*, ch. 7, esp. 235–39).
45 Kegl, "Adoption," 261, 267.

Page, and the Host of the Garter "umpires" (1.1.137), who in actual arbitrations could enforce binding settlements, the regime of control is taken over by the women, who manage to refute a different set of attacks by Falstaff, Nym, Pistol, and Ford.[46]

The result is no foregone conclusion. By sending the two letters and making his actions known, Falstaff has set out to "try" the recipients, both in the sexual sense and in the sense of trying them before the jury of the neighborhood. With letters that are open secrets from the start, he has in effect published a libel against the fame of the two women, whose reputations are put to the test. The trial of two or more wives is a common motif in folktale and jest.[47] Pairs of brothers test and compare their wives' chastity, with boomerang results (*Riche His Farewell to Military Profession*); two neighbors pose as ghosts to scare confessions out of their wives (Brathwait's *Ar't Asleep Husband?*); two friends plot to cuckold each other (Marston's *The Insatiate Countess*); and three dinner guests bet on whose wife will come when called (*The Taming of the Shrew*). Indeed, this is the sort of game that springs into motion in *Merry Wives*: which of the accused wives will show herself most honest before the tribunal of neighbors and husbands?[48]

Although the Windsor wives are longtime neighbors and devoted gossips, the play quickly builds a contrast between them. The differences would have been noted and weighed by audiences, but especially by the women in those audiences because "sexual honor was overwhelmingly a female concern, and as much as women were the targets of the regulation of honesty, they made themselves the agents of its definition."[49] Mistress Page searches her conscience to see if she has given Falstaff any cause. She acquits herself, saying that when she met him she was "frugal of [her] mirth" (2.1.26–28). More important, she is a mother of two and is well treated by her husband, an upstanding citizen and the host of dinners and hunting parties. Even Mistress Quickly, a paid conduit of gossip and an arbiter of the common fame, has only good things to say about her: "Never a wife in Windsor leads a better life than she

46 On arbitrations, see Campbell, *English Yeoman*, 384–85.
47 For examples, see Brunvand, *Taming of the Shrew*, 104–6.
48 This differs slightly from saying that the wives plot to defend their honesty (as Kegl says in "Adoption," 257) because I argue that the two are being deliberately contrasted for audiences who were trained to weigh women's behavior back home in the courts of the neighborhood.
49 Gowing, "Language," 30.

does. . . . truly she deserves it, for if there be a kind woman in Windsor, she is one" (2.2.115–21).

In contrast, Mistress Ford is childless and describes herself as less happy because her husband is jealous. Ford's lack of offspring probably aggravates his peevishness; a childless husband was often the target of jokes about his impotence and probable horns.[50] Mistress Ford grants Falstaff a kiss of welcome in the first scene (1.1.193) and in her next scene enters bawdily joking she could be "knighted" for doing "a trifling" thing, as if she were weighing the offer, along with Falstaff, in her mind (2.1.48–49). Mistress Quickly grants her only the dubious praise that she attracts "coach after coach, letter after letter, gift after gift" when the court is at Windsor (2.2.65). In addition, Mistress Ford conducts herself fairly shrewishly, as was expected of the barren wife of a jealous man. Mistress Page does not mislead her husband in any vital way or oppose him verbally, while Mistress Ford reproaches hers in front of the search party just after crowing, "I know not what pleases me better, that my husband is deceived, or Sir John" (3.3.178–79).

In short, Alice Ford is less honest in her manner than Margaret Page, who is her friend and her first line of defense. Considering her far more solid social position, Mistress Page seems to be acting in a way similar to those women who defended friends and neighbors accused of sexual misconduct. Chastity being unrepresentable, nothing the wives possess or do can function as proof that they did not dally with Falstaff. On the minus side of the ledger, they both have incriminating letters, which they hide from their husbands most suspiciously. Alice Ford almost gets caught with a man hidden in her house, considered proof enough in many presentments for adultery—a very serious charge brought primarily against women and punished by whipping, carting, or standing in a sheet while neighbors jeer. The way they choose to endanger their reputations raises questions about the prevailing opinion that the play uncomplicatedly celebrates the wives' "campaign to defend and rehabilitate the concept of innocent female mirth."[51] The wives' shared pleasure subsumes, or substitutes for, the pleasure of actual adultery, which fills the comic novellas closest to the play. But the wives' delight

---

50 Gossips laugh at a childless husband because he can read, write, and add, "but he cannot multiply" (*Banquet of Jests* (1639), jest 175).
51 Parten, "Falstaff's Horns," 189.

arises from shared female deceit and secrecy and thus cannot have been considered fully innocent to audiences raised on polemics and merry tales about "the deceyte of women."[52]

Female theatricality was assumed to be the sign and seal of that propensity for deceit. *Merry Wives* offers the spectacle of women acting but does not fully condone it, sidestepping the issue with an equivocation. In midplay the two friends exult in the "double excellency" of their plots to thwart Falstaff and Ford (3.3.176–77). Doubling their pleasure requires the duplicity of acting, a fact not banished by the familiar words of Mistress Page:

> We'll leave a proof, by that which we shall do,
> Wives can be merry, and yet honest too.
> We do not act that often jest and laugh,
> Tis old, but true, "still swine eats all the draff." (4.2.104–7)

While usually taken at face value, these lines are rife with paradox, especially in that slippery word "act." Mistress Page uses the word in both its sexual and theatrical meanings at crucial points in the play, which focuses on the uses of performance for women at risk. Without taking action their neighbors would call dishonest, the wives can leave no proof that they have not acted honestly. Without playacting, there would certainly be less female mirth; indeed, the wives revel in becoming jester-players adept at improvisation. Mistress Page stresses the connection in a line that seems calculated to strike horror into an antitheatricalist's heart: "If I do not act it, hiss me" (3.3.38). Despite their disavowal, then, the wives do act, using the erotic duplicity of theater to perform their honesty.

Turning Lechers into Basket Cases

As the chief unwanted suitor of *Merry Wives*, Falstaff furnishes a broad target for women's jests drawn from the rich literature of comic wooing. The "scornful maid" topos extends from Petrarchan lyric, to bawdy wooing ballads, to jest books and plays. From Anne Page's dismissal of Doctor Caius ("I had rather be set quick i' th' earth, / and

52 To brush up on the topic, early modern readers could consult Abraham Vele's exhaustive *Deceyte of women*, (1563).

bowled to death with turnips" 3.4.86–87) to the wives' hilarity over Falstaff's cloned letters, the women of Windsor act as keen-eyed judges of
men's romantic performances. Training in such critical skills came
early in life, and the need for them often lasted for years. Early modern
women married late, and many remarried after a spouse's death; in both
cases they often endured years of courtship. Wooers were expected to
show dogged persistence, and women were expected to "scorn, jeer and
generally discourage the advances of a suitor."[53] They could certainly
find ammunition in jests and ballads, where anti-suitor mocks arise in
all sorts of sexual encounters—from romantic to rapine—between
predatory men and unwilling women, young or old, rich or poor, maid,
wife or widow. Lovesick serenades, for example, always end badly: "A
Gentleman made musick at his Mistress windowe, and sing her a Song
which began this: My secret passions, &c. An other gentlewoman being
then in place, and hearing him begin so, said, Belike your servant is
sicke of the pyles." Another suitor who can play the balidore well but
sings poorly performs under a lady's window. He asks, "how she lik'd
his musicke? She answered, You have played very well, and you have
sung too."[54]

The Windsor wives are adept at detecting amatory pretension. Falstaff initiates one rendezvous with an apostrophe filched from *As-
trophil and Stella*: "Have I caught thee, my heavenly jewel?" (3.3.43)
and continues firing away with Sidneyan paradoxes, to which Mistress
Ford replies with marvelous equivocation: "Well, heaven knows how I
love you, and you shall one day find it" (3.3.80–81). Sidney's verse was
frequently mined by such poseurs. In one jest a suitor tries to impress a
gentlewomen with compliments couched in "pure Philip Sidney,"
which he passes off as the fruits of his own wit. To his ill luck,

> she was so well verst in the Author, as tacitely she traced him to the
> bottom of a leaf, where (his Memorie failing) he brake off abruptly; nay
> I beseech you Sir, (sayd she) proceede, and turne over the leafe, for me
> thinks the best part is still Behinde, which unexpected discovery, si-
> lenc't him for ever after.[55]

Falstaff doesn't take a hint so easily, and his shaming is more physical
and more protracted. His sojourn in the buck basket, changing him

53 Crawford and Mendelson, *Women in Early Modern England*, 117.
54 Copley, *Wits, Fits and Fancies*, 73, 74.
55 Le Strange, *Merry Passages*, item 484.

from a brash, mobile, and erect aristocrat to an infantilized and smelly bundle of household stuff, draws on a centuries-long topos of anti-suitor jest featuring lotharios in baskets. These have a common source in medieval tales about "Virgil the necromancer," whom popular legend transformed into a great magician and trickster. Besotted with a rich man's daughter who is closely watched, Virgil woos her ardently, despite his gray hairs. The maid agrees to smuggle him into her chamber. Never intending to make good, she tells him to get in a basket tied to a rope so he can be hauled up through her window for a night of love. She leaves him hanging halfway up. Dawn's light turns the great man into a laughingstock. When January woos May, January is always fair game, even if he is a mighty magician. In an engraving by Lucas van Leyden, Virgil's object of desire is nowhere to be seen; and a mother stands at the side pointing out the moral to her son, while the great man looks to heaven, shamefaced (see fig. 2). The image is a woman's warning to men about masculine lust and vanity as much as a male warning against women's wiles. "Virgil in a basket" was incorporated into vignettes about "the powers of women" along with the famous tales of Phyllis riding Aristotle and Omphale making Hercules spin, which were reproduced for centuries in woodcuts, jokes, ballads, sculptures, and paintings. Frustrated lovers end up dangling in baskets well into modern times. One eighteenth-century jest book about Margery and Simple Simon recounts how she gets mastery over him on their wedding night by "smoking" him over the fire in a basket.[56]

For the butt of laughter, being the center of attention could feel very much like being hoisted up for all to point at. The target of a jest, the laughingstock in a comedy, and the object of public punishment on a scaffold all suffer from scathing laughter. M. Lindsay Kaplan has demonstrated that the theater was often perceived as a place where evildoers, including defamers, could be publicly humiliated. Being represented onstage, like being balladed, could be a form of slanderous assault: "Theatrical impersonation is also understood as a form of defamation, a function which contemporary plays themselves acknowledge."[57] Falstaff repeatedly calls attention to the minute particulars of his own dousings and drubbings, licensing the play's audiences to revel loudly in his defamation. The greatest indignity occurs when Falstaff, disguised as Mother Prat, plays the witch woman who often bore the

56 Spargo, *Virgil the Necromancer,* 136–97.
57 Kaplan, *Culture of Slander,* 30.

Fig. 2. Lucas van Leyden, *The Poet Virgil Suspended in a Basket* (1512). Reproduced by permission of the National Gallery of Art, Washington, D.C.

brunt of such harassment in early modern neighborhoods. Pretending to be such a woman, he suffers on the stage that defames. "Women" played by boys control these highly ironic stagings, inviting non-elite onlookers to jeer and laugh at their social superior—a ludicrous, greedy, predatory knight played by a socially marginal actor. By exposing his lechery and cowardice to the delighted mockery of their neighbors, two gossips manage to overwrite the scene of their defamation with the spectacle of his shame.

Physical "gests" such as the dousing of Falstaff may have had strong appeal, but for most women the arts of the tongue were more important in daily life. Antifeminist saws derided women's cleverness at explaining away improprieties (*a woman's answer is never to seek*) but no matter how exasperating to men, this quick-wittedness could also be considered a survival skill in a world that constantly called women to account for their honesty. For women, some anti-suitor stories may have served a didactic function; this would not seem a novel concept to early moderns, who heard jests in sermons and read them in conduct books and polemics. Considering the importance of women's sexual reputations and how frequently men accosted women, the mildest joke in which a woman parries a pass may point out the simple lesson, still taught to women today, that safety lies in groups. Protecting one's name also meant being able to spurn a compromising remark with a sharp answer in the hearing of others. In one jest that illustrates this situation, a married woman rides on horseback down the street among her gossips. A stranger, thinking she is alone, leers at her new-shod foot and tries out a jape: you have a very fine foot. Does it have a twin? Were they both born at one time? "No, indeed sir," she shoots back archly, "there hath beene a man borne betwixt them." She says this so her friends can hear: "Wherewith her neighbours that rode by her, falling into a laughing, made him find that she was a married wife." She is on safe ground and knows her audience. As for her would-be admirer, he was "much troubled by her answere, and with lack of wit to reply, galloped away with a flea in his eare."[58]

A sexual aggressor may press money on a woman or threaten rape; in such scenarios jesting women often apply the ancient justice of "the biter bitten." In Marguerite de Navarre's *Heptaméron*, for example, a poor ferrywoman outwits two friars who try to rape her by telling them

58 *Pasquils Jests*, in Hazlitt, *Shakespeare Jest-Books*, 3:22–23.

that they will have a better time by landing on an island, where they
may lie down. She manages to slip away as they clamber off ("she was as
sensible and shrewd as they were vicious and stupid") and mocks them
as she rows away: "You can wait till God sends an angel to console you,
Messieurs! . . . You're not going to get anything out of me today!" She
fetches the law, her husband, and her neighbors, who seize, bind, spat-
ter, and beat the friars.[59]

Horn Mad and Dangerous: Handle with Care

Real wives who were propositioned or attacked usually told their
husbands and friends because quickly resorting to kin and neighbors
could serve as a woman's primary defense against the slanders of a rejected pursuer.[60] The Windsor wives' decision to keep Falstaff's overtures hidden from their husbands would have been unusual in both
common practice and the narratives of the jesting literature. Tales
about wives' liaisons with desired lovers typically show women collud-
ing in secret to achieve their ends. But women who reject advances frequently go straight to their husbands and gossips to report any overture,
recruiting mixed-gender groups of neighbors and kin to play "merry
tricks" to confound them. The accosted wife in the famous *Attowell's
Jig* tells her husband and the seducer's wife, who is a near neighbor, and
enlists them both in a bed trick: the seducer ends up sleeping with his
own wife.[61] A bloodier revenge occurs in *Jacke of Dover his Quest of Inquirie* (1604), a tale in which a doctor tries to seduce a mealman's wife.
After the wife tells her husband, they recruit their neighbors to assist in
a plot in which the husband pretends to be mad when the doctor arrives. He manages to trick and tie down the doctor, whom his neighbors
beat and harry. Finally, a surgeon "cuts both his stones."[62]

A motive for secrecy surfaces in the Windsor wives' hurried sum-
maries of their husbands' contrasting attitudes:

> *Mrs. Ford:* I will consent to any villainy against him that may not sully
> the chariness of our honesty. O, that my husband saw this letter! It
> would give him eternal food for his jealousy!

59 Marguerite de Navarre, *Heptaméron,* 98–101.
60 Quaife, *Wanton Wenches,* 22.
61 Baskervill, *Elizabethan Jig,* 450–64.
62 Hazlitt, *Shakespeare Jest-Books,* 2:349–50.

Mrs. Page: Why, look where he comes, and my goodman too. He's as far from jealousy as I am from giving him cause, and that, I hope, is an unmeasurable distance.
Mrs. Ford: You are the happier woman. (2.1.95–100)

Margaret Page feels safe from her husband's recrimination about Falstaff's letter, but Alice Ford does not. Perhaps her bluster about doing "any villainy" covers the fact she is afraid to tell Ford anything. Certainly her reasons for secrecy are weightier than her friend's. Master Ford is a choleric husband whose reactions to hearing about harassment were to be feared rather than sought, so his wife stands to lose much more than Falstaff or her friend when she decides on her course of action.[63] Mistress Page's high standing, her husband's importance, his regard for her, and his lack of jealousy protect her from rumor, which is why she is able to help her gossip. Nonetheless, the combination of the two male plots almost undoes Mistress Ford. She is playing a dangerous game by agreeing to trysts with Falstaff but one that was not totally unprecedented among wives facing persistent seducers:

> A married woman who rejected the advance and resisted the endeavor was often placed in immediate and long-term jeopardy [of slander and violence]. . . . Some women took tremendous risks—to their own safety and their reputation. They, by their own account, initially encouraged the proposition in order to draw the man out into the open so that his desire might more easily become public knowledge.[64]

Ford's main interest is avoiding being known as a cuckold, not clearing his wife. In fact, he hopes to prove her a whore before he can be called cuckold, as if the two were separable. So he develops his absurd scheme to pay Falstaff to cuckold him—a plan worthy of the Wise Men of Gotham or, even more pointedly, the legendary fool who castrated himself so that, if his wife become pregnant, he would know she had committed adultery.[65] After Ford is thwarted in his goal of showing himself a cuckold, his threats grow violent against his wife and his neighbors:

63 The few wives in Quaife's study who were propositioned or attacked but chose not to tell their husbands "were afraid of the unpredictable reaction of the husband or the dire economic consequences that might follow." They usually told a friend or relative instead (*Wanton Wenches*, 139).
64 Ibid., 138. Also see Capp, "Separate Domains?" 136.
65 Bracciolini, *Facetiae*, 34–35.

Good plots! They are laid; and our revolted wives share damnation together. Well, I will take him, then torture my wife, pluck the borrowed
veil of modesty from the so-seeming Mistress Page, divulge Page himself for a secure and willful Actaeon; and to these violent proceedings
all my neighbors shall cry aim. (3.2.34–9)

His brutal litany ends with his fantasy that his neighbors will shout
"bravo" to his deeds. He hopes to gain their respect and admiration by
ruining the common peace and torturing his wife; and his rage quickly
finds an outlet in Falstaff, who serves as a substitute whipping post.
This switched violence bears a strong resemblance to the gruesome
group of merry tales in which a wife escapes a beating by bribing or beg-
ging a servant or an old woman to disguise herself and suffer the beating
in her place, while she slips out to meet her lover.[66] The horn-mad husband in his blind tantrum always beats the wrong woman, just as Ford
does in beating "the Witch of Brainford."[67] The lesson in neighborhood
urged by Ford's example is clear: the jealous man is a bad neighbor and
a sick man whose disease is contagious. Richard Brathwait's character
of "A Jealous Neighbour" suggests why:

> He heares all that neighbours neare him, or resort unto him, say, They
> never saw children liker their Father; and yet (he replies) not one of them
> al is like an other. . . . How like a sillie man hee looks in the presence of
> his wife and a proper attendant? What a dejected eye hee casts upon him-
> selfe, and how jealous he is of this strangers Count'nance? . . . hee bids
> his Apprentice look to his foreman . . . and calls the Shoomaker knave
> for pulling on his wives shooe, and offering to beate him with his Last.[68]

Horn madness is a social disease that, like a fire, threatens an entire
neighborhood. Its combination of pudeur and self-loathing isolates the
afflicted person from men and women alike. Gibbering before the buck
basket, Ford paints his own sexuality as fouled linen: "Buck! I would I
could wash myself of the buck! Buck, buck, buck!"(3.3.143–4). This is
not approved behavior. As Page and others repeatedly remind him, "you

---

66 For example, see the first story in *Westward for Smelts*, sigs. Br-B3v.
67 Russell-Morgan explores the association of Brainford with assignations and female mirth in "No Good Thing." To Master Ford, the Witch of Brainford represents a
dreaded "world of concerted and secret female power" (Helgerson, "Women's World,"
esp. 172, 180, n. 13).
68 Brathwait, *Whimzies*, 186–87.

wrong yourself too much" (3.3.151–52)—a phrase that also meant "befouling oneself with excrement." Page stays "clean" by ignoring the rumors peddled by Nym, whereas Ford laps up the lies offered by Pistol—malicious male gossip performed in retaliation for another slight offered by men, between men. Luckily his own neighbors find Ford absurd despite his fervent appeals, which work instead to prompt them and the audience to ridicule him to their hearts' content: "Pray you, come near. If I suspect without cause, why then make sport at me. Then let me be your jest; I deserve it" (3.3.137–39).

In other passages Ford's failure to turn up any evidence for his "jury" emboldens Mistress Ford and Mistress Page to taunt him. Ford takes his medicine from them, from his neighbors, and no doubt from the audience as well:

> *Ford:* Come, wife, come, Mistress Page, I pray you, pardon me. Pray, heartily, pardon me.
> *Page:* Let's go in, gentlemen; but trust me, we'll mock him. (3.4.207–9)

Scholars have remarked that Falstaff endures a kind of charivari, but the mocking laughter that Ford's wife and her neighbors lavish on him is also a form of "rough music" expressing communal censure. Ford is a wife beater in his own mind; and as E. P. Thompson pointed out in a landmark essay, by the eighteenth century the skimmington was used against wife beaters as well as against domineering or cuckolded husbands. There were scattered instances of charivari-like behavior against wife beaters much earlier, in the form of raucous ballading, dirt throwing, and name calling.[69] Master Ford's rough treatment at the hands of his wife, her best friend, and his neighbors serves as a reminder that popular culture sometimes does enable "rehearsals of vengeance" against dominant figures long before those actions emerge as expressions in above-ground culture.[70] Considering the close relationship between stage comedies and the culture of the street, it is entirely appropriate that this rehearsal occurs in the shared space in which gender and authority were performed and identity shaped: the vital playing space of the early modern neighborhood.

---

69 See Thompson, *Customs in Common*, 504–5; and Foyster, "Male Honour," 222.
70 Molly Smith makes similar points in her important study *Breaking Boundaries*, 68–80, esp. 70–71.

2 Ale and Female
Gossips as Players,
Alehouse as Theater

If the lofty pulpit, the lectern, and the judge's chair were reserved for men, there were humbler spaces marked out for women: the threshold and yard, the alehouse bench, the birthing chamber, the gossip's stool. Within the restricted realm allotted them, middling to poor women were mobile and interdependent. The neighbor hurried to her friend's childbed or sickbed; herbwives trudged from door to door; servants carried messages back and forth; the alewife opened her house to customers or sold ale from her back door. The poorest were constantly on the street as hucksters or out on the road as vagrants and gypsies, itinerant entertainers and chapwomen.[1]

Women's constant interactions among other women strongly suggest that they had "a popular culture of their own" in early modern England, though few scholars have paid it much attention.[2] Women sat separately from men in church, for example, and were alone together during labors and lyings-in and at the gossipings and churchings afterward, held at homes and in alehouses. They also met in the course of marketing and doing other chores. One London satirist set about to derogate the chatter of women in these everyday settings. *Tittle-Tattle: Or, the several Branches of Gossipping* (1600) bemoans women's noisy and

---

1 On poorer working women in London, see Willen, "Women in the Public Sphere"; on vagrant women, see Woodbridge, *Vagrancy,* 9, 252–53.
2 Sharpe, "Plebeian Marriage," 80.

bothersome ubiquity on the city scene. Crammed within its frame are scores of women working their way from bakehouse, laundry, and conduit to bathhouse, church, market, and alehouse—chatting, hawking, or flyting as they go (see fig. 3).[3] Some fight and curse, while others lean their heads together and gossip. That the print is satiric does not imply that it is completely inaccurate: it would possess little legibility as satire if women did not commonly gather in these places. In its mapping of value, the woodcut insistently links the culturally low with the female body and female speech.[4] The lower-status bakers work on the same level as women; the higher-status men at top either preach to or stand above the sitting women. One male observer stands at a window at the left, gazing at the crowded scene below and directing our eyes to the naked women of the "Hotte-house." The ideological freight of the image forces the symbolic onto the social, literally putting women in their place: stripping them, preaching to them, spying on them.

Nonetheless, it is possible to break the frame that tells us what is right in front of our eyes. Formulaic antifeminist satire fills the verse caption below; but the print abounds in details that do not quickly translate into attacks against mouthy, whorish women. Only a fraction of the image shows incontestably unruly women: the vignettes of women fighting at "conditte" and river and the church scene, in which women ignore the preacher. The title above and satiric verse below direct the viewer to condemn every branch of gossiping, but the image does not fully comply. Such a disjunction between image and text is common in popular imagery,[5] but a further discontinuity would have been furnished by many viewers. As Margaret Ferguson points out, women who were illiterate or partially literate must have interpreted woodcuts and engravings in ways different from the fully literate.[6]

When this image is considered without the satiric stanzas at the bottom, it loses much of the point of its lecture, offering a far different set of signs to the curious interpreter. The verses tell women to stay at home

3 The English print appears to be based on an earlier French print, *Le caquet des Femmes* (1560), reproduced and discussed in Davis, *Fiction in the Archives*, 90–91. In *Le caquet*, the church scene shows a priest raising the Host; it also presents a scene of women at a mill at top right.

4 My argument is informed by the discussion of gender, spatialization, and value in Stallybrass and White, *Politics and Poetics*, 1–26.

5 Luborsky, "Connections."

6 Ferguson, "Response," 270. Important studies of popular imagery include Kunzle, *Early Comic Strip*; and Moxey, *Peasants, Warriors, and Wives*.

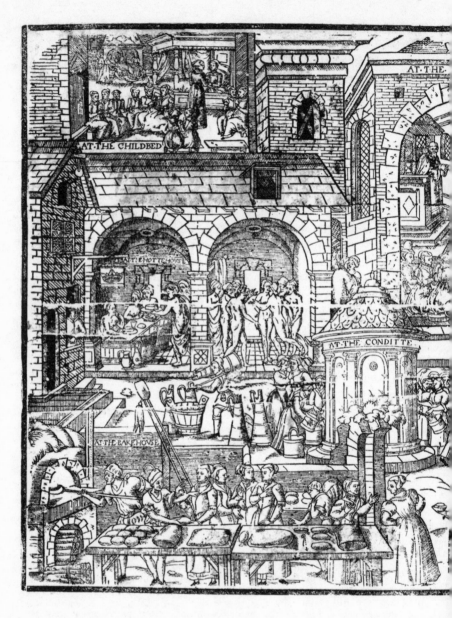

Fig. 3. City of women. *Tittle-Tattle; Or, the several Branches of Gossipping* (1600). © Copyright The British Museum.

to "knit, and sew, and brew, and bake"; but if all widows, wives, maids, and maidservants obeyed, who would go to the market, fetch water and bread, and do the laundry? To anyone who does not read the caption, could the image paradoxically privilege female labor through its detailed representation? Could it engage women by showing them scenes of female leisure? The cutaway walls in the image seduce the eye into gazing at naked bodies. Who are the naked women in the "hotte-house"? Are they simply gossips, as the text states, or are they whores or urban graces? Might some women have enjoyed the voyeurism that the image invites? Does it appeal to lesbian desire? Whatever the woodcut means, certainly that meaning is hermeneutically diffuse and cannot be restricted entirely to the normative masculinist satire of its frame.

Like the woodcut, jests are full of verbal and physical violence, gossip, buying and selling, alehouse carousing, sexual byplay, voyeurism, preaching, street scenes, and a few mysteries. Some are bracketed by titles and captions that shout the moral. But as with a play text or a ballad, no one can force the performer to deliver—or listener to credit—exactly those lines in the way in which the writer intended. Reading jests, like looking at *Tittle Tattle*, provides glimmers of a captioned and therefore disregarded multiplicity, a messy miscellany with an alluring concreteness.

What News? Gossip as Female Subculture

Antifeminist jest and satire against alewives, shrews, and gossips—often grouped together as gossips' literature—provides a rich site for this sort of excavation. The word *gossip* itself requires more careful treatment than it is usually given. Respectable for centuries, gossip (from *godsip*) referred primarily to a godparent of either gender. By the sixteenth century the word was being applied to any close female friend, though it was sometimes used for male friends as well. In the late sixteenth century "gossiping" described a "merry meeting" of women to drink, laugh, and talk; it was not until a century later that Johnson's *Dictionary* equated gossip with the obnoxious woman "who runs about tattling like women at a lying in."[7]

Early modern speakers drew important distinctions between scold

7 Melanie Tebbutt describes this shift in detail in *Women's Talk?* 19–22. Also see Woodbridge, *Women*, 124.

and gossip. The words were by no means equivalents. Unlike talking about one's neighbors, scolding was a chronic, legally actionable offense; and the connotations of shrew varied from mild to damning.[8] In Brathwait's *Essaies upon the five senses* (1619), a scold "goes weekly a catter-wauling, where shee spoiles their spice-cup'd gossiping with her tart-tongued calletting."[9] Whatever those gossips are up to, the scold is wrong to spoil it. Such a distinction suggests that women had certain rights of assembly—despite all the injunctions that women should stay indoors, avoid all gadding, and strive for silence.[10] Traveler Emmanuel Van Meteren marveled that Englishwomen spent so much time

> visiting their friends and keeping company, conversing with their equals (whom they term *gossips*) and their neighbours, and making merry with them at child-births, christenings, churchings and funerals; and all this with the permission and knowledge of their husbands, as such was the custom.[11]

Daniel Rogers warned husbands that they would be foolish to forbid their wives to attend gossipings and even advised them to give wives money "to bestow upon the meetings and lawfull merriments of their kind, which it were a poore thing for a husband curiously to enquire after." Robert Cawdrey urged moderation rather than abstinence: gossips should meet only as often as "the law of good neighbourhood doth require."[12]

John Stephens's character "A Gossip" predictably conflates a woman's volubility and mobility with sexual and bodily incontinence:

8 Dolan, *Taming*, 288. When Jardine "subsumes" gossips under shrews/scolds "for convenience," the grouping is common enough, but still misleading (*Still Harping*, 134, n. 5). Though gossips and shrews are often allied in popular literature, not every shrew attracts gossips, as Kate's friendlessness shows in *Taming*. Proverbs about shrews are often ambivalent, unlike those about scolds (e.g., *a shrew profitable may serve a man reasonable*, versus the old saw *a smoking chimney and a scolding wife may not be endured*). It is the chronic scold, rather than the companionable shrew or the clever and headstrong wife, who creates the most conflict at home and in the neighborhood.

9 Brathwait, *Essaies*, 135.

10 Thomas Becon advised wives "not to meddle in other folks' business abroad, but diligently to look upon her own at home; not to go unto her neighbours' houses to tattle and prattle after the manner of light housewives; not to be tavern-hunters; not idly and wantonly to gad abroad" (*A New Catechism set forth dialogue-wise in familiar talk between the father and the son*, quoted in Thorp, *Triumph*, 85).

11 Van Meteren, quoted in Houlbrooke, "Women's Social Life," 172.

12 Cawdrey and Rogers, quoted in ibid., 173.

Her knowledge is her speech; the motive, her tongue; and the reason is
her tongue also: but the subject of her eloquence is her neighbours wife,
and her husband, or the neighbours wife and husband both. Shee is the
mirth of marriages, and publicke meetings. . . . Shee carries her bladder
in her braine, that is full; her braine in her tongues end, that shee empties. . . . Shee emulates a Lawyer in riding the circuite, and therefore
she keeps a circuit in, or out of her own liberties: striving to be both
one of the judges, Jury, and false witnesses: that is her freedom only, to
censure. . . . Her truth is, to make truths and tales convertibles: tales be
her substance, her conceit, her vengeance, reconcilements, and discourse. . . . If she railes against whoredom it savours not of devotion; for
she is only married to escape the like scandall; from the doore outward.[13]

The irony, of course, is that the author rails in the catty tones of a
censorious neighbor. Despite the formulaic hostility in this character,
one may glimpse a shadow portrait of a neighbor and a neighborhood.
Like *neighbor*, the term *gossip* implies a relationship between peers. Always on hand for disputes and interventions, she also serves as a chief
relayer of news and knowledge within the community. As the sarcastic
phrase "one of the judges" indicates, she operates as an informal social
arbiter. Ironically, it is precisely her narrative skill that qualifies her for
this role. No matter how caustically "tittle tattle" was scorned, gossip
"gave women a particular standing in neighbourhood social relations,"
as Gowing puts it. "Telling stories and judging morals made women the
brokers of moral reputation."[14] While Stephens derides his gossip for
gadding and tattling, he fails to suppress an uncomfortable social fact:
such women can never be excluded from the crucial labor of maintaining social order.

Pamphleteers and playwrights devoted much energy to trivializing
women's talk at gossipings, betraying their fear that the effects on
men's reputations could be far from trivial. In a merry meeting in
Thomas Deloney's *Thomas of Reading*, some gossips "talkt of their
husbands' frowardnes, some shewed their maids sluttishnes, othersome
deciphered the costliness of their garments, some told many tales of
their neighbors."[15] Some jest gossips are two-faced, greedy, and leaky,

13 Stephens, *Satyricall Essayes*, 308–9.
14 Gowing, *Domestic Dangers*, 123.
15 Quoted in Houlbrooke, "Women's Social Life," 173.

such as those in Middleton's *Chaste Maid in Cheapside*.[16] Others are almost witchlike. The author of *The Gossips Greeting* (1620) rants against "the proud, peevish, paultry, pernicious shee-pot companions, those curious, careless, crafty, carping curtizanicall Gossips . . . dangerous as hell, / None of you beare a modest womans mind / You do infect even with your smell."[17]

These representations must be read alongside gossips' texts that are more nuanced and altogether less bilious. Samuel Rowlands's best-selling *Tis Merry When Gossips Meet* (1602) and *A Whole Crew of Kind Gossips* (1609) painted alehouse meetings with a mix of humorous voyeurism, mild satire, and unusually candid social realism. In the first pamphlet a wife and widow give a maid fairly standard advice about men and marriage. The widow buys them rounds with an evident pride in her ability to pay, providing a strong contrast to the many jests in which drunken men cheat the hostess. Satire is directed largely at the widow, who gets tipsy and garrulous. But for the most part, the pamphlet leaves the impression that it offered readers a glimpse of women indulging in a merry pastime that formed an important and familiar part of neighborhood socializing.[18]

To repeat Wrightson's argument, the ideal of "good neighborhood" required everyone to accept neighbors "as a reference group in matters of behavior and to promote harmonious relations among them." How could a woman fulfill this obligation without asking, "What news?" The surprising answer is that she couldn't. What we now call gossip was, in fact, essential to being a good neighbor, and talking about neighbors and strangers was not considered the prelude to scolding or near kin to slander.[19] The obligation of neighborhood made constant comment not only normative but a prime regulating device. To use *Merry Wives* as an example, the Windsor wives' censure of Falstaff and gossip about Ford initiates action that will eventually involve their neighbors

16 On women's verbal and bodily incontinence in the play, see Paster, *Body Embarrassed*, 52–63.

17 From the preface in *Gossips Greeting*.

18 Susan Gushee O'Malley's chapter on Rowlands in *Custom Is an Idiot* discusses the unusual features of *Tis Merry*, such as its emphasis on the gossips' pride in paying their way. I thank her for showing me her work before publication.

19 On the definition and prosecution of scolding, see Ingram, "Scolding Women." He takes issue with Underdown's thesis that scolding became a national obsession in the period ("Taming of the Scold"). Boose draws on Underdown's thesis in her influential essay "Scolding Brides."

in neutralizing the threats to the common peace posed by a sexual ad-
venturer and a horn-mad husband. Their joint consultation and campaign of mockery lie firmly in the bounds of "good neighborhood."

Censorious gossip "could be an effective informal method of control:
it indicated community disapproval, and shamed its subject. If the subject of gossip did not stop the behavior, at least everyone else knew
what to think about it."[20] Gossip, defined this way, could maintain and
reiterate social boundaries. Fueled by curiosity and pleasure in ridicule,
gossip also primed audiences to recognize the more cutting forms of wit
and the aesthetically engineered moral judgment known as satire. Pro-
ficiency at this narrative form, so often salted with jests and proverbs,
promoted rhetorical efficacy in life and art, while skill at telling believ-
able stories about one's life and neighbors held much weight in the
courtroom and on the streets.[21]

Gossip was not always conservative in effect. By asking "What
news?" women also had a chance to learn about and talk over events in
the larger world, out of the hearing of husbands, fathers, and masters.
According to historian Steve Hindle, gossip is both a "female subcul-
ture" and a "formative stage in the development of 'public opinion' over
a whole range of issues, local and national, private and public, personal
and political. To ignore gossip is to ignore one of the few channels of
participation in this 'public sphere' that was open to women."[22] Gatherings during working time or in leisure moments, such as christenings,
may have given women a place in which to articulate opinions and to
plan for common action, such as the many enclosure protests, grain
riots, and religious disputes in which they participated.[23]

Some fictional gossips poach eagerly on male discourses supposedly
closed to them, such as biblical interpretation, the worth of stage plays,
and the fate of kings. In *The gospelles of dystaves* (c. 1510) a group of
women meets secretly to hear a new kind of preaching by "apostles"

20 Quotation from Amussen, *Ordered Society*, 131. Also see Merry, "Rethinking
Gossip," 296.
21 Gowing, *Domestic Dangers*, 42–43.
22 Hindle, "Shaming of Margaret Knowsley," 393. Spacks calls gossip a gender-
coded narrative genre that is harshly derided, enormously effective, politically indispensable, and desired by both men and women, although men often deny they do or
desire it (*Gossip*, 16–17, 38). Gossip is also unsettling because it "provides a resource
for the subordinated" and "incorporates the possibility that people utterly lacking in
public power may affect the views of figures who make things happen in the public
sphere" (5, 7). Also see Halacz, *Marketplace*, 145–54.
23 Houlbrooke, "Women's Social Life," 185.

named Dame Hengtyne and Dame Abunde, while a male scholar transcribes (see fig. 4). Their chat mixes homely proverbs and bawdy laughter, interspersed with more serious challenges to religious teachings about women's subjection. While the pamphlet obviously satirizes ignorant and unruly women, it also suggests that women did talk together about what they heard in church and that they were given to interpreting biblical passages in favor of women's interests. Female association could be dangerous to the state: the weird sisters of *Macbeth* carp about their neighbors, crack jokes, practice riddling prophecy, and rearrange Scottish history. Like gossips in their cups, they "scorn male power" while "their words and bodies mock rigorous boundaries and make sport of fixed positions."[24]

In *The Staple of News*, Jonson attempts to silence and discipline unruly women in his audiences by presenting caricatures of neighborhood gossips. Underlining the close association between the juries of the threshold and the theater, Tattle, Mirth, Censure, and Expectation boldly invade the stage with their stools, sitting down to cavil about the actors and the sweaty playwright, forming a jury of women who judge a play together as if they were judging gossip and scandal at home. Despite the satire, Jonson casts them as the prime producers and consumers of news and rumors; he cannot help but make them sharp-eyed judges of the staple, which commodifies word of mouth" by printing it.

Occasionally gossips are painted as resourceful and clever. In Dekker and Webster's *Westward Ho!*, citizen wives furnish themselves "a commodity of laughter" by leading their jealous husbands and eager suitors on a wild-goose chase up the Thames. As in *Merry Wives*, this pleasure carries a risk. When they plot to scare their husbands with the prospect of horns and turn the tables on their arrogant suitors, one wife warns the others that they must deflect any resulting slanders using shrewd foresight:

> tho we are merry, let's not be mad: . . . It were better we should laugh at
> these popin-Jayes, then live in feare of their prating tongues: tho we lie
> all night out of the Citty, they shall not finde country wenches of us:
> but since we ha[ve] brought em thus far into a fooles Paradice, leave em

24 Terry Eagleton, quoted in Callaghan et al., *Weyward Sisters*, 131.

Fig. 4. Glossing "the women's gospels." Title page from *The gospelles of dystaves* (circa 1510). Reproduced by permission of The Huntington Library, San Marino, California.

int: the Jest shall be a stock to maintain us and our pewfellowes in
laughing at christning, cryings out, and upsittings the twelvemonth.[25]

Similar scenes of female complicity are rooted in the social reality of
women neighbors and gossips who rely heavily on each other's judgment in matters sexual and romantic. Such interdependence was especially important for unmarried women. Comedies featuring maids satirizing suitors (like Portia and Nerissa in *The Merchant of Venice*) or
coolly ranking types of men (like Franck and Clora in Fletcher's *The
Captain* and Celia and Rosalind in *As You Like It*) probably did stoke
masculine anxieties about patriarchy's vulnerability to the desires of
women. On the other hand, the very same scenes may have delighted
women or taught them sophisticated new ways to squelch unwanted
suitors.

The antimasculinist satire and complaint that fill gossips' literature
function in a distinctive way in Margaret Cavendish's *Convent of Pleasure*, which virtually reproduces passages from gossips' literature and
from women's tirades in controversy pamphlets.[26] Poor women meet in
the street to moan about the flaws of their husbands, which include
wife beating, heavy drinking, and gambling away the household funds.
Other scenes show the terrors of childbed and the persecution of a gentlewoman threatened with rape by a married man whose proposals she
rejects. Neighbors and friends cannot stop rapine suitors or worthless
husbands in this dystopia; so Cavendish creates a gender retreat that
takes female complaint seriously, dedicating her earthly paradise to
women's association, education, and delight: a high-toned gossips'
feast.

Uxor's Flood

In English popular culture, the close association between gossips,
shrews, and tippling goes back to medieval drama and jest. In the
Chester play of Noah's Flood, Noah's wife defends her gossips, with
whom she has shared many a gossip's bowl, insisting that Noah take

25 Thomas Dekker and John Webster, *Westward Ho*, in Dekker, *Dramatic Works
of Thomas Dekker*, 2:5.1.156–73.
26 Compare, for example, *Convent of Pleasure*, 3.2, with Rowlands's *Crew of Kind
Gossips*, sig. B2, and *Womens sharpe revenge*, sigs. K4r-v.

them into the ark too. The gossips have speaking parts, calling for one last cup together before they drown:

> *The Good Gossips*
> The fludd comes fleetinge in full faste,
> one everye syde that spredeth full farre.
> For feare of drownings I am agaste;
> good gossippe, let us drawe here.
>
> And let us drinke or wee departe,
> for ofte tymes we have done soe.
> For at one draught thou drinke a quarte,
> and soe will I doe or I goe.
>
> Here is a pottell full of malnesaye good and stronge;
> yt will rejoyse both harte and tonge. . . . [27]

Noah's wife's sons finally haul their mother aboard, and the gossips and the rest of the world are left behind to drown. In the York version of the Flood play, Uxor grieves as she watches her friends perish and later longs so much for their company that Noah rebukes her harshly.[28]

In the Chester *Pageante of Noyes Fludd* Uxor's disobedience is shrewish, but again she shows proper neighborly concern for her gossips:

> *Noe*
> Wyffe, come in. Why standes thou there?
> Thou art ever frowarde that dare I sweare.
> Come, in Godes name; half tyme yt weare,
> for feare lest that wee drowne.
>
> *Noes Wyffe*
> Yes, syr, sett up your seale
> And roe forthe with evell hayle;

---

27 *Thirde Pageante of Noyes Fludd,* in Lumiansky and Mills, *Chester Mystery Cycle,* 52. This scene occurs only in the Chester flood play and was inserted into the text very late, possibly a sign of controversy over a new law against alewives in Chester, the fascinating thesis of Mary Wack's "Women, Work and Plays."

28 [Noah's Flood,] in *York Cycle,* 52–56.

for withowten any fayle
I will not owte of this towne.

But I have my gossips everychone,
One foote further I will not gone.
They shall not drowne, by sancte John,
and I may save there life.

The [y] loved me full well, by Christe.
But thou wilte lett them into thy chiste,
elles rowe forthe, Noe, when thy liste
and gett thee a newe wyfe.[29]

Uxor's skirmishes with Noah—some punctuated with fisticuffs—are
central to four of five versions of the flood play.[30] As a result she is generally treated as a medieval Xantippe, a cartoonish arch-shrew—a significant underestimation. Just as Falstaff is never simply a fat knight,
Uxor is never simply a shrew. First, she was an enormously popular
character who gave the English stage its first "native comic role for
women."[31] Second, she stands up for the familiar world that is threatened with destruction. Third, she never acts only as a bad wife but as a
good neighbor and friend who represents community values in the face
of divine authority. Loud, stubborn, contrarian, appealing, she was
probably played by a woman in some stagings, as were her "good gossips" standing among the spectators.[32] An archetypal jesting woman
with a certain performative doubleness, she represents the homely
worlds of neighborhood and alehouse yet finally crosses to the sacred
space of ark and covenant. She often addresses the audience directly, establishing a close bond with it through asides, proverbs, and jests.[33] In
the Wakefield version she asks the wives in the audience if they, too,

29 *Noyes Fludd*, 50–51.
30 For example, see the Chester, York, and Towneley cycles and the Newcastle
fragment. Only "N-town" has no bout. See Marx, "Problem with Mrs. Noah," 110.
31 Bradbrook, "Dramatic Role," 134; also see Wayne, *Refashioning*, 161–64.
32 On women playing in pageant drama see Davidson, "Women and the Medieval
Stage," Chambers, *Mediaeval Stage*, 2:35, 88–89. Twycross opposes the view that
women acted ("Transvestism"); but for records of women receiving payment for playing roles in pageant and festive drama, see Stokes, "Women and Mimesis."
33 Weimann, *Shakespeare and the Popular Tradition*, 222.

sometimes wish their husbands dead so they can enjoy the gay widow's life.[34]

In contrast to some later shrews in drama and fiction, Noah's wife seems not so much selfish as loyal to the everyday allegiances that have defined her world. She probably garnered more affection than derision in the street spectacle; after all, the townspeople watching were figuratively washed away with the good gossips.[35] V. A. Kolve calls her "a dramatic tradition" who was "familiar and loved," while Arnold Williams observes that her arguments with Noah are all based on "reasonable attitudes," such as her concern for her friends, that "make us sympathize with her just as much as with her husband."[36]

As Peter Womack and others have pointed out, pageant drama recapitulated the beliefs of an entire community in a yearly display of shared tradition and religious belief. Conditions of spectatorship were radically different in the new public theaters, where a variety of fare was offered, plays were replaced constantly, and one paid to get in. Unlike the popular dramatics of shaming on a neighborhood level, the plays in the new theaters presented mere actors, not neighbors known to each other; and as a result, the feeling of shame probably held far less dramatic force.[37] The new amphitheaters gathered together not communities but crowds: "This scene is not part of any community, but takes you *out of it.* . . . whereas the medieval urban audience was the same crowd which assembled for other civic and religious purposes, the audience of Burbage and Marlowe is a casual grouping of individuals, whose coherence must come, if at all, from the show itself."[38]

Womack's vision of an anonymous crowd of strangers seems too sweeping. People do not shed their social identities and longtime habits of spectatorship at an entrance door. It does not follow from Womack's argument that spectators suddenly began to go to the theater alone, to react in complete isolation from each other, or to forsake ingrained

---

34 *The Deluge: Noah and His Sons,* Wakefield Pageant, modernized version in Gassner, ed., *Medieval and Tudor Drama,* 83.

35 Daniels finds her "a spokesman for fallen humanity, for those who are excluded from the ark" (*"Uxor Noah,"* 29).

36 Kolve and Williams are quoted in Marx, "Problem," 110, 119. Storm finds many signs of kinship between Uxor and the wife of Bath, especially in "those unreconciled moments when she bridles, surely to the great delight of the audience, against the constraints of her history" (*"Uxor* and Alison," 319).

37 Bristol, "Shamelessness in Arden," 301.

38 Womack, "Imagining Communities," 108–9.

modes of judgment and participation. Spectators often attended theaters in small groups (women were usually but not always escorted) and the daylight conditions ensured that they saw and reacted to each other as well as to the stage, as they had during pageant and festive drama.[39] Those who paid their pennies still stood at the foot of a platform in broad daylight, judging, jeering, and laughing, but with less occasion for reverence—especially before spectacles that combined didactic intent, funny shrews, and violent conjugal clashes, just as they had in the pageants of Noah's flood.

Audience laughter, as Womack himself points out, is an especially "imperious" form of actor-audience contact, shaping the timing and meaning of stage events.[40] The appeal for audience laughter by *platea* characters is evidence for a kind of continuity between the old and new, its importance indicated by the rapid rise of the stage clown. Indeed, it is in the low figures, such as the descendents of Noah's wife and her gossips, that the greatest continuity with older communal forms exists, along with their own traditions of audience engagement.[41]

Later stagings of the merry shrew often embody the blustering energy and anarchy of Uxor. In Preston's *Cambyses*, Madge May-Be-Good bursts onstage to break up an absurd quarrel between two witless husbands who have been goaded on by the Vice Ambidexter. Madge turns on the Vice and cudgels him until he howls. She is near kin to the alehouse viragoes who function not as selfish shrews but as guardians of public morals and defenders of the weak. This tradition bred comedies such as Heywood's *Fair Maid of the West*, the anonymous *Long Meg of Westminster*, and Middleton and Dekker's *The Roaring Girl*.

Alehouse as Theater

After the pageants were suppressed, the early modern alehouse became a prime place for the cross-fertilization of everyday jesting and theater. Many forms of popular performance, such as sports, games, morris dancing, jigging, and ballad singing, took place at the alehouse; and in the remoter reaches of the country, traveling players sometimes

39 Gurr, *Playgoing*, 57–64.
40 Womack, *Ben Jonson*, 63–64.
41 Bradbrook, "Dramatic Role," 134, and Rogers, *Troublesome Helpmate*, 90.

gave plays and interludes in alehouses.[42] Satirists were fond of accusing
playwrights of culling material there; one called the tavern

> a broacher of more newes then Hogs-heads, & more jests then newes,
> which are suckt up here by some spongy braine, and from thence
> squeaz'd into a Comedy. . . . Tis the best Theater of natures where they
> are truly acted, not plaid, and the businesse as in the rest of the world
> up and downe, to wit, from the bottom of the Seller to the Great Cham-
> ber.[43]

What part did women play in this "Theater of natures"? Historians
take a narrow view. Many agree with Barry Reay's statement that alehouses were "male-dominated milieus, then as now."[44] Peter Clark
maintains that "respectable women" did not go to the alehouse alone
and that many people bitterly resented all alewives for profiting from
husbandly drunkenness and harboring prostitutes. From the 1590s onward, alehouses certainly faced growing competition from male-headed
breweries, while misogynist prejudice fueled the campaigns of social reformers who pummeled home brewers with killing fines, as Judith Bennett has shown.[45]

Nonetheless, the alehouse was far from an all-male space. The issue
is an important one because the alehouse was often the real social center in a neighborhood, the place where news and rumors flew, where
people traded jokes, jigged jigs, sang and bought ballads, and heard chapbooks read aloud.[46] Furthermore, it served as one of the few places one
could speak one's mind, offering "a sanctuary for relative freedom of
speech, for cathartic release in story and song, jest and mockery."[47] If
women were there, they could hardly have been segregated from this
rich circuit of text, speech, and performance. Wrightson argues persuasively that many women ran alehouses or worked in them, while wives
went there with husbands, maidservants and young women gathered
there, and lovers met and were even wed there.[48] Thomas Platter, as-

42 See Watt, *Cheap Print*, 30; and Rosenfeld, *Strolling Players*, 22.
43 Earle, *Microcosmographie* (1629), sigs. D9–D11.
44 Reay, *Popular Culture in Seventeenth Century England*, 11.
45 See Clark, *English Alehouse*, 131–32; on licenses and fees, see 170–71. Judith
Bennett argues that systematic misogyny, in addition to market forces, motivated attacks on home brewing and alewives ("Misogyny").
46 Spufford, *Small Books*, 66–67. Also see Watt, *Cheap Print*, 32–33.
47 Fox, "Ballads, Libels," 72.
48 Wrightson, "Alehouses," 6–9. Also see Houlbrooke, *English Family*, 70.

tounded by the number of drinking places in London in 1599, wrote,
"what is particularly curious is that the women as well as the men, in
fact more than they, will frequent the taverns or alehouses for enjoyment."[49] In ballads, jests, and woodcuts, the alehouse is often shown or
described as a mixed-gender space. Maids huddle with their sweet-
hearts, while wives carouse with their husbands or nag them to go
home. Women sitting together gossip, laugh, and sing; complain about
husbands; and escape their domestic chores.

Despite all these signs of female presence, Clark concludes by casting
men as the players—and women as their servants—in what he, too,
calls "a neighbourhood theatre":

> The enduring reason for the success of the English alehouse in the cen-
> turies before 1830 is that it was quintessentially a neighbourhood the-
> atre in the widest sense, in which ordinary people could be actors and
> observers. Against the backdrop of its flickering fire men could gossip
> and rant, joke, laugh and posture, sublimate their miseries in drunken-
> ness, applaud their own success in generosity and games. [With] their
> pots and tankards kept brimming by an explosive Mother Bunch or the
> serving wench . . . they could discover a further dimension of them-
> selves and their lives.[50]

Clark's scene making shunts women to the margins. When male historians write about popular culture, comments Lyndal Roper, women
are usually "confined to walk-on parts" in precisely this way, with the
result that "most accounts of popular culture are actually about men's
culture."[51] Somehow the alehouse, a vitally important site of social
drama and popular culture in town, village, and city, was often run by
women and patronized by women yet at the same time remained off
limits and off-putting to women. This leaky paradox is built of the
same assumptions I challenge vis-à-vis the jest. Widely believed to be a
discourse available only to men, the jesting literature actually has far
greater female presence than has been noticed. And like the clientele of
the alehouse, not all the women who are players in the jesting culture
are well-to-do, respectable, or literate.

49 *Thomas Platter's Travels in England*, 171.
50 Clark, *English Alehouse*, 341.
51 Roper, *Oedipus and the Devil*, 13–14. Sharpe makes a similar point, faulting
historians for neglecting evidence that women participated in popular recreations
("Plebeian Marriage," 80 and 80, n. 54).

Using available evidence, one can reconstruct an alehouse scene that looks quite different from the mostly male resort created by Clark. In 1600 women could gather in London to drink ale made by another woman, at an alehouse she owned and ran, hear a female ballad seller pitch a song complaining about drunken husbands and impotent lovers, and buy a copy of the penny broadside. They could compose a mocking song together, to be used in shaming a recalcitrant neighbor.[52] This hypothetical but entirely possible group could gaze up at walls and doors plastered with ballad woodcuts of condemned rogues, horned husbands, country lovers, and bizarre births.[53] Women were rarely named as authors of ballads and pamphlets; but in a world of cheap and mostly anonymous print, this consideration recedes in importance next to questions of transmission and reception. Some of the jests they told and heard were undoubtedly the kind Thomas Wilson deplored: "it is not onely meete to avoyde al grosse bourdyng, and alehouse jesting, but also to eschew all foolish talke, and ruffin manners, much as no honest eares can ones abide."[54] My study of jesting culture has convinced me that some women were fully capable of this kind of speech, inside the alehouse and out. Down among the lowliest texts and the smallest transactions, women were undeniably present as sellers, performers, spectators, and buyers.

The key role of the alehouse in the microeconomics of the neighborhood constitutes a running theme in jests and drama. The alewife who drives Sly out of her alehouse in *The Taming of the Shrew* dominates a scene familiar from jests: the tussle between the lackpenny lush and the loud, brash, and muscular alewife. Such bouts were not always decided in favor of the male customer, perhaps because there were too many alewives listening. In one jest a hostess confronts a rude justice who always insists on taking leftovers with him. Fed up, she pours ale and pottage into his saddlebag. When he rails at her, she is ready:

52 Fox, "Ballads, Libels," 52, 58–59.
53 On alewives, brewsters, and brewing, see Clark, *Working Life*, 209, 221–33; Hanawalt, "Of Good and Ill Repute," 104–23; and Bennett, *Ale*. On women ballad sellers see Rollins, "Black-Letter," 308, 315; and Watt, *Cheap Print*, 29. On women as ballad audiences and customers see Wiltenburg, *Disorderly*, 25–31, 38–39. On the ubiquity of ballads, which were pasted over chimneys, walls, and doors of alehouses and posted on cleft sticks, see Rollins, "Black-Letter," 327; and Watt, *Cheap Print*, 12–13. For images of alewives and mixed-gender alehouse scenes, see Clark, *English Alehouse*, plates following 176. For ballad woodcuts, see the *Roxburghe, Euing,* and *Pepys* ballad collections.
54 Wilson, *Arte of Rhetoricke*, 280.

"Oh sir," quod the wife, "I know well ye are a judge of the realm, and I perceive by you, your mind is to do right and to have that is your own, and your mind is to have all things with you that you paid for. . . . I have therefore put in your [bags] the pottage that ye left because ye have well and truly paid for them. For if I shold keep any thing from you that ye have paid for, peradventure ye would trouble me in the law another time." Here ye may see that he that playeth the niggard too much sometime it turneth him to his own loss.[55]

In the brief moment of a jest, a humble alewife can get the better of an educated and far more powerful man. This is not to imply that women's active role in ale culture escaped censure. Vital yet often derided, the alehouse was an especially fraught social and economic arena; and women who kept alehouses were often subject to misogynist attacks.[56] Although her product was crucial to subsistence survival, and although ale was the daily drink of every man, woman, and child, the alewife had been the special target of satire since early medieval times. Everyman is seduced in an alehouse. Pageant drama satirized a lusty, boozy alewife, who appeared as a ghost sent to hell, clashing her "cuppes and cans" and lamenting her cheating ways.[57] Skelton's notorious Elinor Rumming mixes up her scummy brew, and an entire neighborhood of grotesque gossips comes running. With her mountebank claims for its rejuvenating effects, Rumming is close kin to the cheating alewife of the pageants; the poem trades on deep biases against alehouse keeping in particular and women's work in general.

While many popular ballads paint in lurid detail the brawling and whoring that took place there, the humble ordinary was often the only meeting place available, a favorite spot for lovers' rendezvous—and not only for those between women and men.[58] Fletcher draws on these contradictory elements in a scene of bawdy mock warfare in *The Captain*, which blends homoeroticism with the rites of female festive play and proceeds through conflict, crisis, confession, and purgation. The

---

55 *Hundred Merry Tales*, 85.
56 Bennett, "Misogyny," 166–88.
57 *Chester Mystery Cycle*, 50–51.
58 Wrightson, "Alehouses," 6–7. Mario DiGangi identifies taverns and alehouses among the "geographically and socially accessible" places where homoerotic activity took place. In one ballad a husband tells his wife that he isn't consorting with whores, but his male friends: "these are the sweet honies that I kisse and hugge" (*Homoerotics*, 48–49).

woman-hating Jacomo spurns Franck again and again. Finally Franck
and her witty friend Clora meet him in a tavern, where they carouse
with him, getting him very drunk. As he thrashes about making passes
at men and women alike, the women mock him mercilessly and pour a
chamberpot over his head. At one point Jacomo takes Franck's brother
for a woman and tells him he loves him madly. Franck sees this as a pro-
pitious moment. She and her friends tie him to a chair—an urban hocking—and force him to listen to her impassioned declarations, ending in
her weeping aloud. This display convinces him of her sincerity and
cures him of his misogyny. Resounding with female laughter and recep-
tive to all kinds of sexual desire, the tavern is a fitting choice as the
"theater of natures" where female allies can stage their own brand of
comic drama.

Over the Top: Mother Bunch and Long Meg

In the jesting literature, not all alewives are Elinor Rummings, targets
of laughter and contempt. Some legendary alewives and barmaids are
agents of mirth whose feats of wit and brawn are drawn in bright colors,
larger than life. The fame of Long Meg of Westminster led printers to
produce a jest biography about her, just as they had with Scogin, Howleglas, and Tarlton; the redoubtable Mother Bunch was cast as the author
of a series of jest books in which she played the starring role of jester,
tapster, and mistress of ceremonies in her London alehouse. Illustrating
the close connection between printed jests and professional theater,
both Mother Bunch and Long Meg were also brought to the stage in
plays.

Like old wives and gossips, alewives were important transmitters of
culture; but unlike them, their storytelling held a recognized value in
the market because attracting and entertaining customers helped build
the alehouse keeper's fortunes. Popular texts situated an alewife such as
Mother Bunch firmly at the center of the interconnected (and quickly
commodifying) worlds of local gossip, print culture, orality, and performance. Margaret Spufford calls Mother Bunch "the most magnificent
teller of tall stories amongst the alehouse keepers," who are "key figure[s] in the process of disseminating news and stories and therefore in
the world of cheap print."[59] The Epistle to Pasquils Jests and Mother

59 Spufford, Small Books, 66.

Bunches Merriments (1629) tells us that Mother Bunch once ran a renowned tippling house in Cornehill, London, where she dispensed jests and aphrodisiac ale. The "merriments" or jests are supposedly all hers, just as *Tarlton's Jests* are supposedly his. Unlike Tarlton, her legend involves a gigantic explosion of flesh, voice, and wind:

> Now for Mother Bunch, the onely dainty, well favored, well proportioned, sweet complexioned and most delightful Hostesse of England, she was squared into inches, being in height twenty thousand and a halfe, wanting a fingers bredth jump, in bredth eleven thousand and two inches and a nails breadth just: she spent most of her time in telling of tales, and when she laughed, she was heard from Algate to the Monuments at Westminster, and all Southwarke stood in amazement, the Lyons in the Tower, and the Bulls and Beares of Parish-Garden roar'd (with terrour of her laughter) lowder then the great roaring Megge. Shee was once wrung with wind in her belly, and with one blast of her taile, she blew down Charing-Crosse, with Pauls aspiring steeple. . . . Shee was an excellent companion, and sociable; shee was very pleasant and witty, and would tell a tale, let a fart, drink her draught, scratch her arse, pay her groat as well as any Chymist of Ale whatsoever. From this noble Mother Bunch proceeded all our great gresie Tapsters, and fat swelling Ale wives . . . But shee died, and left behind her these pleasant tales following, which she used to tell those nimble spirits, which drank deepe of her Ale, and as she changed their money, as was generally related.[60]

No matter how implausible the description, one may discern in it the outlines of social type. Hazlitt even finds it "probable enough that the lady in question was some well-known ale-wife of the period" whose name helped sell books because her "celebrity [was] extreme." (Printers traded on her fame with *Mother Bunch's Closet New Broke Open*, among other titles.)[61] Her huge body sometimes attracts satire, but she is no mere butt of japes. Though she is laid open to laughter she is strikingly unscathed by it, flourishing as a seller of ale and teller of tales, both of them salable and appetizing commodities. Huge and invincible, she appears to enjoy what Hegel called "that blessed ease of a subjectiv-

---

60 "Epistle to the Reader," reprinted in Hazlitt, *Shakespeare Jest-Books*, 3:112–13. Mother's Bunch's gigantism may be rooted in festive culture: Wells and Coventry paraded figures of female giants as well as male ones through the streets during holidays. See Mills, "Chester's Midsummer Show," 132, 154.
61 From Hazlitt's introduction to *Pasquils Jests* in *Shakespeare Jest-Books*, 3:5.

ity which, as it is sure of itself, can bear the dissolution of its own ends and means."[62]

Like Tarlton and Scogin, Mother Bunch revels in moments when she flouts all rule. In one jest set during Lent, a local busybody searches every nook and cranny of her alehouse for forbidden meat, pestering her to lead him to the two legs of pork he suspects she has hidden. She leads him down the dark cellar steps. At the bottom she lifts up her skirts and then "laid her hand on her tayle, saying to the Promooter, There bee the two legs of Porke, come smell if they will keepe while Easter."[63] Mother Bunch manages to ring a change on a hoary old motif from fabliau: the "kiss my tail" joke, traditionally placed in the mouths of women.[64] Her retort combines jest and gest, dramatizing her improper tale/tail set against a "proper" narrative of compliance.

Mother Bunch has her way with promoters and roaring boys because she has full control over her alehouse and the bodies within it. With its gamblers and roarers, the alehouse could erupt in violence at any time. A strong alewife was bound to keep a more orderly house, combining the functions of bouncer, neighbor, and hostess.[65] Sometimes keeping the peace entailed some well-aimed blows, and popular fictions comically exaggerated an alewife's martial prowess. The tall, brash barmaid Long Meg of Westminster, whose story takes place in the time of Henry VIII, keeps order at the alehouse, protects poor maids from harassment, cudgels lechers who ogle her, duels roaring boys who challenge her, and fights valiantly against England's enemies, decapitating a French soldier in single combat (see fig. 5). Chapbooks and ballads about Long Meg appeared over a forty-year period, and plays showcased her famous "merry pranks." She performs her great deeds not for glory alone but to protect neighborhood women and the organic society symbolized by the alehouse itself, both a "microcosm" and a magnet for "nostalgic nationalism."[66] Her status as an unpretentious local girl is signaled by her sub-

62 Weimann applies this phrase to Falstaff in "Laughing," 36.

63 *Pasquils Jests* (1639). Hazlitt does not reprint this or several other bawdy jokes by women in his edition.

64 In jests the "kiss my tail" motif is almost always a riposte by women against men that cuts off an answer. See, for example, "An Old Gentlewoman's answer to a flowting Gentleman" in *Pasquils Jests*, sig. C2. *The merriments of Mother Bunch* (included in *Pasquils Jests*) contains four jests in which women confound men with this obscenity.

65 Clark, *English Alehouse*, 83–84, 87.

66 Waage, "Meg and Moll," 106, 117. Her legend may be thoroughly sentimentalized, argues Bernard Capp, who claims that Long Meg's original was a bawd named Margaret Barnes, whose alehouse was a front for a brothel ("Long Meg of Westminster").

mission to her husband at the conclusion of the chapbook account of her life.

Middleton and Dekker's *The Roaring Girl*, based on the life of the anomalous Moll Frith, shows Moll Cutpurse "on top" among the roaring boys, drinking, smoking, dueling, trading barbs, and canting, inside the tavern and out. The play also draws on the earlier chapbook biography of Long Meg, with special emphasis placed on her interest in shielding a poor seamstress from the depredations of a corrupt suitor. Long Meg's fame has been long-lived: in England today, the phrase "she's a real Long Meg" is sometimes used to describe a tough and boisterous woman. Seen in the context of a popular culture that applauded some women as famous jesters, one of the first "real Long Megs," Moll Frith, does not seem such an absolute anomaly. In 1611 Frith (dubbed a "female humourist" in one 1662 chapbook) appeared on the stage of the Fortune in breeches and hat. There she smoked her pipe, played her lute, and jested with the audience, sitting comfortably at the edge in the manner of Tarlton and Kemp, who had ruled the same space with their jigs and banter. When a man demanded to know if she really was a woman, she invited him to her chamber to see for himself, a Tarltonizing riposte that brought down the house and rankled the authorities.[67]

Probably the best-known tavern scenes in early modern drama are in Shakespeare's *Henry* plays, making Mistress Quickly of the Boar's Head Tavern the most famous stage hostess. But compared with the doughty Mother Bunch, Mistress Quickly seems meek and muddled. She rails impotently at Falstaff that her bill as been "fubb'd off, and fubb'd off, and fubb'd off, from this day to that day."[68] Mother Bunch outfaces all deadbeats and outjests them too; but when the Hostess trades barbs with Falstaff, she hasn't got a chance, undermined by her own romantic credulity and verbal fumbling. In *1 Henry IV* Shakespeare makes Quickly a laughing spectator to the witty play of Falstaff and the Prince, whereas the jest book author places Mother Bunch squarely on center stage, in the position marked for laugh getting and applause. It is no coincidence that Mother Bunch shows no interest in romance and mar-

---

67 Orgel, *Impersonations*, 146–47. My thanks to Mary Lovell for informing me that brawny or loud women are sometimes called "Long Megs" today, though the phrase's referent is obscure to most. The nickname "Long Meg" also has been applied to cannon and to "articles of unusual size," including a standing stone in Cumberland (Brewer, *Dictionary*, 770).

68 *2 Henry IV*, 2.1.34.

Fig. 5. Long Meg, armed and ready. Title page of *The life and death of Long Meg of Westminster* (?1635). Reproduced by permission of the Houghton Library, Harvard University.

riage, while the Hostess has matrimony in mind. When it comes to pass in *Henry V*, the Hostess (now married to Pistol) is no longer funny, nursing Falstaff in his illness and witnessing his death. Furthermore, the comic turns and stories of Mother Bunch live on in a textual monument after her death, much as the *Henry* plays and *Merry Wives* do for Falstaff, centuries after his.

With the antics of Uxor, the vaunting of Long Meg, and the scatology of Mother Bunch, the female body explodes into the powerful field of jesting, using spectacle, sound, and gesture to vault over the top toward the worlds of carnival and the grotesque.[69] Yet the very homeliness of somatic jesting and its firm bonds to the worlds of women's work and neighborhood routine conquers the urge to read them through the lens of festivity that Bakhtin uses to theorize carnival and the marketplace. For some of the women who made their living there, the marketplace seems to have been far from festive. Rather than a place of unbridled expression and collective laughter as Bakhtin describes,[70] it was a place where whores and bawds were whipped, the fishwife was hounded from corner to corner by zealous licensers, alewives were harassed out of business and into poverty, and many women subsisted as beggars and peddlers. This kind of market is not the newly abstract and "placeless" market of capitalism described by Jean-Christophe Agnew, either.[71] It is the noisy physical place summoned by the proverb "three women make a market," from a village square filled with hucksters and tripewives to the great docks and grocers' stalls of Billingsgate.

In *Tittle-Tattle*, the women drinking together at the local alehouse are part of the market yet seem slightly removed, as if the alehouse grants them a respite from the raucous goings-on nearby (see fig. 6). The scene may have appealed to women who saw the print, reminding them of pleasant times with their neighbors and friends. At such meetings a woman could combine sociability with neighborhood duties; an alewife

69 On those topics my work is deeply indebted to Michael Bristol, *Carnival and Theater*; C. L. Barber, *Shakespeare's Festive Comedy*; Robert Weimann, *Shakespeare and the Popular Tradition*; Francois Laroque, *Shakespeare's Festive World*; and Mary Russo, *Female Grotesque*.

70 Bakhtin calls the medieval market a place for simultaneous commerce and celebration, filled with the frank laughter of the collective social body, and sees its performances (including hawkers' cries, Billingsgate, and organized shows) as "imbued with the same atmosphere of freedom, frankness and familiarity" (*Rabelais*, 38).

71 Agnew, *Market and Theater*, esp. 17–46.

Fig. 6. "What news?" Gossips at bakehouse and alehouse. Detail from *Tittle-Tattle; Or, the several Branches of Gossipping* (1600). © Copyright The British Museum.

could combine labor and play. Gossips might hear a bawdy tale of Mother Bunch or marvel at Long Meg, hear about a court scandal or compose a mocking verse about a priest, exercising judging laughter in a society that held them officially powerless. The effects of such inversionary humor could extend far beyond the holiday pleasures of "women on top" into day-to-day life: "The riot of carnival, the impudence of inversion, the cackling of iconoclasm: these for historical materialism are moments within, not alternatives to, that deeper comedy which is the joke of contradiction and its pleasurable release."[72]

Jesting culture indeed offered women "the joke of contradiction," which sometimes threatened to turn gender hierarchy upside down. When jesting texts are considered as an important part of oral culture, the instant comeuppance that jesting women visit on deadbeats, cuckolds, and roarers probably held out a measure of pleasure and solace for real women who exchanged these tales during their everyday rounds— no matter how much their tittle-tattle grated on men's listening ears.

72 See Davis, *Society and Culture,* 143. Quotation from Eagleton, *Walter Benjamin,* 170.

3 Between Women, or All Is Fair at Horn Fair

A Company of Schollers were talking of an impudent wife
that hit Her own husband in the teeth with his hornes; a
puny among them saith, what a foole was hee to let his
wife know that he was a Cuckold.

Gratiae Ludentes

In 1614 a Salisbury woman named Alice Mustian gave a one-woman
show featuring the irregular sexual lives of her neighbors. She set up her
stage on two barrels with boards set across them and charged admission
of "pins and points" for her performance. Acting and singing all the
parts herself, she quickly attracted attention and an audience. The resulting complaint indicates that she was successful in her ridicule: she
made her friends laugh and her enemies angry.[1]

Mustian's tale of a tub may have been a complete anomaly; but it is
far more likely that her show was a satiric jig about cuckoldry, a performance firmly rooted in common culture. Whether in jest or earnest,
horning filled hundreds of ephemeral texts. Those that survive ring
variations on a theme enacted by neighbors for neighbors, by singers
and dancers as part of holiday license, and by actors and clowns. Cuckoldry farce linked street theater and professional theater: Martin Ingram comments that the "humble performance" of Mustian had "obvious affinities with the bawdy, satirical jigs found on the London stage."[2]
As her choice of venue indicates, the most basic playing space was the

---

1 Ingram, "Ridings," 166–67.
2 Ibid., 167.

neighborhood, with its inviting thresholds, windows, yards, and passages. These ordinary stages provided all the props and cast needed for the occasions of horning, whether festive, hostile, or both—from full-blown horn fairs and ridings to scribbled libels and mocking jigs—and produced a public theater audience fully versed in cuckoldry lore.[3]

Our age disdains this rich layer of cultural detritus, finding it boring and unfunny, "the most remote and distasteful of all bygone fashions in humour."[4] Yet the weight of evidence points to a culture that saw horn jokes as a source of dependable delight, fuel for a bullying laughter that grates on our ears. As a key element in a skimmington, for example, horning was meant to spur "mocking laughter, sometimes light-hearted but often taking the form of hostile derision which could, on occasion, escalate into physical violence."[5] Horning was an insult that could draw blood: with just two fingers, one could prompt a charge of libel or provoke a fatal stab. All this makes the horn jest even more intriguing, if no more amusing. As Robert Darnton points out, the most significant artifacts of the past are often the most opaque and inexplicable. His prime example is the joke that is no longer funny.[6]

In early modern England, horning was part of a much larger cultural field than that delimited by jest and insult. During special entertainments, such as plays, and in times of holiday license, horning offered a focus for nonspecific, collective festivity and cathartic hilarity. The meanings of this laughter, which erupted from an aural field of wrangling voices, gossip, and backtalk, cannot be fully understood through recourse to theories of Bakhtinian festivity, Foucauldian subversion and containment, or safety-valve theories about laughter or comedy. Such approaches close off the ideological rifts that threaten to crack open this impenetrably "remote and distasteful" comic subject.

One way out of this impasse is to pay closer attention to the gender of those who took part in cuckoldry culture. Women were not always

---

3 Brand provides a detailed history of the horning gesture, usually made with the index and little fingers (*Observations*, 2:116). For more on the customs of horning and the etymology of *cuckold*, see 113–27. Horns signify cuckoldom in cultures on every continent, causing much anthropological speculation. Major interpretations focus on the devil's horns, the rutting time of bucks, the scapegoat, the myth of Actaeon, the castration of bulls to produce oxen, the lantern made of horn, and the horn of plenty.
4 Thomas, "Place of Laughter," 77.
5 Ingram, "Ridings," 168.
6 Darnton, *Great Cat Massacre*, 5.

silent spectators to male clowning, and they could not have been neu-
tral spectators to stagings of cuckoldry. Like Alice Mustian, they sometimes created this mocking and dangerous laughter. Although women
participated in the cuckoldry-rife modes of jesting, shaming, rude
rhyming, and jigging, their activity has never been used to assess cuckoldry as a cultural phenomenon.[7] Women's horning humor enriched the
dramatic repertoire of the early modern neighborhood, where they
traded gossip and jokes about cuckolds, wrote mocking rhymes heavy
with horn wit, and bought and sang ballads about the cuckold and his
woes. Women pointed their forked fingers or brandished real horns,
sometimes in teasing mockery, sometimes as part of a frontal assault or
a counterattack. After a man harassed one London woman in the street,
for example, she ordered her apprentice to hang horns on her accoster's
door, intending to shame him with the scornful laughter of neighbors
and passersby.[8]

Acknowledging female participation should alter our perspective on
horning's present-day cultural opacity, a problem that Keith Thomas
equates with the genre's cruelty: "For us it is hard to understand why
deceived husbands should have been objects of ridicule rather than
sympathy."[9] This view, while representative, fails to take the gender of
hearers and tellers into account or to frame such jesting in relation to
the harsh subordination under which women lived. Considering the
grinding inequities of legal wife beating, scold bridling, and the double
standard, some women may have found the spectacle of the horned husband more deserving of laughter than pity.

When scholars turn to the question of why English drama was so sat-
urated with cuckoldry, they almost always limit their inquiries to the
psychology of the male spectator. According to Katharine Eisaman
Maus, men were so thoroughly trained to perform close readings of
women's speech, dress, and actions that plays about cuckoldry and tests
of chastity gave them "voyeuristic satisfaction" and a feeling of superiority over the stage cuckold. Nonetheless, spectators strongly resembled stage husbands in their "combination of awareness and ignorance,

7 On women taking part in rough music and skimmingtons, see Ingram, "Ridings," 191; and Brand, *Observations*, 2:120. On women composing mocking rhymes,
see Ingram, "Ridings," 166, 187; and Fox, *Oral and Literate Culture*, 305, 306, 312.
On women jigging, see Baskervill, *Elizabethan Jig*, 11, 13, 19, 33, 41, 110, 124.
8 Gowing, *Domestic Dangers*, 72.
9 Thomas, "Place of Laughter," 77.

marginality and power, distanced superiority and voyeuristic submission to the blandishments of spectacle."[10] Mark Breitenberg even maintains that "a certain mastery over a threatening and helpless situation may have been provided by the very representations of cuckoldry" in stage plays and pamphlets.[11]

Both Maus and Breitenberg speculate about male spectators alone, and both maintain that the reactions of women are somehow unknowable. Such a stance ignores the cues for female responses in the plays themselves and in the manifold texts and performances that made up the cuckoldry culture of early modern England. As the theatrics of Alice Mustian indicate, women were at play in this field of signification, using the props and words of cuckoldry for good and ill. Because of the age's remarkable obsession with horning and bewhoring, both women and men came to the theater fully primed in the processes of surveillance, accusation, and control, keenly attuned to spying out signs of dishonor in both men and women. Again, it is crucial for feminists to challenge the too-common practice of creating a "pre-existing meaning" for a given text by "assuming that the audience is male."[12] Living out their lives under the double standard, women spectators arguably had just as much reason to be fascinated and threatened by the cuckoldry complex as their male counterparts did.

"Sum boy began this game"

One of the seductions of horn logic was its power to make short work of complex and contested narratives. When Thersites reduces the Trojan War to "All the argument is a whore and a cuckold" (*Troilus and Cressida* 2.3.72), he slyly mocks the spectators who flocked to play after play about precisely that argument. On the street and at the theater doors, ballads aired news of local and homely adulteries, while the stage offered plays about sexual betrayal in elevations low (*Johan the Husband*) to middling (*Arden of Feversham*) to lofty (*King Lear*), many of them preceded by a clown's horning gibes at the audience and capped with bawdy jigs about cuckoldry. If sated playgoers decided to pick up

10 Maus, "Horns of Dilemma," 578.
11 Breitenberg, *Anxious Masculinity*, 187.
12 McLuskie, "Feminist Deconstruction," 39.

an Arthurian romance or a volume of English history, they would find more monitory examples of infidelity, male and female. In the Arthurian legends and in chronicles by Speed and Holinshed, "the king's adultery is an immediately familiar emblem for the defilement of the purity of the state and the abdication of responsible government."[13] In accounts of Edward II's horning and murder, Henry VIII's fatal accusations against his queens, or the explosive rumor of Lord Darnley's horning and murder by Mary Stuart, chroniclers and popular authors warned princes to beware the love of women. As Phyllis Rackin observes, "the patrilineal genealogy" that organized both history and society "required the repression of women, and of heteroerotic passion as well, because the invisible, putative connection between fathers and sons that formed the basis of patriarchal authority was—as Shakespeare's cuckold jokes endlessly insist—always dubious, always vulnerable to subversion by an adulterous wife."[14]

Not even religion was free of the horn. During Queen Mary's reign, Catholics bewhored English nuns who had converted to Protestantism under Edward and married. In taking the veil, they had espoused themselves to Christ; wouldn't he be "stirred up to wrathe and indignation" like any other cuckold?[15] Pageant drama, too, had its share of horn jokes. In the "N-Town" *Joseph's Doubt,* spectators have a good laugh at the expense of Joseph, who moans that he'll be ridiculed back in Bethlehem as an "old cokwold" whose "bowe is bent." When Mary explains that the Holy Spirit impregnated her, he angrily cuts her short: "It was sum boy began [th]is game."[16] It takes a miracle for him to believe her: a cherry tree bows down to give Mary its fruit, finally satisfying him that he is not horned but holy.

Like Joseph, many critics who have considered early modern cuckoldry suspect it was "sum boy began this game" and that the prime mover behind the age's obsession was intense male concern about "the other man." Relying on analyses of property transfer in marriage derived from the work of Marcel Mauss and Claude Lévi-Strauss (theories that Gayle Rubin drew on in "The Traffic in Women"), critics as diverse as Coppélia Kahn, Katherine Eisaman Maus, and Eve Kosofsky Sedg-

13 Butler, *Theatre and Crisis,* 41.
14 Rackin, "Foreign Country," 79.
15 Crawford, *Women and Religion,* 35.
16 Play 12, "N-Town" Cycle, cited in Hines, *Fabliau,* 211–12.

wick forward the proposition that cuckoldry narratives focus chiefly on
the flow of homoerotic and political power "between men," in Sedgwick's famous phrase.[17] Douglas Bruster asserts that only the male
lover, never the wife, is "the one who cuckolds" and that women are
"helpless counters" in a transfer between males.[18]

While the cuckoldry paradigm is certainly about male-male
economies of desire, it seems futile to deny that it is also about female
pleasure and will. In some tales the "helpless counter" is not the wife at
all but the lover, who is hidden, coached, and directed by the wife.
Many tales name the wife as "the one who cuckolds," while the husband is the object. One lame jest puns on this relationship:

> Q. Why doth the man weare the hornes whereas the woman doth make
> them?
> A. Because the man is the head.[19]

More often than not, the merry books feature women who act on their
desires for revenge, love, or sexual satisfaction using the weapons of allies, wit, daring, and timing. A surprising number of tales direct no criticism at the wife or lover but instead upbraid the husband and his faults:
impotence, jealousy, brutality. Finally, some comic narratives give
prominent play to a husband's lechery as the cause of his wife's infidelity
or her threat to give him horns. The author of *Jane Anger, her Protection
for Women* (1589) certainly thought her readers would enjoy hearing why
skirt chasers so often became cuckolds: "some of them will follow the
smocke as Tom Bull will runne after a town Cow. But, lest they should
running slip and breake their pates, the Gods, provident of their welfare,
set a paire of tooters on their foreheads, to keepe it from the ground."[20]

To explain all such narratives by recourse to the theory that women
are counters passed from male to male is to accept a monolithic, one-
sex model of drama and social power. This is unwarranted in light of the
abundant popular materials that dwell on women's abilities to manipu-
late and subvert, if only in fantasy, a sexual marketplace that urged

17 See Sedgwick, *Between Men*, esp. 21–27; and Rubin, "Traffic." Kahn maintains
that "cuckoldry, like rape, is thus an affair between men, rather than between men
and women or husbands and wives" ("Savage Yoke," 150). An exception to the scholarly consensus is Morgan-Russell, "No Good Thing," 70–84, esp. 82–83.

18 Bruster, *Drama and the Market*, 84.

19 *Gratiae Ludentes*, 65.

20 Henderson and McManus, *Half Humankind*, 176.

them to be pliant commodities. Too many stories show the commodity striking back, besting husbands described as deserving cuckolds or proving them hypocrites. More important, the favored genres of the horn—ballad, jig, novella, and jest—often portray women as storytellers and performers, which is not so surprising given that real women engaged in precisely these forms of popular mimesis.[21]

Why would women enjoy these tales? First, many tales assert that women possess a satiric weapon in a world that continually denies them agency and wit. They offer harsh judgment fitting to the harsh conditions of most women's lives, inviting readers to mock abusive, alcoholic, or philandering husbands, all of which were in ample supply. Second, within the jesting literature, poverty and beatings at home are cited as motives behind many extramarital encounters. The narrator in *Cornu-Copiae* (1612) reasons that, by taking lovers, women may be looking for something more than sexual pleasure:

> Sometimes the golden prey doth make the theife,
> And women yeeld for further maintenance:
> Sometimes short commons makes them seeke reliefe:
> And stubborn usage and sterne countenance,
> Perforce constraine a woman now and than
> To seeke for comfort of a kinder man;
> And sometimes want of heartes, when hands are married,
> Is one great cause, that many have miscarried.[22]

It is remarkable how often such passages occur in texts that are otherwise crudely antifeminist. (*Cornu-Copiae* goes on to show a man trapped into marriage, with her family's collusion, by a woman impregnated by another man.) Other jests and ballads target hard-handed husbands who drink to excess. Narratives about tavern-haunting, foul-

---

21 See note 7. I borrow the phrase "popular mimesis" from Jim Stokes, who is documenting a rich tradition of female performance and creativity ("Women and Mimesis," 176–96). Boccaccio paid homage to women's storytelling skills in the *Decameron*, the west's principal trove of cuckoldry tales. Basile's *Pentamerone* features crusty old wives who compete to make an agelastic princess laugh, while Marguerite de Navarre expanded ingeniously on the Boccaccian model in *Heptaméron*. English popular texts are more ambivalent: old wives are belittled as garrulous crones, yet they are also sought after entertainers skilled at telling juicy tales of horror, magic, and sexual pranks. On unlettered women as storytellers, also see Reay, *Popular Culture in Seventeenth Century England*, 11–12; Fox, *Oral and Literate Culture*, chap. 3; and Lamb, "Taken by the Fairies," 301.

22 "Pasquil Anglicanus," in *Cornu-Copiae*, sig. D.

mouthed husbands sometimes show a bias toward the female reader. These may function as ripostes to the more misogynist specimens of the gossips' literature, in which drunken shrews plot how to beat and cuckold their husbands. *Pasquils Palinodia*'s "Muse of Sack" warns men that a husband's brutality can drive a wife to adultery:

> And blame her not for shee is not of steele,
> Nor made of iron, brasse, or such hard mettle,
> Neither so senseless that she cannot feele
> But she is us'd as tinker doe his kettle. . . .
> Then straight he calls her half a dozen whores,
> And to the Taverne gets him out of doores. . . .
> Then druncke, at midnight, home the knave doth creepe,
> And beats his wife, and spues, and falls asleep.
>
> Shall a vast unthrift with a false pretence
> Wrong his poore wife, and be exempt from blame?
> And shall a woman, who hath a just offence
> And forc'd by dogged usage to her shame,
> If she another friend doth entertaine,
> To give her some content, and ease her paine,
> Shall she be censur'd with disgraceful speeches,
> And he stand cleere because he wares the breeches?[23]

The answer goes without saying—she'll be censured, and he'll "stand cleere"—but at least the text identifies and questions the double standard, an example of the counterhegemonic articulation that is sometimes audible in popular texts.[24] Such a passage does not offer up the ventriloquized voice of a female subject. Rather, it is a beckoning slot in discourse, an invitation to debate that may be taken up by multiple voices, including women's. Frances Dolan argues that popular representations of cuckoldry "constitute the wife as a subject only to the extent that they qualify [the] husband's claim to subject status by silencing and immobilizing him and casting doubt on his authority and potency."[25] This restricts the meanings of fictions of cuckoldry largely to

23 *Pasquils Palinodia,* reprinted in Collier, *Illustrations,* 1:9. The pamphlet has been attributed variously to Nicholas Breton and William Fennor.
24 See Thomas, "Double Standard," and Capp's important revision of its conclusions, "Double Standard Revisited."
25 Dolan, *Dangerous Familiars,* 36.

effects on two key players, with the wife gaining only a partial and limited hold on subject status at any one moment. Dolan suggests but underplays the key role of the audience in apportioning social power. Laughers judge and shape the struggle, conferring agency ambiguously yet palpably. In comic interactions the social nexus does more to constitute subjects than does the status of the players or the texts they choose. As Rosaline says to Berowne, "A jest's prosperity lies in the ear / Of him that hears it, never in the tongue / Of him that makes it" (*Love's Labour's Lost* 5.2.861–63). The proliferating jests of cuckoldry do not simply reproduce gender ideology: they also provide contestatory narratives that invite women's participation.

"All Is Fair at Horn Fair!"

The "multitudinous and indecorous" jests and props of horning were readily available for those indulging in noisy excess during festive play.[26] The prime example is Horn Fair at Charlton, held every year on St. Luke's Day (October 18). Although it seems counterintuitive that women would celebrate symbols that impugn their sexual honor, in fact this famous fair was a carnival for, and dominated by, women.[27] For three days boisterous crowds of "roystering matrons and swaggering blades" with horns in their hats and hands paraded through the streets, trading ribald jokes and bawdy songs and doing their best to obey the rule of misrule: "All is fair at Horn Fair!" Despite the rough music and rude gestures, the revelry apparently bred few brawls or scandals. Names were named and fingers pointed "all in jest." [28] Women and men wore masks or appeared in cross-dressed disguise. Playing kings, queens, millers, shrews, and cuckolds, fairgoers went from tavern to alehouse to green, shouting "Horns! Horns!" Some women brought props and mimed the skimmington or flocked to fairbooths, where they

26 Quotation from editor's note in *Roxburghe Ballads*, 7:196.
27 Reay, *Popular Culture in Seventeenth Century England*, 11. *Horn fair* has several meanings. A skimmington aimed at a cuckold was sometimes known by this name, but more usually a horn fair was a festive local gathering with horn motifs and sometimes an actual cattle market. Charlton was the most famous of the festivals. See Thompson, "Rough Music," 483–84.
28 *Roxburghe Ballads*, 8:668.

could buy "every kind of toy made of horn; even the ginger-bread figures
have horns."[29]

The transgressive release of playacting, cross-dressing, and making
light sport with symbols of illicit desire may well have had considerable
appeal for women; in any event, the Charlton Horn Fair managed to survive into the early nineteenth century.[30] For both married and unmarried women, the festival offered them a chance to escape the round of
domestic duties—to joke, flirt, dance, and sing. One ballad advertises
these pleasures:

> At *Charlton* there was a Fair, where lads and lasses did meet;
> Young *Johnny* and *Jenny* came there, to dance to the fiddle so sweet.
> Brisk *Sue*, she led up a Dance, and called for *Sellenger's Round*,
> And *Nelly* to *Will* did advance, and neatly trip't o'er the ground;
> Fair *Frances*, with her fine meen, and *Dorothy*, gay as a Queen,
> With *Fanny* and pritty-faced *Nanny*, the glory of all the Green.
> The *Wives* from their houses fled, and thither with joy did repair,
> Forsaking their Husbands' dull bed, to find out Gallants at *Horn-Fair*,
> There kisses with glasses go round, upon the Maids' Marmalet cheek,
> And many sweet pleasures were found, which vainly their Husbands
>   did seek.[31]

Women's merrymaking during horn fair incensed Daniel Defoe, who
carped that they behaved "as if it was a day that justify'd their giving
themselves loose to all manner of indecency and immodesty, without
any reproach, or without suffering the censure which such behaviour
would deserve at another time."[32] A fanciful bit of Charlton lore required all cuckolds to dig gravel to make smooth paths for their wives
to walk on to the fair. In a stark reversal, this tableau creates a world upside down in which husbands suffer in silence, laboring on while their
mobile and haughty wives crow over them. One ballad, *The Scolding
Wife's Vindication*, bears a woodcut of two grim men at their shovels;
in the text an angry wife bewails her husband's sexual inertia:

> He's lain like a log of wood, in bed, for a year or two,
> And won't afford me any good, *he nothing at all would do.* . . .
> I am in my blooming prime, dear Neighbours, I tell you true,

29 Brand, *Observations*, 2:121; and Thompson, *Customs in Common*, 483–88.
30 *Roxburghe Ballads*, 7:196; and Thompson, *Customs in Common*, 483–84.
31 "Hey for Horn Fair!" (circa 1685), in *Roxburghe Ballads*, 8:661.
32 Quoted in Reay, *Popular Culture in Seventeenth Century England*, 11.

I am loath to lose my teeming time, *yet nothing at all he'll do*. . . .
Long, long have I liv'd at strife, I kick'd, and I cuff'd him too,
He's like to live no better life, *since nothing at all he'll do*.
I solemnly do declare, believe me, this is true!
He shall dig gravel at next Horn Fair, *and that he is like to do*.[33]

As this ballad suggests, cuckoldry humor tends to dwell on the horned man's powerlessness and social humiliation. While many songs and jests ridicule the scold and shrew who make men's horns, the jesting literature lavishes far more attention on those who wear them: the jealous husband obsessed with spying out his wife's "privie secrets," the spineless wittol who turns a blind eye, or the impotent old pantaloon who bores his young wife. The latter spectacle evokes sneers of contempt. The narrator of *Cornu-Copiae* savagely lampoons "old Mopsimus" as a "rotten horse" and an "olde cock sparrow" and pities his young bride, who "falls in longing for the Thing":

No marvell then if that a lusty Lasse,
That looks as fresh, as flower doth in May,
When she is mated with a foolish Asse,
Which storms like Winter on his wedding Day,
Sometimes seek change of pasture and Provant,
Because her commons be at home so scant?
For in a dri'd herring, and poore John,
Remaines more vertue then in old men's bones. (sig. B2v)

Cuckolds' clever or bloody deeds of revenge are quite rare in a narrative field crowded with tales of wives and lovers outwitting husbands, most of whom have little wit to begin with.[34] A few tales trade on "bottom up" satire, in which wives take lovers of lower rank and then taunt proud lords who are uncrowned *and* horned. In Marguerite de Navarre's *Heptaméron* the King of Naples seduces the wife of a gentleman, who realizes the insult and then informs and seduces the Queen, urging her to take revenge. The two rival couples trade horning taunts, to the court's amusement, until the King is finally bested, his crown turned to

---

33 *Roxburghe Ballads*, 7:196–97.
34 In Painter's *Palace of Pleasure*, horned husbands get nasty revenges. In tale 43 (1:190–96) a wife is sealed in a dungeon with the stinking corpse of her lover, and in tale 58 (2:171–73) an old man tricks his adulterous young wife into eating poison. The book was aimed at a more upscale subset of readers compared with the audience for ballads and jest books, in which cuckolds rarely end up on top.

horns that evoke ridicule in his subjects. Both men act like idiots in the course of cuckolding each other, while the wives are satisfied with the arrangement they have chosen. One reader concludes that "Marguerite's feminist project, highly comic by definition and in execution . . . is to portray both the male deceiver and the deceived male as butts of infidelity, of nature, of culture, of comedy."[35]

Considering the combined weight of religious doctrine, law, and local mechanisms enforcing the regulation of wives, it is truly remarkable that so many tales reward sinning wives without laying down a moral condemning them. Cuckoldry discourse is rife with such paradox and aporia. For example, the spectacle of husbands who are the last to know sometimes seems designed to make women smile and men feel their foreheads. Even a domestic tragedy such as *Arden of Feversham*, based on a notorious husband murder and ending with executions, "can be seen as an extended cuckoldry joke," as Dolan points out. "Like such jokes, and like popular shaming rituals such as the charivari, the play holds the cuckolded husband responsible for his wife's adultery and insubordination."[36] Such popular satire reasserts patriarchal authority by urging vigilance over wives, but it also highlights the tenuousness of male claims to that authority. The laughter evoked is always ambiguous, not to say corrosive of tragic dignity.

In the jesting literature, adultery—the most aggressive act of wifely treachery short of murder—sometimes serves as payback for mistreatment. When Emilia justifies adultery in her famous speech in *Othello*, her reasons would have been as familiar as Iago's barbs about women being "bells in their parlors" and "huswives in their beds." She reads chapter and verse from the jesting literature, listing all the usual faults of husbands:

> Say that they slack their duties,
> And pour their treasures into foreign laps;
> Or else break out in peevish jealousies,
> Throwing restraint upon us; say they strike us,
> Or scant our former having in despite:
> Why, we have galls; and though we have some grace,
> Yet we have some revenge.
>
> (4.3.87–94)

---

35 Nash, "Male Butt," 152–53. The story is novella 3 in *Heptaméron*, which is the basis for tale 51 in Painter's *Palace of Pleasure*.
36 Dolan, *Dangerous Familiars*, 36.

By decrying husbands' "peevish" suspicions just before her phrase about striking wives, Emilia links male jealousy directly to wife beating—a particularly live topic of concern to any women listening. Indeed, stage representations of the violently jealous husband, such as Leontes and Othello, seem tailor-made to engage women's interest and contempt.

The horn-mad motif is generically flexible, adaptable to tragic, satiric, comic, and mixed modes, perhaps because it resists all logic. Although horn-mad husbands are not actually cuckolded, they are always classed with true cuckolds in the comic typologies that flowed from the presses. While the wittol wears horns and doesn't care and the unwitting cuckold wears horns and doesn't know, the horn-mad cuckold makes his own horns out of nothing. In *Tarltons Newes out of Purgatorie* (1590), Tarlton's ghost encounters three "cuckold-kings" enthroned in purgatory: the unwitting cuckold, the wittol, and the horn-mad cuckold, whose arms feature "the Asse, with a marvelous paire of long and large eares," which make him the biggest fool of all.[37] The text invites readers to ridicule all such asses for exhibiting the "restless sting" of jealousy, stoking an unruly masculinity that was especially dangerous to their wives and neighbors.

When a jealous tyrant brutalized his wife and wrecked the common peace, female neighbors watched and intervened; they sometimes used mockery and gossip to control the abuse. "Jealous men are either knaves or coxcombs" went the proverb, but onstage they are often both.[38] Every horn-mad husband in Shakespeare threatens his wife with violence or murder, and in each case the transgressor is humiliated by his wife or her allies. Master Ford of *Merry Wives* is an inept fool without the wit to torture and bewhore his wife as he wishes; King Leontes of *The Winter's Tale* rages in a manner that out-Herods Herod; and Othello draws gibes from Emilia, and perhaps from original audiences as well, in his quick dissolution into homicidal frenzy.[39] Women spectators were well aware of the dangers such men posed. The spectacle of their comeuppance may have tempered women's laughter with suspense and fear, alternating tension and release.

---

37 *Cobler of Caunterburie*, 161. The author tried to top *Tarltons Newes* by naming eight kinds of cuckolds and describing them in tedious detail (159–62).
38 Stevenson, *Home Book*, 1263.
39 In "*Othello* and Italophobia," I argue that the play invites women to show scorn rather than sympathy for the horn-mad stranger Othello (189–90).

For women living in a world of blows and accusations, plays and merry tales may even have furnished them with a few quick answers. Some present the pleasing spectacle of a raging husband stymied by a wife's well-timed vow to horn him. *The Bachelors Banquet* warns men not to resort to blows because a beaten wife will "become shameless, converting into deadly hate the love that she should bear him" and lead her to tell her neighbors he's a cuckold.[40] This fate is supposedly worse than the pain of living with an unfaithful wife. The jesting literature exaggerates the leverage this possibility supposedly gave to wives. Often a wife's threats seem to be mere bravado, but within the dream-work of a stage fiction it does the trick. In John Fletcher's *The Woman's Prize, or The Tamer Tamed*, Maria boldly answers Petruchio's promise to beat her:

> I defie you.
> And my last loving teares, farwell: the first stroke,
> The very first you give me, if you dare strike,
> Try me, and you shall finde it so, for ever
> Never to be recall'd: I know you love me,
> Mad till you have enjoy'd me; I doe turne
> Utterly from you, and what man I meet first
> That has but spirit to deserve a favour,
> Let him beare any shape, the worse the better
> Shall kill you, and enjoy me.[41]

This confounds Petruchio, who stamps and swears but stops talking about cudgels. Real women may have hurled this threat, but the extreme danger of carrying it out surely mitigated its impact.

More common, and possibly more useful, were jests in which wives got the better of husbands who hounded them verbally about their fidelity. Ignoring friends' warnings about the futility of their quest, fretful husbands seek sexual and linguistic certainty, often by demanding riddles of their wives or forcing them to take oaths.[42] Sometimes the

40 *Bachelors Banquet*, 60. This 1603 work is based on the fifteenth-century *Les Quinze Joies de Mariage*. Its authorship is uncertain, but strong arguments have been made for Thomas Dekker and Robert Tofte (23–24).

41 Fletcher, *Woman's Prize*, in *Dramatic Works*, 4:88–89. Wives make similar threats in *Wit of a Woman* and Middleton's *Family of Love*; see Woodbridge, *Women*, 179.

42 A jealous husband makes his wife swear on a Bible about whether or not he is a cuckold, which he had been called "in company, between in earnest and game." She

trial takes the form of a madcap wager posed by the husband. In *The Mad Men of Gotham*, a fool bets his wife that she cannot make him a cuckold. She hides all the spigots in the house and asks him to plug a running tap for her while she goes to fetch a spigot. She goes next door and has sex with a compliant tailor. Returning, she says, "pull out thy finger out of the tap-hole, gentle Cuckold: for you have lost your bargaine." When he beshrews her, her retort is to the point: "Make no such bargaines then, said she, with me."[43] This kind of jesting is two-edged: antifeminist in casting the wife as innately treacherous and antimasculinist in laughing at the massive stupidity of the husband. But it should also be recognized that women were celebrated in proverbs and jests for their mental quickness in a pinch and their uncanny talent for solving impossible riddles. The idea that female wit was sometimes admired and applauded jars categories that have been cemented into place, yet there are many riddle- and wager-solving women in popular culture. One witty wife in *A Hundred Merry Tales* takes on the challenge of solving a riddling bet her husband made but cannot figure out, winning by using only a pun and a broken jug. The moral: "by this, ye may see that a woman's wit at an extremity is much better than a man's."[44]

Occasionally a woman's wit is cited less as proof of perfidy than as an example of acumen, recorded in the grudging spirit of giving an opponent her due. In a story from *Tarltons Jests*, Tarlton decides to lay a wager with his wife:

> Tarlton, being merily disposed as his Wife and he sat together, he said unto her, "Kate, answer me to one question without a lie and take this crown of gold"—which she took on condition that if she lost, to restore it back again.
>
> Quoth Tarlton, "Am I a Cuckold or no, Kate?" Whereat she answered not a word, but stood silent, not-withstanding he urged her many ways.
>
> Tarlton, seeing she would not speak, asked his gold again.
>
> "Why?" quoth she. "Have I made any lie?"
>
> "No," says Tarlton.

---

resists as long as she can but finally takes the book and swears that he is indeed a cuckold. "By the mass, whore," said he, "thou liest! Thou sayest it for none other than to anger me" (*Tales and Quick Answers*, in Zall, *Hundred Merry Tales*, 255).

43 Hazlitt, *Shakespeare Jest-Books*, 3:16.

44 Zall, *Hundred Merry Tales*, jest 49.

"Why, then, goodman fool, I have won the wager."
Tarlton, mad with anger, made this rhyme
  As women can with speech revile a man,
  So can they in silence beguile a man.[45]

Tarlton's wife outclowns the clown by Tarltonizing with a difference.
She wittily solves the chastity test by parodying the submissive wife—
ambiguously silent, verbally chaste, ironically obedient. Her tactical silence angers her husband and wins her gold, but it also suggests that
keeping mum was a common enough policy when real husbands tried
to pry out admissions of incontinence. Though she spoils her husband's
merry mood, she plays by the rules of the game; her own chastity stays
out of the reach of discourse, while her brief triumph survives.

Playing Dirty: The Cuckold Bewrayed

In jests, foolish cuckolds often end up "bewrayed" with feces or
urine. Such scatology openly associates unfathomable female sexuality
with an intolerable threat to male genital and anal decorum. One jest
starkly sets out this association: "He that is Jealous, and tryes after his
wife, yet with no Desire to find her false; Is like one that comming into
a Darke Privie, groapes with his Hand, to examine the Cleanness of the
Seat, but would be sorry to find it otherwise."[46] A scornful country
maid mocks her lovesick swain by warning him that his too-urgent love
will wreak havoc with his trousers, first because his unrequited passion
will stain them with semen and later because if he does win her, he is
likely to earn horns that will cause him to befoul his clothing and his
honor. Her charming refrain: "Good sir, you'll wrong your breeches."[47]

In *The Parliament of Women* (1640), a royalist pamphlet satirizing
Puritans as cuckolds, a convocation of Puritan shrews discusses how to
cure a drunken spouse who wears the insignia of the fool and cuckold:

> Then spake Mistris Dorothy Doe-Little, and say'd: My good man came
> home drunke the other day, and because I should not see him in that

45 From *Tarlton's Jests*, in Zall, *Nest of Ninnies*, 93–94.
46 Le Strange, *Merry Passages*, item 526.
47 *Pepys Ballads*, 1:41.

manner, he hid himself in the house of Speciall Office, and there he began to ease his stomacke, and to lay about him like a Hogge when hee hath eaten so much he is ready to burst; and because I should not heare him, he thrusts his head into the hole; and whether it was his large Asses eares, or his Bull head and necke I cannot tell, but he could not get his head out againe, but needes must pull up the seat about his necke, so that he looked as if he had been in the Pillory. Upon which, relation they all fell into a great laughter, and withall concluded that it was his horns.[48]

As Susan Wiseman has shown, the scene of bodily undoing and un-control is part of the "porno-political rhetoric" launched against women who attempted to act in the public sphere during the Civil War.[49] The elements for these caricatures are taken from the ranker reaches of the gossips' literature. Even in this dark subcellar of comic misogyny, there are jests in which the leaky body of woman takes its revenge.[50] In Richard Brathwait's *Art Asleep Husband? A Boulster Lecture* (1640), two husbands argue over whether one of their wives is unfaithful. The first husband allows the second to hide in his bedchamber all night, confront his wife in the guise of a spirit, and scare the truth out of her. The ruse works, and the wife confesses to having slept with no less than three lovers. The next night, the cuckolded man sneaks into the bedroom of his helpful neighbor to play the same trick. Hiding behind the arras, he calls out to the terrified wife that he knows she has slept with one, then two, then three men. Finally she explodes:

Never but twice. yea thrice, and thrice, thou mopp-fac'd Incubus (quoth she) and more than all you Haggs have hornes in your lower region. And with that, whipping out a bed, as if this Spirit of phrensy had wrought some strange operation on Her body, and drawing neare to her

48 *Parliament of Women*, sig. B2v.
49 See Wiseman, "Adam." For more on the political import of the antifeminist satire in "Ladies Parliament" pamphlets, see Achinstein, "Women on Top."
50 On female leakiness see Paster, *Body Embarrassed*, 23–63. Nonetheless, male incontinence, whether deliberate or involuntary, surpasses women's in the jest books—for example, in the jest biographies of Scogin and Howleglas. When excrement is used as a comic weapon, women are often on the receiving end. In *The Life and Death of the merry Devill of Edmonton*, a clownish drunkard named Smug trades tricks and blows with his shrewish wife. One night he goes to bed so drunk that he pisses in a sieve instead of the chamberpot, drenching his wife (sig. F3v).

close-stool which stood shrowded under the Arras; instead of it she fell upon the Spirit, on whom for want of stoole of ease, she eased herself sufficiently, till that ayry Spirit resolv'd it selfe to a substantiall body.[51]

In this scatological variant on "the biter bitten," a cuckold who attempts to besmear and deceive receives his comeuppance, while the wife decisively shifts her shaming and punishment onto her tormentor. Forced confession acts as a purge, sluicing out the woman's body as well as her tongue. But in her case she has probably "eased herself" deliberately, as her angry outburst suggests—and the "phrensy" he has provoked merely substantiates the shame he had hoped to escape. As below the belt as this story is, it still directs female laughter at the bewrayed would-be confessor. While the woman is the target of a conspiracy between men to trap her, she retaliates in a way that may have struck home to women who had to endure smearing and terror tactics from jealous husbands or fathers who were haranguing them to confess incontinent acts. Bakhtin refers to such excremental images as a cure for cosmic fear: "Cosmic catastrophe represented in the material bodily lower stratum is degraded, humanized, and transformed into grotesque monsters. Terror is conquered by laughter."[52] The laughter Brathwait's story evokes might conquer terror in some listeners, but its denouement would probably have appealed far less to husbands who made a habit of interrogating their wives.

Through the quick reversals of comedy, stage lechers who cheat on their wives sometimes manage to cuckold themselves, enduring spectacular "disciplines of shame" into the bargain. In Chapman, Jonson, and Marston's *Eastward Ho,* the old usurer Security colludes with Sir Petronel Flash, who wants to ditch his new bride for a lawyer's wife and flee with her to Virginia. Sir Petronel double-crosses him and steals away with Security's wife in a boat. Security pursues them downriver, but all are capsized in a storm. Security comes ashore at Cuckold's Haven, *"without his hat, in a nightcap, wet band, etc."* (4.2.42). The tableau is completed by a pole holding horns, as was once placed at the actual spot on the Thames called Cuckold's Haven.[53] A butcher, Slitgut,

---

51 Brathwait, *Ar't Asleep Husband?* 54–55.

52 Bakhtin, *Rabelais,* 336.

53 In 1598 a traveler saw Cuckold's Point (or Haven) at a spot near Rotherhithe on the Thames and described it as "a long pole with ram's horns fixed on it, the intention of which was vulgarly said to be a reflection on willful and contented cuckolds" (*Roxburghe Ballads,* 7:195).

is on hand to spy on Security's ludicrous condition. Having climbed the pole to attach a new pair of horns, the butcher tells Security where he has landed. The water-logged usurer vows to drown himself but falls down. In this pathetic pose he whimpers,

> Landed at Cuckold's Haven! If it had not been to
> die twenty times alive, I should never have scap'd
> death! I will never arise more; I will grovel here and
> eat dirt till I be chok'd; I will make the gentle earth
> do that which the cruel water hath denied me.
>
> *Slitgut:* Alas, good father, be not so desperate! Rise
> man; if you will, I'll come down presently and lead you
> home.
>
> *Security.* Home! shall I make any know my home that has
> known me thus abroad? How low should I crouch away,
> that no eye may see me? I will creep on the earth while
> I live, and never look heaven in the face more.
>
> > *[Exit, creeping.]*[54]

Security's abjection repeats that of the serpent expelled from the Garden, and Security has indeed sinned by hissing encouraging words of seduction into the ear of a woman he believes is another man's wife but who turns out to be his own (3.4.161–73). The joke on Security is that he is no more secure than the lusty Frauncis in *Attowell's Jig*, who covets Besse, his neighbor's wife, but ends up sleeping with his own wife, believing she is Besse. The lecher-lured-into-a-bed trick is tailor-made for female laughter, especially when the accosted wife comes up with the sexual switch that protects her name and her husband's forehead. Besse gets a public apology and ten pounds from her would-be seducer and, perhaps sweetest of all, the last word:

> *Besse.* He hath paid for this I trow.
> > All women learn of me.
> *Frauncis.* All me by me take heed
> > How you a woman trust.
> *Besse.* Nay women trust no men.

54 Chapman, Jonson, and Marston, *Eastward Ho*, in *Elizabethan Plays*, 4.1.54–68.

> *Frauncis.* And if they do: how then?
> *Besse.* Ther's few of them prove just. . . .
>   And if you stay at home,
>   And use not thus to rome,
>   heere all our quarrel ends.[55]

"Hear my tale or kiss my tail"

If women were encouraged to laugh at the cuckold and the lecher in plays and farces, they were also invited to add their own tales to the mix when they sat down to gossip, spin, sew, or work in the marketplace. Many jests portray the scabrous mockery of the cuckold as a well-defined pastime of women, and several merry books give special prominence to women storytellers. Because such texts circulated mainly through reading aloud and among groups, not through silent, solitary reading, depictions of women as storytellers invite their readers to act as performers as well. One series of merry books that features old wives as authorities for tales of cuckoldry begins with *Tarltons News Out of Purgatorie* (1590). Tarlton's ghost launches into a mock diatribe against "upstart Protestants" for denying purgatory, for it is a place "that all our great grandmothers have talkt of, [and] that Dant hath so learnedly writ of . . . yet if thou wert so incredulous that thou wouldst neither beleeve our olde beldames, nor the good Bishops: yet take *Dicke Tarlton* once for thine Author."[56] Tarlton's ghost goes on to describe the penances of various characters languishing in purgatory, the bulk of whom are characters in cuckoldry stories drawn from jest books, Boccaccio, and Bandello.

Within the year *Tarltons Newes* was answered by an anonymous "invective," *The Cobler of Caunterburie*, which has a Chaucerian frame and Boccaccian contents. This time the female taleteller has a speaking part. The frame is a journey by barge from Billingsgate to Gravesend, and the storytellers are an old wife, a cobbler, a smith, a gentleman, a scholar, and a summoner. Before introducing the old woman who is given pride of place as the first storyteller, the cobbler-narrator courts

---

55 "*Frauncis new Jigge,* between Frauncis a Gentleman, and Richard a Farmer" (or *Attowell's Jig*), in Baskervill, *Elizabethan Jig,* 450–64.
56 *Cobler of Caunterburie,* 146.

his rustic readers and listeners, salting his overtures with gentle satire directed partly against women:

> Here is a gallimaufre of all sorts. . . . When the Farmer is set in his Chaire turning (in a winters evening) the crabbe in the fier, heere may hee heare how his sonne can reade, and when he hath done laugh while his belly akes. The old wives that wedded themselves to the profound histories of Robin hood, Clim of the Clough, and worthy syr Isembras: may here learne a tale to tell amongst their Gossipes.[57]

What is striking is the way gender governs the overlay of didacticism and pastime: the young son reads aloud to show his father his literacy, while the old wives "learne" a tale to tell other women. What this cozy picture leaves out, of course, is the old dame who may have taught the son to read.

After the appearance of *Cobler of Caunterburie,* other pamphlet writers took up this riverine vein, offering tales and jests told by travelers on the Thames. John Taylor, the Water Poet, offered up vivid reports on his journeys on the river and abroad. Maidservants and apprentices were drawn to his works; one writer sneered that such readers indulged in Taylor's "merry wherry-books" in their "kitchen-cobweb-nooks."[58] In one such book, Taylor's wherry companions trade tale for tale to pass the time from Billingsgate to Gravesend. Along the way a woman distinguishes herself by her adroit storytelling.[59] *The Canterbury Tales* was never far in the background in suck works, with writers invoking the name of Chaucer even when storytellers went no farther than the local tavern. In the hugely popular *Tis Merry When Gossips Meet* (1602), Samuel Rowlands boasts that he can offer readers a maid, wife, *and* widow, outdoing Chaucer: "of blithe wenches scarcelie he hath / Of all that crue none but the Wife of Bath"[60]

In 1620, another pamphlet in the Chaucerian mode appeared on the stalls—this time featuring an all-woman cast of fishwives. *Westward for Smelts, Or, The Water-mans Fare of mad-merry Western wenches* (1620, but possibly first published in 1604) opens with six market-

---

57 Ibid., 20.
58 Abraham Holland, quoted in Capp, *World of John Taylor,* 72; on Taylor's readership see 69–71.
59 Ibid., 86–87.
60 "Dedication," in Rowlands, *Tis Merry.*

women hiring a waterman to row them home from London. The time of
year is Lent, and "this company of Western Fishwives, having made a
good market, with their heads full of Wine, and their purses full of
coine, were desirous to goe homeward."[61] After a while "Kinde Kit"
sees his passengers nodding off, so he wakes them up and offers to sing
a song "to continue their mirth":

> They prayed me so to doe: but yet not to cloy their eares with an old Fi-
> dlers Song, as Riding to Rumford, or, All in a Garden Greene. I said, I
> scorned to do so, for I would give them a new one, which neither
> Punke, Fidler, or Ballad-singer had ever polluted with their unsavourie
> breath: the subject was, I told them, of a Servingman and his Mistris.
> They liked this subject well, and intreated me to proceed, promising
> that each of them would requite my Song with a Tale. (sig. A3v)

The serving man in Kit's song dilates on his mistress's charms and
his duty to her but then suddenly confesses that lust drove him to hide
in her closet to spy on her getting undressed for bed:

> Her bright beauty maz'd me
> All her parts well pleas'd me,
> For of pleasant sights I had my fill,
> Then'gan her hand for to uncover
> Her whitest neck, and roundest pap:
> Then gan I to discover
> More pleasing sights, yet way'l my hap
> Still I stood obscured
> And these sights indured:
>   Yet I to this goddesse durst not speake. . . .
> Therefore will I rest contented,
> With private pleasures that I viewed,
> And never with love be tormented,
> Yet love I her, for that she shewed. (sig. A4)

The voyeur's song leaves Kit's listeners cold. He is forced to prod
them for a response:

> I askt them how they liked my Song? They said little to it. At last, Well,
> quoth a venerable Matron (or rather a matron of Venery) that sate on a

61 *Westward*, sig. A3r.

cushion at the upper end of the Boat, let us now performe our promises
to him in telling every one her tale. . . . so the Waterman shall be sure
of his requitall promised by us, which shall bee Fishwives Tales, that
are wholesome, though but homely. (sig. A4v)

The fishwives are deeply unimpressed as their glum expressions in
the title-page woodcut suggest (see fig. 7). Not only does no one look
"mad-merry," but no one is even speaking, creating an ironic visual un-
dertow to the jovial subtitle and its allusion to tongues "like Bell-clappers, that never leave ringing." Of course, popular woodcuts in cheap
print works were often recycled and printed with little regard for the
text; but when one does match so exactly, the relation of image to text
demands to be read. Perhaps this depicts the moment of silence when
Kit asked for reactions to his song, or it may be a sly dig at the conventions of garrulous fishwives and singing watermen. In the text, the
women are certainly depicted as self-assured critics and adept competi-
tors in the storytelling game. The contest is marked by rules of gender,
genre, and status: a male sings in the persona of a servant, in a strained
attempt at Ovidian erotic verse, while the women go on to tell mostly
bawdy tales *in propria persona*, in prose of low to middling elevations.
The song of Kinde Kit—possibly a cutting allusion to Marlowe—broad-
casts closeted masturbatory fantasy and fails to amuse.[62] The women's
tales are dramatic, public, explicit, and even violent, exciting laughter,
applause, and finally controversy. While Kit maintains his role as a
somewhat hostile framer of the tales, introducing several with unflat-
tering verse descriptions, his actions show that he is eager to hear
merry tales from his passengers rather than furnish them. He is no John
Taylor, boasting of his vast stores of wit, as their laconic response
proves.

In similar fashion, Peele's *The Old Wive's Tale* pairs a sought-after female teller with a desiring but patronizing male. Three roaring boys be-
seech Madge Mumblecrust to tell some good ones: "methinks, gammer,
a merry winter's tale would drive away the time trimly: come, I am sure
you are not without a score."[63] As in *Westward*, intergender air time is
not granted without a struggle. When Frolic cuts her off with a jape, she

62 Capp reads similar tale telling by male servants as "the fantasies of a repressed
apprentice about his master's wife," which "helped to compensate for his social and
sexual inferiority within the household" ("Double Standard Revisited," 71).
63 Peele, *Old Wive's Tale*, in *Minor Elizabethan Drama*, 2:78–80.

Weſtward for Smelts.

OR,

The VVater-mans Fare of mad-merry VVeſtern
wenches, whoſe tongues albeit like Bell-clappers,
they neuer leaue Ringing, yet their Tales are ſweet,
and will much content you.

VVritten by Kinde *Kit* of *Kingſtone*.

LONDON,
Printed for *Iohn Trundle*, and are to be ſold at his ſhop in
Barbican, at the Signe of the No-body. 1620.

Fig. 7. Fishwives about to tell "tales that are wholesome, though but homely."
Title page from *Westward for Smelts* (1620). Reproduced by permission of the
Folger Shakespeare Library.

retorts "Nay, either hear my tale, or kiss my tail" (112). In jesting literature, women frequently deploy tongue-in-tail barbs; such an answer is
supposed to be unanswerable. In *Tarltons Jests*, it leaves the famous
clown speechless: "Tarlton meeting with a wily Country wench, who
gave him quip for quip: Sweetheart (saies hee) I would my flesh were in
thine. So would I Sir (saies shee) I would your nose were in my, I know
where, Tarlton angred at this, said no more, but goes forward."[64] The
wench uses misogynist pudeur as a bludgeon; yet the moment of the
anal/genital kiss also summons up a scene of utter capitulation of male
to female, suggesting why "kiss my tail" became so tightly bound to
the female speaker.

Madge Mumblecrust's homely obscenity can't hold a candle to the
bawdry of the fishwives in *Westward*, however. Madge goes on to tell a
tale that cobbles together bits of romance, fairy tales, and ghost stories—the usual associations of the phrase "old wives' tales." One striking distinction separating the average bawdy tale from the average romance is the latter's lack of clever wives and witless cuckolds and the
former's lack of damsels in distress requiring male rescuers. The fishwives aren't all old, and they are certainly not rustics like Madge. Their
stories come from novella and fabliau more often than romance, with
tellers striving to top each other with tales more racy and "homely"
than "wholesome."[65] Their status as urban fishwives—associated more
with Billingsgate flyting than fairy tales—may account for their pun-
gency.

Westward has spawned scholarly controversy because the second tale
has been read as a source for *Cymbeline* despite its date, an idea that is
now receiving renewed support.[66] Predictably, the introduction to the

64 "How a Maid drave Tarlton to a Non-Plus," *Tarltons Newes*, unpaged. Kate
loses a verbal skirmish with Petruchio when he uses this bawdy weapon against her
(*Taming of the Shrew* 2.1.210–20).

65 This is not to imply that old wives never talked dirty. Puttenham knew one
whose repertoire included this riddle: "My mother had an old woman in her nurserie,
who in the winter nights would put us forth many prety ridles, whereof this is one: 'I
have a thing and rough it is / And in the middle a hole Iwis: / There cam a young man
with his ginne, / And he put a handfull in.' The good old Gentlewoman would tell us
that were children how it was meant by a furrd gloove. Some other naughtie body
would peradventure have construed in not halfe so mannerly" (*Arte of English Poesie*,
188).

66 The Stationers' Register lists the pamphlet only once, in 1620, but George
Steevens, writing in 1773, said he saw an edition of 1603 that could have influenced
Shakespeare. F. P. Wilson recently noted that a play of 1604 appears to refer to the
pamphlet. Holger Klein reviews the controversy in *Westward*, v–vi.

modern edition gives no weight to the fishwives' real-world counter-parts; nor are the words "oral transmission" or "folk tale" mentioned, although there are stories from India, China, Wales, and France that strongly resemble both the second fishwife's tale and *Cymbeline*.[67] In-triguingly, the pamphlet depicts a performing community of women exchanging novella-like stories within a semiparodic but not harshly satiric frame. Like a players' company, this storytelling community has standards of performance and a joint stock of typical stories and motifs. The gentlewomen speakers of Boccaccio as well as Chaucer's prioress and wife of Bath are distant precedents, but they are overshadowed by less genteel forbears: the redoubtable Mother Bunch of jest book fame and Skelton's Elinor Rumming, whom the first storyteller, the fishwife of Brainford, strongly resembles.[68] Mimetically, a storyteller like Mother Bunch or the fishwife of Brainford is a far more credible stand-in for a woman than is the spectacle of a cross-dressed boy. In popular prose narratives the female fiction is stylized but not literally cross-dressed, nor is her voice ventriloquized in the same way as it is in a stage play. While early moderns knew no professional English actresses, they did know old women who told stories and alewives who retailed dirty jokes along with their ale.[69]

Of the fishwives' six tales, all deal with sexual intrigue. In two tales an adulterous wife emerges as victor over her husband and enjoys her lover; in three others, a chaste lady is either sexually accosted or slan-dered yet emerges triumphant. In the stories of adulterous wives, the cuckolded husbands are old, nasty, stupid, and brutal; and the wives put

67 See listings under "chastity test" (3:H400) and "chastity tested by ordeal" (3:H412) in Thompson, *Motif-Index*. Linda Woodbridge maintains that male writers who used such folk tales appropriated what was generally a female, oral art form without acknowledging their debt ("Patchwork," 13–14).

68 Kinde Kit describes the fishwife of Brainford: "She stunk of sweat. / Let it suf-fice, / She had large eyes; / And a low brow, / Much like a Sow / That sindg'd had bin, / Appear'd her chin: / For it was hayr'd" (*Westward*, sig. A4). For a Bakhtinian reading of Skelton's creation as a "carnivalesque challenge to male hegemony," see Herman, "Leaky Ladies."

69 Here I allude to Elizabeth Harvey's concept of "transvestite ventriloquism," de-fined as male appropriations of the female voice that accentuate "issues of gender, voice and authorial property in ways that illuminate both Renaissance conceptions of language and their relation to the gendered subject" (*Ventriloquized Voices*, 1). Lamb believes men probably told just as many tales as women; she discusses the "obsessive emphasis" on elderly female narrators as "a crucial signifying element" in the oral tradition ("Taken by the Fairies," 301). On the concept of ventriloquism as applied to plebeian voices, see Patterson, *Shakespeare*, 41–50.

themselves in extreme danger but succeed because they are far richer in wit and friends. One wife wreaks an elaborate revenge on a jealous and sadistic husband who "with the most spitefull words . . . would revile her, calling her so many Whoores, that it were unpossible to make him so many times Cuckold" (sig. D). She comes very close to being beaten bloody while tied to a post in a locked chamber but manages to escape. Eventually she locks him out, dumps a pisspot on his head, and gets approval from kin and neighbors to divorce him. The fishwife of Brainford thoroughly approves: "This was a wench worth talking of; she deserveth as much praise as those women called Amazones, who out of a brave minde cut their husbands throates: and so made themselves, rulers of themselves." All of the chaste women in the tales confound and shame those who assault or accuse them. One slandered wife gains the power of life and death over her suspicious husband, who has plotted to have her murdered: "Your wife shall be your Judge," he is told.[70]

Westward's fishwife storytellers are practiced critics of others who perform in the same vein. After each teller finishes, she asks the others how they liked her tale. Their responses vary from laughter, praise, and admiration to debate and worry over how men might misread the story, a frame that leads the modern editor to call it a "marriage debate among women, with the Wife of Bath party at some advantage over the proponents of virtue and duty."[71] The competition among the tellers mounts, and the final pair of tales creates open dissension. In the tale told by the fishwife of Kingstone, a lady confesses to a priest that because her husband is old and impotent, she has taken a lover. Hearing this, the priest begins to lust after her, too. Posing as the lover, he manages to have sex with her in this disguise. She discovers the deception and lies in wait for him. At their next tryst, her servants bind him and cut off one of his testicles, to her great satisfaction. He suffers a painful ride home bearing a paper that proclaims he is "halfe a man."[72]

The bloody tale pleases everyone except the prim fishwife of Twitnam, who "hates lewdness" and who tells the only tale in which a woman is punished for trying to get the best of a man. In it a cruel maid torments her lover by imposing a vow of silence and provokes his hatred, ending up pregnant, shamed, and abandoned by him. This brings a

70 *Westward*, sigs. D4, C4.
71 From the editor's preface, ibid., viii.
72 Ibid., sig. E3v.

loud protest from her listeners, who think her tale too harsh; but under
the urging of the fishwife of Brainford, they agree to seek out an alehouse together:

> Let us leave this *pro* and *contra*, let every tub stand on its owne bot-
> tome: and so our mirth and journey ends about one time: for yonder is
> Kingstone, whose large and considerable pots are praised throughout
> England. . . . Then since it is so neere, let us not be factious, and con-
> tend for trifles, but let us seeke to enjoy that which we came for, mirth:
> that best preserver of our lives: so land us with all speed, honest water-
> man.[73]

On the Phallible

In court records of defamation suits, a common neighborhood jest
was to pretend that a suspected cuckold actually wore gigantic horns,
with neighbors warning him in mock concern that his horns threatened
to break doorways and walls.[74] This street jape has its parallel in printed
jests. In one, a jealous husband always sticks his head out the window
to check on his wife when she leaves the house, "which she taking in
great endugine [dudgeon], roundly told him that if hee used continually
to looke after her shee would clappe such a paire of horns upon his head
that from thenceforth he would not be able to put his head out of
doores."[75] Her spatial manipulation requires theatrical projection: he
seeks to control her access to the outside world and thus her sexuality,
so she uses an imaginary scene of neighborhood humiliation to control
him.[76]

Allowing space to a woman's wit means allowing for her independent
sexual will. Jests insist that women can always evade the confines of
subjection and surveillance by exercising their intelligence: "Make the
doors upon a woman's wit and it will out at the casement; shut that,
and 'twill out at the keyhole; stop that, 'twill fly with the smoke out at

---

73 Ibid., sigs. Fv–F2r.
74 Gowing, *Domestic Dangers*, 96.
75 *Gratiae Ludentes*, 129.
76 On the association of portals with female sexuality, see Stallybrass, "Patriarchal Territories," 128. Lena Cowen Orlin discusses the difference between the highly
charged window and the safer door as places where women were seen and heard
("Women on the Threshold").

the chimney" (*As You Like It* 4.1.148–51). This lack of fit between abjection and control conflates the sexual and spatial, but it also leaves a gap for women's laughter:

> A lock-smith jealous of his wife, and that not without cause, had often read her lectures, telling her how pretious a womans chastity was, and honorable the state of matrimony. And being best acquainted with his own trade, he would draw his comparisons from that: when thinking to hit the naile on the head, he proceeded to hammer out his mind as followeth, Women ought to keep a latch upon the door, their brests bolted, their hearts lockt, and double lockt, their bodies neither to be wrested by force, nor opened with picklocks, and the like. She being vexed with the tediousness of his talke, broke out into a passion, and said, Here is a coile indeed with your barres, your bolts, & your locks; when there is not a Tappster, nor an Oastler, that I know, but hath as good a key, as the best Smit of you all, to open.[77]

The husband's lecturing is odious, his rhetorical and phallic keys interchangeable. The jest directs the audience to laugh at the possibly betrayed but certainly garrulous husband by using loaded words such as "lecture" and a barb about "the tediousnesse of his talke." Two strains of popular jest are in dialectical play: proverbial wisdom and antimasculinist wit. Both players deal in generalizations about all women and all men, but only one gets the laugh. Hers is perhaps a Pyrrhic victory; but in her retort some listeners may have sensed, with delight or discomfort, that it had derailed phallic pretension with rhetorical efficacy. The passionate retort trumps the old saw.

Props freighted with sex crowd tales of the horn, as if the masculinist imagination *must* transform "deeds of darkness" into objects that can be manipulated and exhibited—for, as a writer of characters put it, "who can distinguish between that which was never foul, and that which is cleanly wiped?"[78] A husband's resort to objects that promise to confirm a wife's chastity inevitably boomerangs. A famous example is "Hans Carvel's ring," versions of which appear in Poggio's *Facetiae*, Rabelais's *Gargantua and Pantagruel*, and Shakespeare's *Merchant of*

---

77 *Banquet of Jests New and Old* (1657), 17. This jest's "lock-and-key" bawdy was deeply familiar: people often used the image in defamation cases to talk about sex (Gowing, *Domestic Dangers*, 70–71).

78 Thomas Fuller, *The Harlot* (circa 1642), in Aldington, *Book of Characters*, 264.

Venice. Its earliest appearance in print in England came in *Tales and Quick Answers* (circa 1535):

> A man that was right jealous on his wife dreamed on a night as he lay abed with her and slept, that the devil appeared unto him and said: "Wouldst thou not be glad that I should put thee in surety of thy wife?" "Yes," said he. "Hold," said the devil, "as long as thou hast this ring upon thy finger no man shall make thee cuckold." The man was glad thereof, and when he awaked he found his finger in his wife's arse.[79]

The political analogy that turned households into kingdoms threw up another unanswerable question: how can a wife have power over the honor of a man who is her absolute ruler? This paradox drives men to distraction in lofty tragedy and raw farce. In one jest, an old husband, married to a pretty young woman, grew "almost mad for feare his wife any way should play false: he saw by experience, brave men came to besiege the castle, and seeing it was in a womans custodie and had so weake a governor as himselfe, he doubted it would in time be delivered up, which feare made him almost frantike."[80] Faced with their vulnerability, men ransack their own homes seeking what cannot be found. Their own eyes betray them.[81] Jest narratives frequently pair castration and blinding, possibly because a wife's adultery impugned her husband's sexual honor and manhood, yet "ocular proof" of her transgression remained maddeningly elusive. Husbands in extremis set fires to smoke out lovers but succeed only in burning down their own houses. In one notorious story, a husband even castrates himself so that he can trap his wife in adultery, having been driven frantic by his failure to catch her in the act.[82]

---

79 *Tales and Quick Answers,* in Zall, *Hundred Merry Tales,* 256. The basic plot continued to trouble the dreams of Europeans in the twentieth century, according to Freud and Oppenheim, *Dreams in Folklore,* 60–65.

80 *Cobler of Caunterburie,* 178–79.

81 In Twyne's *Schoolemaster,* an old woman, aiding a wife whose husband has caught her in flagrante, convinces the husband that he imagined it because he had eaten chervil, which supposedly causes double vision. He apologizes to his wife. In another jest, a husband comes home complaining of a cinder in his eye; his wife washes out his eye while her lover escapes.

82 For the story about an old cuckold who burns down his house trying to capture the lovers and then dies of shame, see *Cobler of Caunterburie,* 178–99. The castration story was included in Poggio Bracciolini's famous *Facetiae:* "An extremely jealous man racked his brain for a way of ascertaining, without the shadow of a doubt, whether his wife had an intimacy with any other man. By a deeply matured contrivance, well worthy of a jealous mind, he emasculated himself with his own hands: 'Now,' he thought, 'if my wife becomes with child, she will not be able to deny her

English jests associating castration and cuckoldry owe much to the medieval fabliau tradition. Fabliaux—verse jests that generally narrate a comic deception followed by a misdeed—often feature a clever wife "on top of the world of play."[83] In *Berangier du long cul* ("Berangier of the Long Ass"), an unhappy lady is married to a craven knight who only pretends to go out and fight. When he returns from these faked bouts, he kicks her and reviles her. One day she has had enough. She cross-dresses as a knight in full armor and follows him into the forest, where she spies on him hacking his own sword. Accosting him, she challenges him to joust. Cowering before her, he cravenly begs for mercy. She forces him to kiss her bare ass. Bending over, he is shocked to see only a long cleft, with no testicles. She tells him in a rough voice that "All other men are beneath my class. / I'm Berangier of the Long Ass / Who puts to shame the chicken-hearted."[84] The fabliau culminates in the wife's confrontation with him at home, where she boldly sits in bed with her new lover. When he rages, she silences him by saying she knows all about his meeting with Berangier of the Long Ass and that she will tell the world if he says another word:

> He felt checkmated. He felt ill.
> And from that day, she did her will:
> She was no common girl or fool:
> *When the shepherd's weak, the wolf shits wool.*[85]

Such tales about tails are short and sharp, a feature that has led Howard Bloch to argue that the analogous French pun on tale/tail (*con(te)/con*) functions as more than an apt quibble. Accepting the Aristotelian rule that comedy is rooted in the defective, he locates that defect in the voice of the *con* (cunt/fabliau), whose "illogical" and "scandalous" speech cuts meaning short. Logic is phallocentric: every child believes in "the ubiquity of the phallus [which] by analogy accounts for

---

adultry'" (134–35). In England it appeared in Edward Sharpham's *Cupid's Whirligig* (1607) and in Burton's *Anatomy of Melancholy*; see Taylor, *Castration*, 253n.34.

83 According to Hines, the fabliaux "show very much less interest in exposing the wickedness of the trickster than in ridiculing the tricked," most often the deceived husband (*Fabliau*, 10–11). Women in fabliaux are "morally no worse than the lecherous men who inhabit these tales, and intellectually much superior to them on most occasions" (32).

84 Guerin, "Berangier of the Long Ass," in DuVal, *Fabliaux*, 105.

85 Ibid., 106.

the presupposition of logic."[86] Laughter produced by a joke or *conte* disrupts this logic and therefore cuts or castrates. His theory has its own
shortcomings. Bloch fails to address the peculiar dramatic form of the
fabliau, which is less punchline-focused and more hermeneutically demanding than a modern joke. In *Berangier du long cul* a new kind of
logic plays out for a full forty lines beyond what he reads as the curtail-
ing "punchline" of the anal kiss, which, rather than ending the narrative, spurs a denouement focused on the wife's triumph and mirth. Indeed, Bloch discounts everything outside the castrating moment; he
cannot allow that the *con* may also result in laughter that is its own
logic, issuing from certain hearers for whom the phallus is not "ubiquitous." If the joke brings forth a "rule ready-made in words," as Freud ordained, the rule of the fabliau is that laughter is already present: if it
symbolically cuts some, it somatically pleases many others.

   In song, jest, and verse, women certainly do take special delight in
hacking away at phallic pretensions. The topic figures large in gossips'
literature, such as the early Tudor *A Talk of Ten Wyves on Their Husbands Ware*. A group of wives drinking in the alehouse vie to outdo
each other in belittling their spouses' equipment. The first wife sets the
terms of the debate:

> Talys lett us tell
> Off owre hosbondes ware,
> Wych of hem most worthy are
> To-day to bear the bell.
> And I schall now begyn att myne:
> I knowe the [measure] well & fyne,
> The length of a snayle,
> And ever he warse is from day to day.[87]

   All ten have a go. One wife moans in anguish that her husband is "the
length of four beans" even when "he was in his most pryde," another
compares her mate's parts unfavorably to those of her cat Gyb, and a

---

86 Bloch, *Scandal*, 110. The fabliaux are "scandalous" because they mask their
own lack of authority using the horrifying loquacity of "le con qui conte," or the tale-
spinning cunt (101–110).
87 *Talk of Ten Wyves* appears in *Jyl of Breyntfords Testament*, 29–33. The subgenre
of willie jokes told by women flourishes today, for example, in the hip-hop song "Short
Dick Man" and the cartoon and jest book by Cathy Hopkins and Alison Everitt, *Revenge of the Essex Girls*. The epigraph runs "She who can lick, can also bite."

third says her spouse's ware is long enough but as weak and thin as her little finger. Narrators in some tales do call lusty women whorish, but in general jests do not; and on closer inspection many are more accurately about women satirizing men, especially for inept lovemaking. Such tales often circle back to cuckoldry because a man who cannot pay his marriage debt is inviting horns. It is too easy to dismiss a narrative such as *Talke of Ten Wyves*, in which women express sexual desire or connoisseurship, as nothing but formulaic satire on vulgar female tongues and women's frightening insatiability. In her foundational study of cheap print, Margaret Spufford takes a minority view by arguing against reading an automatic tone of disapproval or satire in all such references to women's sexual desires: "Women were depicted in the chapbooks . . . as taking positive pleasure in lovemaking. Certainly, the whole tenor of the merry books conveys that seventeenth-century women enjoyed their own sexuality and were expected to enjoy it."[88] Whatever women's experience of their own sexuality—and Spufford's comment raises more issues than it answers—most women would have been familiar with jesting literature that held men responsible for providing them with a degree of pleasure in bed, expressing that expectation through shrewd criticisms of sexual performance.

When placed in a social context of neighborly surveillance, cultural discourses about cuckoldry elicit judgments about female duplicity, to be sure. But as these texts show, the conversation also recruits female pleasure and involves negotiations about the limits of male violence and criticisms of male stupidity, impotence, and hypocrisy. Many tales recruit women's laughter at drunken, jealous, and hateful husbands; and some attempt to discipline men by teaching that such behavior will result in horns. Some jests can almost be considered primers in verbal evasion for harassed women, while others seem calculated to heat hostilities to the boiling point. Sometimes the language of play translates

---

88 Spufford, *Small Books*, 63–64. Also see Reay, *Popular Cultures in Seventeenth Century England*, chap. 1, esp. 24–26. Like many other commentators, Anthony Fletcher reads such texts as univocal, showing male fears of women's vicious, predatory sexuality (*Gender*, 5). Certainly the topic demands a subtler study of issues of voice and authorship, the potential for lesbian or class-transgressive desire, or the ways attitudes about sex and the body relate to discourses about status, power relations, and ethnicity. What can be stated with certainty is that the jesting literature, as well as court records about defamation, show many women using the language of bawdy wit in the arenas of social conflict, sometimes directing their sallies against the sexual failings of men.

struggles ending in blows and blood to contests for linguistic mastery, especially in the jest topos of the forced oath, which turns on the unanswerable riddle of chastity. But the threat of violence is not always hidden. *Pasquils Palinodia* paints an unforgettable picture of cuckolds as sadists and blowhards, egging each other on:

> And what is then his prattle with his mates,
> His fellow drunkards, sitting o'er the pot?
> There he begins the story, and relates
> What an infernall fury he hath got,
> An everlasting scold that's never quiet,
> But checks him for his company and his ryot.
> Why bang her well, quoth one, for by this quart,
> If she were my wife, I would break her heart.
>
> Well, quoth another, fill a cup of Sacke,
> And let all scolds be damn'd as deep as hell;
> Abridge her maintenance, and from her backe
> Pull her proud clothes, for they doe make her swell.
> And thus in divellish counsell there they sit,
> Til of Sherry they have drowned their wit.[89]

The anonymous narrator concludes this remarkable passage by observing that it is "too great a wrong, and most unjust / The weaker to the wall should thus be thrust" and "deny'd the favour of the laws" (10). Perhaps it is this antimasculinist edge in cuckoldry humor—that utter lack of sympathy for the "wronged" husband—that led later generations of critics to disdain cuckoldry so completely. Norbert Elias, Keith Thomas, and others have ascribed the shift in taste to the massive change in manners that occurred in the later seventeenth century; what is less clear is how much this change depended on establishing new standards of female respectability and on restricting the kinds of stories they should hear and tell. In any case, it is important that the vast field of early modern cuckoldry narrative not be dismissed as rank misogyny. Any given tale may be heard as a lesson in amorality, a fable about the subordination of patriarchs, and prime

---

89 *Pasquils Palinodia*, 8.

laughing matter for all—but especially for women. Subject to sexual attacks, slurs, and scrutiny, they knew danger in a physical as well as psychological sense. They were, therefore, even more likely to enjoy a simulacrum of mastery that proved a stage husband wrong or wronged, again and again.

4 "O such a rogue would be hang'd!"

Shrews versus Wife Beaters

But time with pity oft will tell
to those that would her try:
Whether it best be more to mell
or utterly defye.

Isabella Whitney

In early modern England, some forms of "neighborhood" were alien to what our age considers neighborly. Midwives forced unwed mothers in labor to confess the names of the fathers; neighbors spied on each other or took part in shaming rituals to drive unwed mothers and disliked couples from town. Women tormented their neighbors by throwing horns and mocking rhymes into their yards or performed insulting songs and jigs about their flaws. Some women defamed others with the simple word "whore" and with elaborate narratives of incontinence, disease, and duplicity. Many assisted in witch trials, probing for "witch's teats" or testifying about the dark powers of neighbors they had known all their lives, sending some to their deaths.[1]

But it is also worth considering that women sometimes acted to-

---

1 On women spying, see Archer, *Pursuit*, 77; on midwives, Ingram, *Church Courts*, 262. On women horning neighbors, writing mocking rhymes, and performing jigs, see Fox, "Ballads," 52, 58–59, and Ingram, "Ridings," 166. For libels, see Gowing, *Domestic Dangers*, and "Women, Status." For witches' marks and trials, see Paster, *Body Embarrassed*, 247–52, and Thomas, *Religion*, 530–31, 652–59. On the crucial role of gossip and female sociality in witchcraft accusations, see Sharpe, "Women, witchcraft," 108–13, 120.

gether against obnoxious or dangerous male opponents. Ralph Houlbrooke has shown that "groups of female 'gossips' could be a potent
force in the life of the local community, and on occasion they cooperated in order to punish or put pressure on errant men."[2] Women under
attack often turned to friends and neighbors for support and protection;
women often rallied to the aid of other women. One ballad woodcut
shows a group of women beating and drenching a husband "who has
been too liberal with his talents outside the household" while a man
rides skimmington alongside, suggesting that the beaten man's whoring
has led to his being cuckolded and publicly shamed (see fig. 8).[3] Court
records contain instances of concerted action: in one case, women way-
lay and pummel a priest who has been harassing their friend; in a second, a group of women mock and splatter outsiders who had called
their neighborhood promiscuous; in a third, six women bring a male
neighbor to court, charging him with vicious cruelty against a maidservant.[4] Women could and did challenge the dread threat of a skimmington against one of their friends. In Quemerford in 1618, a group of men
and boys planning to subject a local woman to a riding were temporarily
foiled by her gossips, who managed to tear the drum that was to be used
for rough music.[5] While the men eventually went on with their plan—
beating the victim and dragging her through the mud—the women's actions show that rough music and other shaming rites, such as cucking,
should not be read as expressions of local consensus because they could
provoke dissent and opposition among others in the same community.[6]

2 Houlbrooke, *English Family*, 110. They also cooperated to punish other women,
sometimes unfairly and viciously. For an account of one community's role in bring-
ing down severe punishment on a woman who charged a clergyman with sexual harassment and attempted rape, see Hindle, "Shaming of Margaret Knowsley," as well
as Boose's fascinating essay on the case and its afterlife ("Priest").

3 *Roxburghe Ballads*, 2:184. Diane Purkiss argues that this image shows a "symbolic equivalence" between the skimmington and the women beating the man and
that "a perceived inversion of the social order is both represented and corrected by
another, different inversion" (Brant and Purkiss, *Women, Texts*, 81). This interpretation fails to take account of the fact that groups of women sometimes did punish
men for transgressions in a community, performing a policing function that was
never simply inversionary.

4 See Capp, "Separate Domains?" 136–37. Also see Houlbrooke, "Women's Social
Life," esp. 180–81. In a fifteenth-century case, a group of London women chased down
and killed a Breton who had robbed and murdered the widow who had raised him (181).

5 Cunnington, "Skimmington," 287–90.

6 Reay, *Popular Cultures in England*, 161. In nineteenth-century Wales, women
often voiced opposition to rough music and charivari against women; such antipathy
was part of a long tradition of resistance (Hammerton, "Targets," 27).

Fig. 8. Two kinds of rough justice. To the left, a skimmington; to the right, "a gang of women evilly-entreates a Husband who has been too liberal with his talents outside the household." Woodcut from *Halfe a dozen of good Wives: All for a Penny* (1634), from *The Roxburghe Ballads.* Reproduced by permission of the British Library.

On the streets the female posse was spontaneous and extralegal; on the stages of the public theaters, writers sometimes used the comic topos of the women's court to show women interrogating, judging, and punishing male malefactors. In *Swetnam the Woman Hater Arraigned by Women,* gossips and old wives set upon the notorious Swetnam/Misogonous, who has been bound and gagged, and torment him with insults, pinches, and pricks from their needles. A more genteel version of a revenge hocking takes place in Fletcher's *The Woman Hater,* with its spectacle of a bound Gondarino surrounded by laughing gentlewomen who subject him to a teasing dance and mocking caresses. In Fletcher's *The Nightwalker,* alliances between gossips prove even stronger than blood ties: the aunt of a ne'er-do-well recruits a group of women to harangue him for mistreating an abandoned maid, whose death they have just faked. The women find him guilty and threaten to burn down his house, in a scene crackling with the aggressions of charivari.

The coney-catching literature contains a fascinating and often-cited instance of collective action, with older women helping a younger and more powerless one. In "A Walking Mort," an episode from *Caveat for Common Cursitors, Vulgarly called Vagabonds* (1566), Thomas Harman presents a conversation with a female vagrant. She recounts how she once conspired with an irate wife and four "furious, sturdy, muffled gossips" to beat a lecherous husband black and blue.[7] The plotting is remarkable: the husband has browbeaten the vagrant into a sexual assignation, but she goes straight to his wife because (she tells Harman) the wife "is my very friend, and I am very much beholden to her" (113). The wife recruits her gossips, one of whom has also been sexually attacked by the husband. Just as he walks into his barn to meet the vagrant, the women ambush him. Blindfolded and bound, the husband endures a long and bloody beating. As a result, he reforms and lives happily ever after with his wife.

A magistrate who capitalized on his contacts with the traveling poor, Harman treats the vagrant woman's vulnerability and the husband's depravity with prurient relish. His attitude veers from the frown of the public official to the leer of the alehouse tattler, and he ends the disturbing story as if it were an entertaining tale of tit-for-tat. Some readers dismiss the narrative as a fabrication or a jest, but one historian argues that it "probably reflected a real and widespread female refusal to accept the double standard."[8] Is this resistance a mere spice added to the jest, a narratological illusion manipulated by the male author; or is it possible that this tale flashes some fairly sharp teeth, especially for female audiences? Certainly the encounter would not have seemed outside the bounds of possibility. An entry from the diary of Henry Machyn, for example, records how a group of gossips turned the tables on a lecherous London priest in 1563. When the priest pursued an unwilling woman and offered her money for sex, she pretended to agree but then recruited her friends. They hid in the room appointed for the assignation. When he entered and took off his clothes, they jumped out and beat him.[9]

One possibility is to read narratives like Harman's as templates charged

---

7 "A Walking Mort," in Salgado, *Cony-Catchers,* 129–35. Important discussions that have informed my reading of Harman include Carroll, *Fat King,* 89; and Mikalachi, "Women's Networks," 52–69.

8 Houlbrooke, *English Family,* 117. Woodbridge discounts *Caveat* as "a subspecies of the Tudor jest book" with little value or relation to reality, like all works of rogue literature (*Vagrancy,* 40).

9 Capp, "Separate Domains?" 136.

with potential social energy—energy that must be activated by tellers and hearers—rather than authorized possessions of the writer and buyer. The narrator may be "a man speaking to men," the printer may be male, and the buyer may be male. But the story of the "Walking Mort" may be circulating orally among women who have heard it read aloud; it may be available in another form, as a jest, song, or mocking rhyme; or it may even be part of someone's mental attic, matching a bit of first- or second-hand experience. For at least some women who had experienced similar mistreatment and were expected to eat their wrath, the tale may have fed more than their curiosity. Fantasies and stereotypes can conceal land-mines. The songs and jests of the gossips' literature, for example, mean to satirize the women's bawdy and insubordinate talk, but the effect is to put into wider circulation attitudes that cannot be spoken or acted on by most women. Certainly, overt rebellion against male authority could not be safely practiced every day by every woman. The interesting fact is that it was represented. Dismissing these texts as laughable examples of male-authored misogyny not worth examining—as often happens with tales about women's vengeful violence and trickery—is like ignoring all stories in which slaves plot against their masters because such narratives some-times circulate in popular works read by their masters. As James Scott ar-gues, real slaves do harbor such ideas and tell such stories, which reappear in altered yet recognizable forms in above-ground culture.[10]

Popular literature that intends to scoff at shrews and gossips does not lend itself to conventional feminist recuperation, but it does offer scenes of female revenge and passages of female satire that cannot be dismissed as pure products of the male imagination. A male-centered reading assumes far too much authorial originality in patching together elements from oral culture—gossip, invective, jest, insult. While jesting texts cannot provide a faithful transcription of daily conflicts, some do show a high degree of cor-respondence to what social historians have documented about women's lives, and in particular the verbal and physical violence they faced.

"To him Xantippe"

Perhaps the most degrading aspect of woman's subjection in the early modern period was a husband's right to strike his wife. A proverb

10 Scott, *Domination*, 5–6.

recorded in 1475 allowed *ther be iij thyngs take gret betyng: a stock-fish, a milston, a fedirbed, a woman*. A century later, a jest tried to make the most of this mundane and unpromising subject:

> A certayne lytle boy seeing his father beating his mother every daye, and hearing him saye one night when he was abed, that he had forgotten to do one thing: I know what it is quoth the chyld, what sayd the father: Mary (sayd he) to beate my mother.[11]

While the merry books labored to wring humor from the thud of fist against flesh, church courts adjudicated horrific cases of male violence against women, whether maid, wife, or widow.[12] English law allowed husbands to beat their wives as much as they liked so long as severe injury or death did not result. On this issue the law was more conservative than church doctrine, which was firmly, though not consistently, set against wife beating.[13] Many preacher-pamphleteers cited the Pauline precept that husband and wife were one flesh, arguing that it was wrong to seek to harm oneself. Henry Smith held that "these mad men which beat themselves should be sent to Bedlam till their madness be gone."[14] Although the one-flesh argument erases the individual woman on the receiving end, at least it could be invoked to stay men's hands. Popular literature did not fail to register the doctrine's attractiveness to wives. In an early Tudor example of gossips' literature, *The gospelles of dystaves*, women secretly gather to hear the following "gospel" preached by a wise shrew: "He that beteth his wyfe shall never have grace of our lady tyl he have pardon of his wyfe. . . . Mary faith it is great synne as he wolde despaire himself / for after that whiche I have herde our vicar saye it is but one body man and woman togather."[15]

Some conduct-book authors managed to find a loophole even here.

---

11 Twyne, *Schoolemaster*, 12.

12 Quaife documents beatings and sexual violence by men toward girls, pregnant women, and uncompliant wives and widows (*Wanton Wenches*, 26, 137–38, 172, 174). Also see Mendelson and Crawford, *Women in Early Modern England*, 211.

13 For a summary of the debate see Amussen, "Being Stirred." As *The Lawes Resolution of Women's Rights* (1631) informed readers, a husband could lawfully perform "reasonable correction" of his wife (quoted in Amussen, 71). Fletcher maintains that the wholesale condemnation of wife beating was largely confined to the Puritan clergy, remaining "a distinctly minority view before the civil war" (*Gender, Sex*, 198–99).

14 *A Preparative to Marriage* (1591), quoted in Foyster, "Male Honour," 220.

15 *Gospelles of dystaves*, chapter 3.

William Whately's *A Bride-Bush* (1623) called wife beating permissible
after all else failed because it could serve as a healing "corosive" to a
husband's "owne flesh." In this perverse bit of sophistry, wife abuse becomes pious self-flagellation. Other godly pamphleteers urged husbands to be proactive. Robert Snawsel's *A looking glass for maried
folkes* (1610) told husbands they had every right to control their wives
by firm discipline, "including beating and deliberate changes of
mood."[16] One extremist even offered his readers lessons in wife beating,
showing how husbands could measure and justify their blows.[17] Certainly, the church did not fully or logically enforce its own strictures. In
1618, for example, an episcopal court judge chastised a Lincolnshire
vicar for beating his wife in the churchyard. The offense lay not in his
beating her but in doing so on holy ground.[18]

Faced with such acts of Christian instruction, wives were told to endure with patience and thank their husbands for the correction. Henry
Bentley's *The Monument of Matrones* (1589) contained this prayer "to
be used by the wife that hath a froward and bitter husband":

> O most wise and provident GOD . . . if it be thy good pleasure with
> frowardness, bitternes, and unkindnesse, yea, the hatred and disdaine of
> my husband, thus to correct me for my fault, I most hartilie thanke
> thee for it . . . and that I for my part may quietlie beare the frailtie, in-
> firmitie, and faults of my husband, with more patience, mildnesse and
> modestie, than hitherto I have, so that mine example may be to the
> comfort and commoditie of other to doo the like.[19]

Many women refused to serve as comforting examples of patience,
fighting back when attacked and crying out for help. Neighbors were
their first line of defense because local authorities could not be counted
on to prevent severe or mortal injury.[20] Gowing has shown that women
under attack turned to women neighbors first and there is evidence that
all members of the community expected women to risk their own safety

---

16 Quoted in Stallybrass, "Patriarchal Territories," 126.
17 Moses a Vauts, *The Husband's Authority Unvail'd* (1650), quoted and discussed in Gowing, *Domestic Dangers,* 222.
18 Hajzyk, "Little-Known Ladies," 40.
19 Henry Bentley, *Monument of Matrones,* quoted in Hull, *Chaste,* 93. This massive anthology is composed almost entirely of prayers written by women, some famous (Elizabeth I, Anne Askew) but many unnamed, like the author quoted here.
20 Amussen, "Being Stirred," 78–81.

for the well-being of other women. Some beaten women filed complaints against their husbands in church courts or (more rarely) in civil
courts. Not surprisingly, women who sued men for violence usually
brought other women to court as witnesses.[21] Though many husbands
bitterly resented the women neighbors who intervened, neighbors continued to act as a vigilant and moderating force. Because of the wider social conflicts wife beating engendered, the extent of a husband's right to
correct his wife was a live issue in the courts and in neighborhoods.[22]

In one of the many jests about the long-suffering Socrates and his
wife Xantippe, the wise man explains his diffidence in the face of his
wife's assaults:

> Upon a time, when Xantippe in the open marketplace had plucked his
> cloak from his backe, and such of his friends as saw it, said unto him,
> why Socrates do you not correct this impudent outrage in her, and chas-
> tise her soundly for it? replied to them, Yea marry, that were a jest in-
> deed, that we two be together by the eares, all the whole market folke
> looking upon us, may cry, *Hold thine own Socrates, To him Xantippe:*
> by which meanes wee shall be made a derision to all men.[23]

Socrates is not to be seen simply as a milksop but as a wise fool with superior understanding. When the whole world is watching, the best recourse is stoicism—especially among those who might side with Xantippe. To early modern audiences of this jest, it would have seemed
natural that some onlookers would recognize Socrates but root for his
wife, shouting, "To him Xantippe." Though the gender mix in the marketplace is not specified, it is easy to imagine some of Xantippe's gossips in the crowd, ready to take up her cause.

As Socrates' reticence suggests, the threat of being jeered at could
sometimes curb male violence. Ballads show irate husbands grousing

21 Gowing, *Domestic Dangers,* 217–19, 230–31. On wives' resort to the Court of
Requests to sue husbands for violent treatment and other abuses, see Stretton,
Women Waging Law, 143–54.
22 When neighbors sued each other the offense was usually against peace and
quiet. In a typical case neighbors complained that one man drunkenly "beat his wife
about the street so as the neighbours could not rest in their beds he kept such a disorder" (Amussen, *Ordered Society,* 123). On local debates over the proper use of violence by men and women, see Dolan, *Dangerous Familiars,* 33; and Amussen, "Punishment," esp. 15. Margaret Hunt speculates that in the eighteenth century, women
intervened so often because they were used to violence, both as recipients and perpe-
trators ("Wife Beating," 23).
23 Heywood, *Curtaine lecture,* 244.

that their hands are tied, although they itch to pound their wives, because their wives' friends will criticize and slander them. Neighbors upbraid the harshest wife beaters with terms leveled at their sense of honor and rationality: vicious or repeated beatings could raise the cry that a man was "bedlam" or "unmanly." Being known as a wife beater could shame some men, but others ignored such pressure until either a wife's death or the law stopped them.[24]

Faced with intransigent offenders, neighbors sometimes escalated countermeasures. In a case from Bristol in 1667, a group of neighbors surrounded a notorious wife beater and threw dirt at him, creating "a loud mocking demonstration" that strongly resembled charivari.[25] Another example of neighborhood discipline concerns a child beater rather than a wife beater—making it a rare case because parents' right to administer beatings was seldom questioned—but it does shed light on the verbal arsenal that communities could deploy against transgressors. In 1622, neighbors of a prominent Essex citizen named Richard Turner wrote rhymes to mock him for brutally beating his daughter Anne. Among its many verses:

> Hye thee home Anne,
> Hye thee home Anne,
> Whippe her arse Dicke,
> Will have thee anon.
> All those that love puddinge,
> Come unto Parke Street,
> And learne the songe,
> Whip Her Arse Dick.[26]

As if that weren't enough, the song goes on to compare Turner to a child murderer who had just been hanged.[27] Written by artisans and tradespeople, the song spread from town to town through the posting of

---

24 Foyster, "Male Honour," 217, 221.

25 Ibid., 222. As Foyster notes, the use of charivari against a wife beater is unusual at this early date; there are few traces in England before the nineteenth century. In France, however, the practice was established before the sixteenth century as part of holiday license. May was a "women's month" during which "wives could take revenge on their husbands for beating them by ducking the men or making them ride an ass" (Davis, *Society and Culture*, 100, 141).

26 Fox, "Ballads, Libels," 74.

27 Amussen, "Being Stirred," 76.

copies and constant singing so that even children came to know the song and torment Turner with it. For a time he was forced to stay indoors, hoping the "balleting" would abate.[28]

Visual culture bears evidence of the social pressures that functioned to limit male violence and to succor the abused. "Patience Baited," an emblem by George Wither, spells out collective limits on patriarchal privilege, warning that even the meekest wife will finally turn and fight. The image shows a sheep attacking its tormentor, a young boy. The poem informs readers that anyone who mistreats a friend or spouse runs the risk of social ostracism:

> Thus, many times, a foolish man doth lose
> His faithfull friends, and justly makes them foes. . . .
> And by abusing of a patient Mate
> Turne dearest Love, into deadliest Hate:
> For any wrong may better bee excused,
> Than, Kindnesse, long, and willfully abused.[29]

Male drunkenness was a leading cause of "kindnesse long and willfully abused," and jests involving domestic violence are generally alcohol-sodden. Many merry tales strongly criticize alcoholic husbands who ruin their health and pauperize their families. *Pasquils Palinodia* (1619) blames husbands for driving wives to other men's arms because of their own alehouse haunting and violent drunkenness, while Thomas Heywood's *Philoconothista, or the Drunkard, Opened, Dissected, and Anatomized* (1635) shows brawling, puking asses and goats served by an alewife who looks on with a touch of scorn (see fig. 9).

In some jests, wives seize the position of agency in the narrative, in a brief but significant moment of linguistic mastery.[30] *The womens sharpe revenge* contains a jest in which a husband

---

28 Fox, "Ballads, Libels," 73–74.
29 Wither, *Collection of Emblemes*, 4:252.
30 The phrase "linguistic mastery" is from Susan Purdie, *Comedy: The Mastery of Discourse.* A speaker achieves this mastery when he or she wins the teller position in relation to an audience, within a discourse that denies discursive potency to a butt whose power is at first assumed (58–59). Purdie concludes that "all joking 'masters' discourse, and thereby seizes ideological power" (147).

Fig. 9. Sots satirized. Title page from Thomas Heywood, *Philocothonista, or, the Drunkard, Opened, Dissected, and Anatomized* (1635). Reproduced by permission of the British Library.

came home Delicately mad drunke, and pluckt a ropes end out of his Pocket, wherewith hee most forcely beate his wife; which shee poore woman was faine to suffer with griefe and impatience; but within a week after, they being friends, she provided him the same Ropes end for his supper, boyld in Broth, like an Eele, and when hee had eaten the Broth out of the Platter, hee took his knife, with intent to cut part of the Eele, and finding it to be hard for his cutting, hee asked his Wife what it was? Truely Husband, said shee, it is no worse than what you gave mee; and therefore I thought good to make it ready and Cooke it for your Supper.[31]

In "A tale of the revenge of a scold" from *Pasquils Jests,* a wife devises an elaborate practical joke to punish her husband for coming home drunk. Night after night he lurches in and she gives him harsh words, promising to drown their newborn child ("whom he dearly and tenderly loved") if he does it one more time. On an icy winter night, the wife "having intelligence from her scouts" that he was carousing at the tavern, hides the baby and wraps a cat in its blanket. When he comes in staggering, she snatches up the bundle and throws it in the moat outside, striking terror into her spouse:

> the poore man much affrighted, leaves to pursue her, and leapes into the water up in mud and water to the very chin, crying, Save, oh save the childe: now waded he in the moat in a very bitter cold frost, till he brought out the mantle, and with much paine and danger comes to the shore, and still crying alas my poore childe, opened the cloathes; at length the frighted Cat cryed Mew, and being at liberty leapt from betwixt his arms, and ran away. The husband both amazed and vexed, the woman laughed heartily at her revenge, and the poore man was glad to reconcile the difference, before shee would either give him fire or dry linnen.[32]

It seems entirely possible that women of the neighborhood may have relished such tales, seeing in them examples of justified vengeance rather than wifely treachery. What is certain is that this particular jest

31 *Womens sharpe revenge,* sigs. K4–5v.
32 *Pasquils Jests,* sigs. G3r-v.

wife seems to have little use for conduct books and sermons that offer her only the patience of Griselda as a model.

Brawls between men and women in early farces such as *Tom Tyler and His Wife* (circa 1558) and *Ralph Roister Doister* (circa 1567) play out within a frame of neighborly observation and side taking, with alliances splitting along the fault line of gender. The incorporation of female allies into connubial battles harks back to comic scenes between Noah and his wife in pageant plays about the Flood. They trade insults, threats, and finally blows. She emerges the victor from their farcical bouts, literally sitting on top of her vanquished mate.[33] *Tom Tyler and His Wife* contains many of the timeworn elements from the Flood plays: long stage bouts between weak husband and strong shrew and scenes of tippling and singing by the shrew and her gossips. The play begins with a battle royal between Tom and Strife, which Strife wins. Afterward, Strife carouses with her friends Tipple the alewife and gossip Sturdie, crowing about her triumph. Sturdie praises Strife and wishes to imitate her but fears her husband's wrath. Meanwhile, Tyler asks macho Tom Taylor for advice, wailing that his wife "is so well schooled with too many shrowes / To receive any blowes."[34] Eager to help, Taylor disguises himself in Tyler's clothes and pummels the astonished Strife. She tries to shame him with the charge of cowardice: "Ah knave, wilt thou strike thy wife? . . . Hold thy hand, and thou be a man." Taylor ignores this and beats her black and blue.

The next scene opens with the neighbors having heard all about it and marveling that "such a simple fool" as Tyler could manage such a feat. They rush to comfort Strife when she enters "fair and softly, wailing and weeping":

> *Sturdie* Though all this be with you Gossip,
>   discomfort never.
> *Tipple* He watched ye once for ever.
>   But trust his hands no more. . . .
> *Sturdie* Bind this about your head,
>   And hardly lay you down. (sig. C)

33 *The Deluge: Noah and his Sons* (Wakefield Pageant), in Gassner, *Medieval and Tudor Drama*, 83.

34 *Tom Tyler and His Wife*, sig. C. Antifeminist satires often depict female friends schooling each other in ways to defy and exploit their husbands; see Woodbridge, *Women*, 27.

When Strife learns from foolish Tom Tyler that she was tricked, she leaps out of bed and gives Tom such a beating that the gossips hear the noise and, as good neighbors must, rush in to part them.

Strife and her gossips go on to sing a merry song proclaiming "how the Tylers wife of our Town / Hath beaten her man." The women's song ends on a bravura note of defiance:

> If Tom Tiler give a stroke,
> Perhaps if he be stout,
> He shall then have his costard broke,
> Till blood go round about.
> Though some be sheep, and some be shrowes,
>   Let them be fools that lust:
>   Tom Tilers Wife will take no blows,
>   No more than needs she must. (sig. C3v)

Such popular forms suggest that few Englishwomen actively aspired to sheephood. "Our womanish spirits are too virile to endure such affronts. . . . no modern eare can endure such break-necke love," observed Richard Brathwait a bit sourly, as he compared Englishwomen to Russian women, who felt neglected unless they were beaten, in the xenophobic stereotype of the period.[35]

Not all husbands in popular culture were Tom Tylers, however, unable to pummel their wives into submission. Some narratives feature brutal shrew beaters, like the new husband in *A Merry Jest of a Shewd and Curst Wife Lapped in Morel's Skin;* yet even these texts often contain passages that undercut a univocal reading of the husband's mastery. The anonymous author of *Wife Lapped in Morel's Skin* hints that the bride turns shrewish not simply because her mother is a shrew but because her spouse is crude, rough, and boorish on their wedding night.[36] Thomas Heywood's antifeminist *A curtaine lecture* (1637) contains a story about a battling couple who nearly kill each other. After the husband beats his wife to a pulp for scolding, he goes out to boast about his victory. She feigns cowed submission, and wins a vow from

35 Brathwait, *Ar't Asleep Husband?* 117.
36 *A Merry Jest of a Shrewd and Curst Wife* (circa 1550), reprinted in *Taming of the Shrew,* ed. Dolan, 254–88. The husband beats his obstreperous wife with rods until she bleeds and then wraps her in a horse's skin, which "cures" her shrewishness. Dolan points out that readers may find themselves "rooting for the feisty wife" in spite of the text's raw antifeminism (257).

him not to beat her again. Then she waits patiently to take her revenge. Opportunity strikes a few weeks later:

> It happened of a summer evening, he and his wife, sitting among others of the neighbours and their wives, she made the motion that they should goe to a sport called All-Hid, which is a meere childrens pastime; to which they, then being set upon a merry pin, agreed. Now shee had perswaded her husband to creep into a sacke, which he, in regard of her late conformitie suspecting nothing, was willing to do: and when she had tied the Sackes mouth fast, she call'd in two or three of her like conditioned Gossips, to whom she had acquainted her project, and they every one with a good cudgell did so bast the gentleman, that hee thought his very bones to rattle in his skin; and notwithstanding all his intreaties or fair promises, they would not let him out, or suffer him to take breath, till he had sworne unto them, not to take up so much as a small sticke to strike her ever after; to which (being almost stifled) he was forced to swear; nor did he offer the lest blow after, in regard of his oath.[37]

But the husband has spoken with forked tongue. He lies in wait; and when she expects nothing, they go to a party together. While dancing with her, he lifts her above his head and throws her down a steep flight of stairs, "and great odds she had not broken her neck; and this he did laughing."[38] His violent act is described quickly and with a slight coolness in tone; when he laughs, he laughs alone. In short, the husband ends up on top but not without violating the spirit of his oath, losing face and enduring a shameful public struggle, raging in a sack like a trapped beast while being basted by his wife and "her like conditioned Gossips"[39]—neighbors and friends with similarly hard-handed husbands. Despite all odds, and the hostility of the author, they have been smuggled into a text that is supposed to illustrate the perfidy of women.[40]

37 Heywood, *Curtaine lecture*, 208.
38 Ibid., 209.
39 Joy Wiltenburg (personal communication) suggests that part of the joke is that he has found a way to hurt her without hitting her, thus saving him from breaking his vow.
40 On ways in which images of violent revenge can be smuggled into above-ground culture from below, see Scott, *Domination*, 157.

"What woman can be such a Tame fool"

Satire is notoriously double-edged: it can cut both ways. In jesting literature and stage comedies the bonds of loyalty and shared desire among women attract much male-authored satire, of course, as with the shrews' man-baiting victory song in *Tom Tyler* and the culturally voracious gadding of Jonson's Ladies Collegiate in *Epicoene*, to name two very different works. But such satire raises to view scenes and pleasures that some spectators might prefer to replicate rather than scorn. The vehemence of the attacks suggests the feared strength of women's alliances, while their prolix specificity may have provided useful information to women who heard or read them. As Frances Dolan points out, referring to merry books about the nagging curtain lectures that wives gave husbands in bed, "It is also possible to imagine a female reader who finds encouragement in all this female complaint or who picks up tips about things she might resent or insults she could level."[41]

Such a reader would find more than a few tips in the gossips' literature. These songs and tales often "discover" seditious shrews gathering to plot insurrection and to seduce meeker wives into open rebellion. Wives in their cups trade complaints about their violent husbands, with a shrew taking the lead in urging the others to give as good as they get. Even meek wives are stirred to combat:

> My husband is so fell
> He beteth me lyke the devill of hell,
> And the more I crye,
> The lesse mercy
>
> Alis with a lowd voys spake then:
> Evis, she said, littill good he can
> That betith or strikith any woman,
> And especially his wyff
> God geve myn short lyff
>
> Margaret meke said, so not I thryve,
> I know no man that is alyve

41 *Taming of the Shrew,* ed. Dolan, 325.

That giveth me iii strokes but he have v!
I am not fered
Though he have a berde.[42]

In Rowlands's *A Whole Crew of Kind Gossips, All Met to Be Merry*
(1609) the bold wife hits back, as her mother taught her, boasting
about a scuffle in which she struck her husband with a "Faggot-
sticke" until the blood ran down. Then she "brake his head, and all
bescratch'd his face: / Then got him downe, and with my very fist / I
did bepommell him until he pist."[43] The second wife is not strong
enough to protect herself from beatings, so she curses her husband and
taunts him for his drinking. She thinks about cudgeling him when he
comes in staggering drunk but doesn't have the courage. She proudly
reports a trick she played on him one night, setting a stool in front of
the door and laughing in her sleeve when he tumbles down and cuts
his shins.[44]

Rowlands's gossips scorn wives who choose sheepdom over shrewdom, calling anyone who humbly suffers a husband's drunken fury "a
tame fool." This epithet surfaces in many jests, always conveying
women's anger at other women's mute and useless patience. "Mary Tattle-well and Jone Hit-him-home" use the insult in *The women's sharp
revenge:*

And what woman can be such a Tame Foole, as to hold her tongue in
her mouth (like a dumb beast) say nothing to her unthrifty Husband,
that shall day and night wash down his throat, with all, or the most
part of her maintenance, and pisse against the Wall his health, wit,
money and credit; and all her comfort is, that hee comes home, stinking, spewing, belching, spetting, spawling, slavering, and (being once
laid) snoring, like a Hogge in a Stie; or if he be not in that veine, perhaps
he is in a worse mood to sweare, curse, fight, fling, and throw.[45]

42 "The Gossips' Song," quoted in Anderson, "Gossips," 37.
43 Rowlands, *Whole crew of kind Gossips*, sig. B.
44 Ibid., sig. B2. Such scenes seem comically paranoid; but "while culture imagined women's violence as a laughing matter, women did assault one another, [and]
husbands did fear being killed in the night" (Gowing, *Domestic Dangers*, 229).
45 *The womens sharpe revenge*, sigs. K4r–v. Capp argues for Taylor's authorship
(*World of John Taylor*, 118–19). If Taylor is the author, his mimicry has allowed a dissonant fiction to emerge. Or as Barbara McManus says, "If John Taylor actually used
that feminine subject position . . . it was the masculine authorial voice that was effectively silenced" ("Whose Voice Is It Anyway?" 237).

Similarly vivid passages of pragmatic invective occur in other stories that contain recipes for female insurrection. Such is the treacherous power of satire: in order to purge recognizable vices, it opens a mimetic space for representing dissident voices.

Playwrights certainly recognized the dramatic appeal of staging female collusion and rebellion. In Fletcher's *The Wild-Goose Chase* the lover Bellure, fed up with Rosaura's teasing and tricks, threatens her with "swingeing" and catechizes her on a woman's inferiority to man, ordering her to grovel and cry before him. She pretends to comply; but at her cue her friends rush in and surround Bellure, jeering at him as an unmanly coward.

> *1 Woman.* Let him do his best,
>   Let's see the utmost of his indignation;
>   I long to see him angry. Come, proceed, sir.
>   Hang him, he dares not stir; a man of timber!
> *2 Woman.* Come hither to fright maids, with thy bull-faces?
>   To threaten gentlewomen? Thou a man? A Maypole!
>   A great, dry pudding!
> *3 Woman.* Come, come do your worst, sir,
>   Be angry, if thou darest.
> *Bellure.* The Lord deliver me!
> *4 Woman.* Do but look scurvily upon this lady,
>   Or give us one foul word—we are all mistaken,
>   This is some mighty dairy maid in man's clothes . . .
> *Lil.* And hired to come and abuse us. A man has manners,
>   A gentleman civility and breeding.
>   Some tinker's trull, with a beard glued on![46]

This angry chorus of women makes its unkindest cuts using the language of class, which trades heavily on gender-based notions of worth. He is impotent and trivial ("a great, dry pudding"), rustic and ignorant ("A Maypole"), and simultaneously effeminate and whorish ("tinker's trull," "dairy maid"). By bullying a woman, he bastardizes his own "breeding." By Fletcher's day some people were questioning the idea that a husband could discipline his wife with as much freedom as he did his children or his servants; furthermore, wife beating was slowly com-

---

46 Lister, *Critical Edition of "The Wild-Goose Chase,"* 4.2.77–92.

ing to be associated with vulgar drunkards and rough-handed artisans.[47]
The jesting literature, however, registers some doubt that gentlemen
and gentlewomen actually could or did exercise greater control than
their inferiors. With considerable irony, Heywood tells a tale about gender violence and the shallow civility of the elite:

> a basket-maker in the country, having with his best care and cunning
> made the end of an extraordinary Basket, which had been bespoke, &
> finding it finished to his own desire and fancy (his wife then sitting by
> him), he said, *Now God be thanked I have finisht my Basket, and I
> pray thee wife say so too*. But shee being refractory and obstinate, held
> her tongue; and the more he entreated her, the more adverse shee was
> to him, giving him foule and coarse language. Which he was not able to
> endure, fell upon her with a good cudgell, and beat her till she was for-
> c'd to cry out. A Noble man comming then by accidentally, with a great
> traine at his heeles, finding her weeping, began at first to commiserate
> the woman, and to chide the man for striking her: but being by him tru-
> ely informed of the cause, he commended the fellow for justly correct-
> ing her disobedience, and told her shee had her mends in her own
> hands: so left them, and rid home to his house. At supper he related
> all . . . to his Lady, and asked her opinion of the matter. Who answered,
> *The Basket-maker was a knave to offer to beat his wife upon so sleight
> an occasion*. Who replied unto her, *Why Madam, would you be so per-
> verse and obstinate unto me, if I should command you to speake those
> words?* Indeed my Lord, answered she, *I would. How*, saith he? *I charge
> you to say these words before all this company, God be thanked. I
> have finisht my Basket*. [She] answered againe, *my Lord I will die be-
> fore I will doe it*. At which he mightily enraged, rose from the table,
> and taking his battoone upon his hand, had he not been held by main
> force by his noble guests and his Gentlemen about him, there had been
> as great a fray betwixt them, as there was with the Basket-maker and
> the shrew his wife. Now what manner of Lecture she read after to him
> I cannot relate, being then not present to heare it.[48]

Heywood coyly refuses to give readers the scorecard at the end of this
round, withdrawing before the lady delivers her "Lecture," leaving his
listeners poised at the moment of keenest curiosity and inviting them
to dispute the case themselves.

47 Detmer, "Civilizing Subordination," esp. 274.
48 Heywood, *Curtaine lecture.*

Early moderns seem to have found basketwork an excellent trigger for domestic disputes. A sixteenth-century broadside ballad also associates this humble craft with escalating violence and teases listeners by withholding the final outcome. *A merie newe Ballad intituled, the Pinnyng of the Basket* climbs down and up through three discrete social worlds: that of apprentices and maidservants, artisans and their wives, and a justice and his wife. A joiner's apprentice overhears a battle between a chandler and his wife. He tells her to "pinne" a basket but she refuses, angry that he has been out drinking at the alehouse. A battle ensues, and the husband "bumde her well" with "a bastian that stood by" so that she "pinned" the basket "passing fine." The apprentice goes home and tells his master and mistress. The joiner enjoys the tale, but the wife frowns and sides with the beaten wife: "The knave the basket should have pinde / Himself, spight of his nose!"[49] Her husband asks her the fatal question: would *you* have pinned the basket if I had asked? This creates a new battle, which angers the maid who has seen all. She beats the apprentice, who beats her.

Next day the war grows so hot between the joiner and his wife that she runs to her friend nearby, the wife of a justice. The joiner's wife seeks the protection of her gossip and the law:

> And to the joylly Justice wife
> > Discovering all,
> Betwixt her spouse and her what strife
> > Did late befall.—
> Tantara, tara, tantara,—
> > Whom she would faine have bounde
> Unto the peace, if by the happe
> > There might suche meanes be founde.
>
> Of this her friende the francke consent
> > She soone had wone,
> To do for her incontinent
> > What might be done,—
> Tantara, tara, tantara,—
> > This Justice wife now gose,
> Her gossipps sute in haste unto
> > Her housband to disclose.

49 From *A Collection of Seventy-five Black-Letter Ballads,* 105–11.

> Her housband hearing by the tale,
>   How all thynges stood,
> In mynde he at this jeste so stale
>   Did laugh a-good;
> Tantara, tara, tantara,—
>   A little more adoe,
> The Justice wold have taught his wife
>   To pinne the basket too.

With its "tantara, tara, tantara" evoking both rough musicking and marital boxing, the ballad cues listeners to laugh along with the justice at "this jest so stale." But it is also quite possible that the ballad invites some to read against the masculinist grain, "the clean contrary way" (a popular royalist ballad that seems to support the opposition but reverses itself with each repetition of the refrain). On the narrative level, the ballad presents a tale of news flying from one household to another, causing strife and dissension among all who hear it; but on the level of performance, it also directs a similar challenge to the mixed-gender ballad audience.[50] In other words, the ballad represents and instigates opposing reactions by men and women to the same drearily familiar event, a man beating his wife for complaining about his drinking. A normative masculinist reading might run like this: by acting the shrew, the chandler's wife has bred unruliness in her neighbors, whose reactions range from frowns to blows, to curtain lectures, to the recruitment of neighborhood allies and a treacherous appeal to the rule of law. On the other hand, women listeners may well have identified with the beaten wife and her gossips rather than with the alehouse-haunting chandler; the voyeuristic, sadistic servant; or the irritable joiner. Violence begets violence within a neighborhood, threatening more than one woman as battles erupt. Female alliances and eventually "a gossippes suite" are ways in which women neighbors try to contain it. In its final stanzas the ballad spells out the right of a wife to appeal to the courts to force a husband to post a bond for his good behavior, as real women in danger sometimes did.[51] At each level the women are overmastered, but only with an effort.

50 Wiltenburg notes that the ballad author "makes no excuses for the treatment meted out to unruly wives, but apparently expects that women will be included in his audience" (*Disorderly Women*, 120).

51 See Mendelson and Crawford, *Women in Early Modern England*, 143; and Amussen, *Ordered Society*, 130.

At the end the narrator rather uneasily laughs away the alliance of the middling wife and her influential neighbor under the cover of an ideology of class difference. By erasing the logical final step of having the justice bash his own wife, the ballad author trades on the comparatively recent concept that higher status brought greater self-control—although even a justice could easily lose his head and unleash his hand with just "a little more adoe." The idea that a true gentleman does not strike women is, of course, the weapon that Katherina pulls out in *Taming of the Shrew*:

> *Petruchio.* Good Kate, I am a gentleman—
> *Katherina.*   That I'll try. *(She strikes him)*
> *Petruchio.* I swear I'll cuff you if you strike again.
>   *(He holds her.)*
> *Katherina.* So may you lose your arms.
>   If you strike me, you are no gentleman.
>   And if no gentleman, why then no arms.
>
> (2.1.213–17)

The rest of the play shows that Katherina may quibble but Petruchio disarms. Despite his "bedlam" behavior, Petruchio's social standing is only enhanced by his ability to tame this particular scold. Padua admires him for his unusual methods, but *Taming of the Shrew* gives small indication that he would have been any less admired *had* he used force on his chattel. Indeed, Kate's family and acquaintances make no attempt to protect her from Petruchio when he disrupts the wedding and abducts her from the feast, having their own strong reasons for wishing her gone.[52] By beating her sister and raging at her father and suitors, she puts herself in the dangerous position of being entirely without allies. Indeed, Petruchio quickly establishes complete hegemony over his new wife and household, ignoring any contravening force of neighborhood. His bride's shrewishness proves weak and superficial compared to that of the wives in jests and ballads who preferred death to capitulation.[53] *The Taming of the Shrew* seems to have been deliberately fashioned to spawn debate and to challenge "rules of love and neighborhood." Kate may seem "a

---

52 Detmer, "Domestic Violence," 287.
53 In an ancient story a shrew keeps calling her husband a louse. Enraged, he tries to drown her. She keeps miming lice killing with her fingers even as the waters close over her head, until he finally gives up (cited in *Taming of the Shrew*, ed. Dolan, 325–26). For more on Kate's lack of shrewish grit, see my essay, "Fie."

second Grissel" to the men who marvel at her abrupt metamorphosis, but she estranges all the women onstage and offers little for women in the audience to pity or admire. Seeing her sister throw away her cap and grovel before Petruchio, Bianca recoils in disgust—a reaction that may have appealed to the kind of spectators who would complain furiously when a preacher such as Gouge told them they had no rights to any property, not even their own clothing.

Kate and Petruchio had not been forgotten by 1611, when John Fletcher wrote *The Woman's Prize, or the Tamer Tamed*, in which Petruchio is reduced to a sputtering fool in the mold of Johan the Husband, Ralph Roister Doister, and the hapless Noah. Petruchio has married a second wife named Maria who, knowing his reputation for brutality, refuses to sleep with him on their wedding night. Her cousin Byancha, reminding her of Katherina's recent suspicious death, urges her to defend herself and accompanies her when she locks herself in Petruchio's house with all her gossips. Because the threat of harsh retaliation drives the play's action, the women's stratagems demand to be read as something more than laughing matters. Scott's "hidden transcript of resistance" is partially visible in the play's complex pattern of female jest/gest, which appears to demonstrate that shrews may be wiser than sheep when the butcher comes.

The rebels in Fletcher's comedy exploit the weapons available to them, especially those that seek to exert social control through shaming. Gossips publicize male vices; neighbors and kin ridicule wife beaters as crazed, unmanly tyrants; women hurl filth at assailants and hound them with rough music; wives withhold sex from their mates and threaten to cuckold them; maids laugh at impotent old lechers; and viragoes revel in waging "women's war." Flush with victory, they drink, sing, and vaunt their triumphs over men. One male spy who has peered in at their feast reports

> [They] daunce with their coats tuckt up to their
> bare breeches,
> And bid the Kingdom kiss 'em, that's the burden,
> They have got Metheglin, and audacious Ale,
> And talke like Tyrants. (2.4.36–42)

Each element springs from the traditional worlds of female jesting, reverberating through mocking rhymes and jigs, visual imagery, ballads, and jest books as well as plays. Beside the obvious parallels with *Lysistrata*, the siege scenes draw on the long tradition of "women on top" available to Fletcher and his audience from common culture. The women's boisterous blockade has its roots in the shaming rituals and mocking jigs in which women took part; the Hocktide games in which women captured and tied up men, demanding money for their release; and the legends about the martial cross-dresser Mary Ambree or the brawling barmaid Long Meg, who protected other besieged women. The bare-bottomed dance may glance at the licentious games of the Bessy in the May Games or the gambols of female mummers and Horn Fair revelers.[54] As heinous and "mankind" as all this might have seemed to a male spectator, scenes of female riot and rebellion may have greatly pleased women who knew far too many Petruchios for their liking.[55]

Despite its festive slapstick, *The Woman's Prize* raises grim questions about men's rights to maim and even kill wives. As in *Taming of the Shrew*, bruises and broken bones do not mar its gay surface; but Fletcher manages to invoke wife beating far more than Shakespeare's play did. The opening scene is full of tense banter. Petruchio's male friends gossip about his new wife Maria and her likely fate. One bets that she'll be dead within three weeks. It seems that Kate had reverted quickly to shrewdom and that the couple fought constantly until she died. The men hint strongly that Petruchio killed her. One says that if *he* were the new bride he would come out swinging, in simple self-defense: "I would eate Coales with an angry Cat, / And spit fire at him. . . . There is no safety else, nor morall wisdome, / To be a wife, and his" (1.1.24–29). Of course Kate's scolding is what made Petruchio turn tyrant, they agree—just the thought of her causes him to "Cry out for Cudgels, Costaves, any thing" (34). Still, they express sympathy for the bride and hope that he will forbear from whipping her.

Maria has other plans. Her cousin Byancha has just convinced her that Petruchio will batter her, no matter how meek she is: "Let not your blushes, / Your modesty, and tenderness of spirit, / Make you continuall Anvil to his anger" (1.2.56–58). Women neighbors have gathered to-

---

54 See Davis, "Women on Top," in *Society and Culture*, 135, 137–38, 140, 148; Houlbrooke, "Women's Social Life"; Hutton, *Rise and Fall*, 120–21; and Ingram, "Ridings."

55 For the intriguing argument that the women's riotous celebration resembles May Day festivities and political uprisings such as Kett's Rebellion, see Smith, *Breaking Boundaries*, 68–80, esp. 70–71.

gether to help Maria defend the house so that no man may enter. The men sense that something is up. As a servant says,

> I have observ'd, all this day; their whispers,
> One in anothers eare, their signes, and pinches,
> And breaking often into violent laughters:
> As if the end they purpos'd were their own.
>
> (1.2.209–15)

Barricaded with her gossips, Maria engages Petruchio in a parley. Their dialogue is punctuated with popular sayings batted back and forth (Petruchio: "Well, there are more Maides than *Maudlin*, that's my comfort." Maria: "Yes, and more men than *Michael*" [1.3.221–22]). Women pour down the fragrant contents of chamberpots, and carnivalia reigns as "gay matter" sails through the air. Turds and urine are time-honored missiles that women wield in jests, going back to the famous facetiae about Xantippe, who empties a pisspot on her husband's head after scolding him furiously. Socrates comments that he expected no less: "after so loud a thunder there must needs follow a violent raine."[56]

The play's staging underlines the idea that control of space implies the control of power and sexuality, with the house and its portals symbolizing the female body and its orifices, calling for eternal male vigilance.[57] For much of the play, the "uncrowned" men occupy the stage level; and the women appear above at windows and balconies of Petruchio's house, now a besieged castle. Such a squaring-off is a classic formation in comic fictions. In one version of the lockout trick, an aged husband discovers that his wife has been sneaking out at night, so he bars the door. She comes home late and begs him to let her in. He refuses, promises to beat her, and calls her a whore, telling her to stay outside all night so that everyone will know what she is. She says she is going to drown herself and then throws a stone in the well. This brings him running out. Of course, she runs in behind his back and locks the door. He tries to climb in the window; but she slams the window on his arms, scratches and beats his face, then pushes him out. Next day she points to his bloody scars and accuses him of consorting with ramping

---

56 Heywood, *Curtaine lecture*, 247. In *Westward for Smelts* a furious young wife pours "cuckold's urine" on the head of her old husband, whom she has locked out (sig. D3).

57 See Stallybrass, "Patriarchal Territories," 127–28.

whores, winning her sympathy from neighbors and kin, who denounce him roundly.[58]

Early modern women may well have taken these tales in the spirit of *sawce for the goose is sawce for the gander.* The scenario, after all, was not so far-fetched: in several cases in church court records, a husband locked his wife out in the cold to punish her.[59] *The Woman's Prize* adds to this basic *agon* a group of gossips above and a crowd of male onlookers and allies below. In this game of cat-and-mouse, the mouse is better prepared, more resourceful, and more mobile. She also has more to lose. Maria continues to provoke Petruchio without his being able to lay a hand on her, although he tells other men that he will beat her like a drum if she continues to rebel:

> She should ride the wild Mare once a week, she should,
> (Believe me friends she should.) I would tabor her,
> Till all the Legions that are crept into her,
> Flew out with fire i' th tailes.
>   (2.4.20–24)

As the last lines suggest, Petruchio understands that Maria has girded herself with the strength of her gossips, just as his house is fortified by their bodies. By the third act Maria has left the security of the house but shows that she is still internally fortified. She quickly succeeds in getting Petruchio locked up in his own house by telling people he has been stricken with plague; and eventually he has to force the door open with a gun, looking every inch the fool. The resolution is brought about by liberal applications of social pressure through threats of gossip and loss of male honor. As one of Petruchio's friends puts it: "Now you must grant conditions or the Kingdom / Will have no other talke but this" (2.4.84–85).

"Hold Your Hands, Honest Men!"

When the women warriors sing a drinking song proclaiming their victory, they do it in terms that invite the audience to join in: "Let this health be a Seal, / For the good of the Common-weal / the woman shall wear the breeches" (2.6.48–50). Ballads often featured a rousing call for

58 *Westward,* sigs. D3–D5.
59 Mendelson and Crawford, *Women in Early Modern England,* 211.

participation by customers, which "not only increased [their] market appeal but also enhanced [their] potential as a medium for the statement of communal statement."[60] By singing along, as playgoers were known to do, Fletcher's female audiences could take an active role in the pleasurable duty of shaming the men for making violent threats.

The gossips' song recruits spectators to function almost as neighbors, positioning them in much the same way that street ballads did when they showed neighbors swarming in to protect a woman under attack. As Wiltenburg points out, "in some broadside ballads, spirited wives yell murder when beaten by their men, in hopes of attracting neighbors to intercede. The surrounding community is seen as playing an important role in maintaining or modifying the balance of marital power."[61]

In the dialogue ballad *A merry discourse twixt him and his Joane* (circa 1620), a tinker and his wife argue about his drinking and profligacy. After she scolds him roundly, he promises to "amend his drunken fit" and stay at home, thus letting her have her will—but he begs her not to let the neighbors know:

> *Man.*
> Well, do what you wilt, I am at thine command,
> But let not my neighbours of this understand,
> For that if thou dost, I know it will be
> A shame to thy selfe [and] disgrace unto me.

> *Woman.*
> No matter for that, Ile make you to know
> What 'tis for to injure a loving wife so,
> In pawning her goods, and making her be
> A scorne to her neighbours, and all long of thee.[62]

In *By west of late as I did walk*, a couple comes to blows inside a house. The wife beats the husband, but both know that their neighbors will mock them if they hear what's going on. So the clever wife covers

60 Clark, "Economics." I thank Sandra Clark for allowing me to see her paper.
61 Wiltenburg, *Disorderly Women*, 103. The increasing detachment of neighbors plays a key role in the rise of husbandly violence in the United States today, reports Peterson del Mar in *What Trouble I Have Seen'* which documents a modern trend away from active intervention beginning in the nineteenth century. By the 1970s, some people were turning their backs on husbands' public beating of their wives, calling it "a private matter."
62 *Roxburghe Ballads*, 1:251.

the sound of her blows by screaming—as if *she* is the one receiving them. She feigns pain so well that the neighbors beat down the door to rescue her. When they burst in, she runs out of sight, leaving her husband sprawled on the floor, beaten to a pulp. Raising his head, he manages to swear that he would have killed her if they hadn't stopped him! With this ruse they save face in front of the neighbors, where it really counts. The reversal produces an irony that serves to satirize both the comic convention and neighborhood values.[63]

Paired ballads by opponents on a given topic echo the push and pull of community judgment. *Keep a Good Tongue in Your Head*, a warning for scolding wives by a shrew-ridden husband, was soon matched by a ballad in the persona of an abused wife, *Hold Your Hands, Honest Men!*[64] The refrains counter each other neatly, with the woman singing "but he cannot rule his hands" and the man singing "but she cannot rule her tong." Both are addressed by a neighbor to neighbors of the other gender, and both seem to seek to foment discussion among a mixed-gender crowd. The female narrator in *A Married-womans case* charges that wife abusers are cowards who are afraid to fight men, warning maids that a wife in her predicament "shall not want blowes, though vitle she lacke, / Although from a man hee'l perhaps turne his backe."[65]

In a pair of mid-seventeenth-century answer ballads by Martin Parker, there is every indication that he wishes to offend some hearers and to make others laugh but at any rate to gather a crowd. *Have among you! good Women* presents the "high-way discourse" of old William Starket and young Robin Hobs, two men gossiping about the shrews of the neighborhood as they walk to market. Using a familiar formula, the subtitle warns women that they may not like what they hear, but they'd better keep quiet or risk detection:

> Good Women before hand let me you advise,
> To keepe your owne counsell, and so be held wise.
> If any one take in ill part what here's said,
> Shee'l shew by her kicking that she's a gauld jade.[66]

---

63 Quoted in R. Boedekker, "Englische Lieder und Balladen aus dem. 16 Jahrundert," *Jahrbuch für romanische und englische Sprache und Literatur* 14 (n.s. 2) 1875, 220. I am grateful to Joy Wiltenburg for sending me this ballad and providing the citation.

64 *Roxburghe Ballads*, 3:237, 343.

65 Quoted in Wiltenburg, *Disorderly Women*, 94.

66 *Roxburghe Ballads*, 1:435–40. On the often-used metaphor "galled horse" to describe angry women, see Williams, *Just Anger*, 1–2, 25–28, 49–50.

The younger man asks the older what should be done with Alce the butter woman, who scolds and fights with her neighbors; Jone the spinner, who picked her husband's pocket; Ruth the seamstress, who domineers over her husband; and "Jone that cries pins," who beats her husband. In his litany of punishments that were in fact used on women, sage old William says with glee that the first "should be cuck't," the second "kickt," the third "tam'd," and the fourth "tam'd in the stocks."

The gossiping men roundly criticize husbands for failing to beat these wives into compliance. But the two men reluctantly acknowledge that their neighbors will not allow husbands to indulge in the degree of savagery they would like; these wives have allies who will intervene. In the case of the wife who has "broken her husband's shins," young Robin questions why her husband puts up with it. Old William sets him straight:

> "Why wherefore all this doth he suffer?"
> "Why, if he should give her a check,
> She tels her friends how he doth cuff her
> and threatens to break her neck:
> So hee, for feare shee'll cry out,
> dares neither to strike her nor chide her,
> For shee'll give the word all about
> that his Queans will not let him abide her."

Jone is safe, for the moment at least, because her friends can help her shame her husband with a charge of consorting with whores. The conversation continues; the polis itself appears to be at risk as the list expands from venal sins such as scolding to mortal ones such as whoring, stealing, and murder. The nose of "Peg the Pie-Woman" has been slashed by the jealous wife of her lover ("Oh! such a Queane should be lash't"); and "snuffeling Kate" has been selling "maidenheads at a rate" ("Oh! such an old Trot would be carted"). For cozening and stealing, "Madge who cries wheat" should be hanged. "Quarreling Nan" tops the list by threatening the ultimate treachery:

> ". . . What thinke you of quarreling Nan,
> that will to no goodness be turn'd?
> She threatens to kill her good man!"
> *"Oh! such a Queane would be burned."*

With its sadistic refrain and its covert invitation to buyers to compare the characters to their own neighbors, the ballad may have angered or frightened at least some of the women who heard it. Unfortunately, such extravagant cruelty was not outside the bounds of possibility. In a case from 1619, a violent husband tormented his abused wife with threats ranging from breaking her bones, to jailing her for disorderliness and lunacy, to deporting her as a slave, to having her executed—a grim litany "whose force is weighted by the very real possibility of men's manipulation" of some of these punishments.[67]

As a print ballad meant for popular consumption rather than for individual terrorizing, however, the most intriguing characteristic is of *Have among you! good Women* is its status as a male response to a female gossips' song.[68] Two women meet by chance in the street, just as William and Robin do. The original ballad, *Well Met, Neighbour*, bears the subtitle, "A Dainty Discourse betwixt Nell and Sisse, / Of men that doe use their wives amisse: / Then all you good women their cases pitty, / The cause you shall heare if you list to this ditty."[69]

Nell says she's hurrying to another woman's bedside to assist in her labor, so Sisse joins her:

> For I have a thing in my head
> That will hold us talking a mile:
> Heard you not lately of Hugh,
> How soundly his wife he bang'd?
> He beat her black and blew—
> *O such a rogue would be hang'd!*

Sisse and Nell agree that wife beating should be answered with husband thrashing: "If my husband should / Not use mee so well as he ought," says Sisse, "My hands I should hardly hold, / For I'de give him as good as he brought." They both deplore the cowardice of men who "dare not, with swords or staves, / Meet men in the field for their lives," but prefer to harass and beat their poor wives instead. Next they castigate "Kett the

---

67 Gowing, *Domestic Dangers*, 227. For example, husbands could and did have their wives arrested for disobedience.

68 Although neither is dated, both ballads are by Parker, who died in 1656. *Have Among You! good Women* names as its tune ("To the tune of O such a rogue") the refrain of *Well Met, Neighbour*, showing that the women's ballad probably came first.

69 *Roxburghe Ballads* 3:98–103.

baker" for threatening to abandon his wife. When Sisse asks what could
be his reason, Nell responds that his drinking causes them to fight:

> ". . . when hee's drunk as a rat,
> Then shee'l act the part of a shrow."
> "Tush! Thats such a catching disease,
> Few women their silence can keepe:
> Let every one say what they please,
> *But a shrew's better far than a sheepe.*"

In both the men's and women's exchanges, proverbs abound. As with
many scenes showing "jurors" of the neighborhood in open debate, they
enlist proverbs to appeal to common sense and the precedent of past experience, similar to a lawyer's use of previous rulings in a law case.[70]
Like a legal precedent, an aphorism is mobile: adaptable to differing
(and even opposing) rhetorical purposes. In this instance, the proverb
preferring a shrew to a sheep is put in a woman's mouth—which is,
after all, just where it belongs.

According to Diane Purkiss, *Have Among You, Good Women* and
other ballads about women offer "the pleasure of locating disorder in
femininity and expelling both from man. They constitute the male
group and the male subject as those from which femininity has been
excluded."[71] Her view fails to consider the possibility that ballads may
have helped constitute a female group and a female subject; and it
erases the other half of the conversation (audible in songs such as *Well
Met Neighbour*) in which disorder is located in unruly masculinity.
Women singing along with the refrain "O such a rogue would be
hang'd!" spell out this view to anyone listening. As Sandra Clark points
out, a male ballad singer might undercut such ballads in performance,
"but equally it can be argued that the ballad's public and communal
mode, and the likely encouragement of audience participation at the
point of delivery, would function to reinforce any message explicitly expressed."[72]

---

70 Proverbs were often used by lawyers in court, and villagers "expected an exchange of proverbs to have some role in legal argument and probably used them
themselves before manorial courts and in village disputes" (Davis, *Society and Culture*, 244).
71 Brant and Purkiss, *Women, Texts*, 81.
72 Clark, "Economics," 2.

It is important not to overvalue such ephemera by claiming that they could somehow fully articulate female resistance. Ballads, sayings, and jests are never weapons in and of themselves: it takes a sense of timing, delivery, occasion, and audience to make them rhetorically potent. In many cases, voicing open opposition could have resulted in broken bones or worse. My only claim is that the jesting literature could furnish scripts and cues, ready for the taking from common culture. Turning them to use was the role of the speaker and depended entirely on her talent or her desperation. Such phrases and sayings were cues for a kind of female speech that did not always condone, comply with, or submit to the double standard's achingly crude violence. Anonymous culture alerts all listeners, high or low, meek or mannish, that *he that will make himselfe a sheepe, it is no matter though the wolf eate him.*[73]

73 Le Strange, *Merry Passages*, 161, no. 611.

5 Scandalous Pleasures
A Coney-Catcher and Her Public

In a note to his edition of *Jacke of Dover his Quest of Enquirie, or His Privy Search for the Veriest Foole in England* (1604), W. C. Hazlitt speculated that "the title was perhaps recommended by the popularity of a tract, which appeared in 1595 under the title

> A Quest of Enquirie,
> For Women to Know,
> Whether the tripe-wife were trimmed
> By Doll, yea or no."[1]

On inspection the title page actually reads: "A Quest of Enquirie, by women to know. . . ."[2] The small misreading turns a stray preposition into a proposition: the pamphlet and the scandal it magnified were by and for women, though not in ways that required female literacy, authorship, or ownership. Instead, these texts figure women as a generative force, combining the roles of publisher and public in recirculating sensational acts of female roguery and satire.

The "Doll" of *A Quest of Enquirie* went by the name of Judith, Dorothy, or Doll Philips and by her married name, Doll Pope. Posing as a fortune-teller, she apparently conned a well-to-do London widow who

---

1 Hazlitt, *Shakespeare Jest-Books*, 2:312.
2 *A Quest* (title page). That it sold well is suggested by the fact that this was the second printing in a year.

had a thriving trade selling tripe in St. Nicholas Shambles. According to the highly imaginative details of *A Quest*, Philips promised to divine which of the widow's suitors she should marry, but first she required a bit of her victim's pubic hair. The widow complied, propping her leg upon a trivet while Doll "lopt off a lovers locke."[3] Afterward, Doll contrived to rob her of gold and household stuff. A second caper prompted a crime pamphlet, *The Brideling, Sadling, and Ryding of a Rich churl in Hampshire* (1595), which reports how Philips robbed a farmer after using him as a beast of burden. For these crimes she was finally caught, tried, and whipped.[4] In the mock-solemn pages of *A Quest*, the tripe wife suffers in a different way: after being balladed and jigged about her "trimming," she is tried before a court of hostile neighbors, who judge her a fool.

While ignoring the presence or absence of pubic hair in *A Quest of Enquirie*, Alexander Grosart commented that it merited attention because it called up a specific locale and a particular kind of resident:

> [It] seems to the Editor of quick interest for its . . . presentation of the "simple" or vulgar aspects of "the commonalty." Regarded broadly, it reminds us how very small our now great London then was and how provincial in its tone, when such a "quarrel" and "quest" could so excite the community and inspire (as it would seem) abundant "ballads" and keen passion all around.[5]

Given the traditional gendering of gossip and ballad-buying as female pastimes, one may hear in these words a male intellectual's condescension toward the clacking tongues and vacant minds of women. Despite Grosart's disdain, one may also sense his "quick interest" in the indispensable fascinations of the vulgar, which he displays by editing and publishing the pamphlet.[6] For modern scholars, as Dolan points out,

---

3 Ibid., sig. C2.

4 On January 9, 1594, sergeant-at-law Thomas Fleming examined Judith Philips and her husband in Newgate Prison on the charge of cozening a rich widow after promising to help her choose a suitor. This incident apparently produced the *Quest* pamphlet, in which the widow became a tripe wife, the husband's role was reduced, and enticing details were added. The examination appears in *Historical Manuscripts Commission (Salisbury 5)*, 82, cited in Foley, "Falstaff," 246. Also see Baskervill, *Elizabethan Jig*, 73, n. 4.

5 Grosart, *Grosart's Occasional Issues*, xxiii.

6 "Low domains" such as the vulgar and obscene are "apparently expelled as 'Other,' [but] return as the object of nostalgia, longing and fascination" (Stallybrass and White, *Politics and Poetics*, 161).

sensational chapbooks and ballads about women and crime are most valuable "not as records of particular crimes but as evidence of the processes of cultural formation and transformation in which they participated."[7]

Along with their engrossing display of a female trickster, the pamphlets' appeal for women's laughter is intriguing and potentially illuminating. At the time of the tripe wife's troubles, phobic male discourse about women's garrulous mouths and stabbing tongues was a an admission of women's power to wound through language, prompting elaborate and even violent countermeasures.[8] This disturbing power bore a political valence reflected in the genres that represent it. *Brideling* and *A Quest of Enquirie* are satires aimed at the rich and dull, brought about through the agency of a poorer but wittier woman, and eliciting bottom-up mockery. Such irreverent laughter—rarely revolutionary but definitely not obedient—pervades stories about women's courts, mock testaments, jokes in which old women confound cheaters, and "witty servant" plays in which maids run rings around masters and seducers. All these comic forms depend on a knowing audience that acknowledges through its laughter (however briefly) the view from below and the articulation of the unauthorized.

While they do satirize "tittle-tattle," the texts discussed here markedly attribute a sense of skepticism and judgment to women whose sharp tongues and laughter play a central role in a collective small-scale drama. *Brideling* and *A Quest* derive their energy from that gendered verbal art, gossip, seeking to represent and stimulate it using specific genres of popular satire: a burlesque trial, juicy and imaginative libels, and, above all, a mocking ballad jig. The busy street and talkative neighbors that figure so largely in the tripe wife's trials provide both market and seedbed for new deeds, new texts, and new speech. Taken together, these motley texts provide a satiric portrait of the open-eared and voluble populace that generated such scandals: "Farewell till within this fortnight," concludes *A Quest* invitingly, "by which time we shall either be all friends, or make our fude endlesse" (sig. D3v).

In short, these works suggest the practices and desires of those who mocked the churl and the tripe wife for themselves. Given the reading practices that prevailed until the mid-seventeenth century—non-elites

---

7 Dolan, *Dangerous Familiars*, 3.
8 See Boose, "Scolding Brides," 179–213; and Underdown, "Taming," 116–36.

used printed texts mainly as prompt books for speaking or scripts to read aloud to a group—these texts are artifacts not of solitary silent acts of reading (or of sole ownership) but of the sounds and sights of bodies speaking to others.

News "whereat everie true meaning maid may smile"

Curiosity about Judith Philips was probably sparked by her arrest, trial, and public whipping on two occasions, the latest occurring on February 14, 1594. Her crimes were taken up by pamphleteers, including the anonymous author of *Brideling*.[9] The full title is tantalizing:

> The Brideling, Sadling, and Ryding of a Rich churl in Hampshire, by the subtill practice of one Judith Philips, a professed cunning woman, or Fortune teller. With a true discourse of her unwomanly using of a Trypewife, a widow, lately dwelling on the back side of S. Nicholas shambles in London, whom she with her confederates, likewise cosoned, for which fact, she was at the Sessions house without Newgate arraigned, where she confessed the same, and had judgment for her offence, to be whipped through the citie, the 14 of February, 1594.

Under a veneer of moralizing, the pamphlet provides laughable details of these crimes and paints the coneys as covetous fools. While Philips is roundly denounced, her victims are the targets of the concluding moral: "Of al the seven deadly sinnes, there is none so common in the flourishing realme of England as the grievous sin of covetousness." The spectacle of the coneys' shaming takes far more space than do the details of capture or punishment, and the text provides copious cues for the attitude to be taken toward them. They are termed "poor fooles" and "simple," and the churl is called miserly and suspicious yet "fantasticall and given to beleeve every tale he heard" (sig. A3v).[10]

9 Three items about Philips were entered by Josiah Parnell in the Stationers' Register on February 25, 1595: "*ij bookes the One intituled a trew Discoverye of ij notable villanyes practised by one Judith Phillips the wyfe of John Phillips of Crowne Allye in Bishopsgate strete / and the other entituled the notorious cousenages of Dorothie Phillips otherwise called Dol Pope,*" and "a ballad thereof" (Baskervill, *Elizabethan Jig,* 73, n. 4).

10 According to the *Oxford English Dictionary, churl,* while not yet the stinging insult it would later become, was assuming pejorative weight at this time, with secondary significations ranging from "peasant" to "boor" to one who is "sordid, hard, or stingy in money-matters."

The text quotes the rogue's speeches directly, inviting mimicry, while the gestures of her victims might well have been repeated by the reader-performer:

> then this Judith caused him and his wife to go into the yard, where she set the saddle upon his back, theron girded it fast with two new girths, and also put a bridle upon his head, all which being done, she gat upon his backe in the saddle, and so rid him three times betwixt the chamber and the holly tree, then said this cosoning queane, you must lye three houres one by another groveling on your bellies under this tree, & stir not till I charge you, until I come back againe, for I must goe into this chamber to meete the Queene of the Fairies and welcome her to that holy and unspotted place, so this churle and his wife were left quaking in the colde, casting many a long looke for the comming of this woman. (sig. Bv)

The title-page woodcut of Philips vaunting on the churl's back is especially intriguing (see fig. 10). Part of an instantly readable tradition based on the tale of Phyllis and Aristotle, the image does not stay safely in the realm of myth. This "woman on top" is no legend (or is she?) Just as we don't imagine real women fighting with men over real breeches, we don't usually take the notion of women on top literally; so it is startling to confront an image that illustrates an actual event rather than legend or jest. The story of Aristotle's riding was as much a visual lesson as a verbal one, and each medium relayed a subtly different message. For one thing, the visual text is arguably more comic and asks for scorn at the ridden rather than horror at the rider. In the original story, Aristotle warns Alexander away from his paramour Phyllis, so she gets even "by coquettishly persuading the old philosopher to get down on all fours and, saddled and bridled, carry her through the garden."[11] Early modern England mingled other scenes and other associations with the classical tale: Noah's wife sometimes mounted Noah during their bouts in pageant drama, while a shrew's husband was proverbially so tame he could be "ridden to Rome in a bridle."[12]

Churl riding and tripe wife trimming are not necessary to Philips's larcenous ends, but her motives are never explained in these pamphlets. Her peculiar wit erupts into discourse as an attention-grabbing surplus,

11 Davis, *Society and Culture*, 135–36.
12 Rogers, *Troublesome Helpmate*, 87.

THE

Brideling, Sadling and Ryding, of

a rich Churle in Hampſhire, by the ſubtill practiſe of one
Iudeth Philips, a profeſſed cunning woman, or
Fortune teller.

VVith a true diſcourſe of her vnwomanly vſing of a Trype wife, a widow,
lately dwelling on the back ſide of S. Nicholas ſhambles in London, whom ſhe with her conferates, likewiſe coſoned:

For which fact, ſhee was at the Seſſions houſe without New-gate arraigned,
where ſhe confeſſed the ſame, and had iudgement for her offence,
to be whipped through the Citie, the 14. of February, 1594.

Printed at London by T. C. and are to be ſolde by
William Barley, at his ſhop in New-gate
Market, neare Chriſt-Church. 1595.

Fig. 10. Title page from *The Brideling, Sadling and Ryding, of a rich Churle in Hampshire* (1595). Reproduced by permission of The Huntington Library, San Marino, California.

a burst of creative energy in the manner of the jester or clown. An earlier narrative that appears to recount Philips's exploits stresses her Sco-
gin-like delight in turning the world upside down. In Henry Chettle's
Kind-Hartes Dream (1592), an old tooth drawer dreams that a female
rogue bridles, saddles, and rides a farmer in the course of cozening him;
but in this telling she is not named, the farmer is "honest and simple,"
and the riding takes place in a locked room. After she is captured, she is
asked about her reasons for saddling up and replies, "faith . . . only to
see how like an Asse hee lookt."[13]

Woodbridge has recently argued that popular texts about roguery and
coney catching are thinly disguised jest books. Knowing that a funny
crime featuring a female rogue atop a bridled man was already circulating in a Chettle's merry book does make *Brideling* look less credible as
news.[14] Skepticism grows the more one studies its woodcuts, which
start to resemble single-panel comics. Did Judith Philips actually sad-
dle up the rich farmer?[15] Assuming that we can't know exactly what
happened (even if additional documents were found, the "facts" could
be archival fictions), can we assume that the story is meant to give
more pleasure than instruction? If the picture and tale are meant to be
titillating and entertaining, whose pleasure is being courted?

The second woodcut in *Brideling* is even more mysterious (see fig.
11). The text doesn't say who these women are, what the scissors are
for, or why one woman points down; the pubic trimming isn't explained
here but in the *Quest* pamphlet printed a year later. This is a strong
clue that the tale of the trimming was already widely known via word
of mouth or from a lost publication or performance because the woodcuts seem purposely commissioned for the Philips story, a rarity with

---

13 Chettle, *Kind-Hartes Dream,* 62–65; Chettle may have drawn on similar exploits by Philips rather than the Hampshire incident (see Foley, "Falstaff in Love,"
228, 234). Levin argues that Chettle describes the same events as in *Brideling* ("Another 'Source,'" 215).

14 Woodbridge, *Vagrancy,* 49. Certainly, *Brideling* is meant to peddle both merriment and scandalous news, but most jest biographies (of Scogin, Howleglas, and Long
Meg, for example) don't end with their protagonists being caught and branded as
criminals. An exception is *The Twelve Merry Jests of the Widow Edith,* about a female vagrant who infiltrated the household of Sir Thomas More, where she was exposed and humiliated. See Woodbridge's discussion in *Vagrancy,* 193–204; also
Prescott, "Crime and Carnival."

15 Rollins maintained that ballads were generally "far more trustworthy and far
less absurd on the facts" than were the sensational news pamphlets, many of which
feature exotic crimes ("Black-Letter," 275).

crime pamphlets and ballads, which usually reused generic woodcuts.
A likely possibility is that songs and jigs about Philips were already
common currency in the weeks between her whipping and the *Brideling* pamphlet. Baskervill notes that, "jigs on the well-known characters
of the London underworld were commonly sung both among the people
and on the stage," with the usual trajectory going from the street—
where people sang songs learned from singers or devised their own—to
the stage, with "the comedians merely giving a professional turn to
what was common enough in everyday life."[16] Rogues and whores were
favorite subjects. A bawd in *Kind-Hartes Dream* complains bitterly that
the players had exposed all

> our cross-biting, our conny-catching, our traines, our traps, our gins,
> our snares, our subtilties: for no sooner have we a tricke of deceipt, but
> they make it common, singing jigs and making jests of us, that everie
> boy can point out our houses as they passe by.[17]

To anyone who had heard a few details of the story, the pamphlet offered the thrill of hearing more about how a notorious female rogue
could have ridden a man and "trimmed" a woman—a highly suggestive
phrase to sixteenth-century ears, connoting cheating, satirizing, and
sex.[18] There is no reason to assume that such pleasures were the sole
province of men. A certain complicity with Judith Philips is encouraged
by her knowing, sly half-smile, so different from the blank, even stupid
looks on the faces of her prey. She directs the action, using firm gestures
in contrast to her victims' diffident ones. The tone throughout varies
from formulaic sermonizing to onrushing colloquialism. There are loud
hints that neither tale nor moral is to be taken with a completely
straight face, particularly in the direct address to the readers, who are
identified as women. The anonymous author names maids and dames
as the desired readers and buyers in words that provide them with a
face-saving excuse for their interest.[19] Philips is nothing less than

16 Baskervill, *Elizabethan Jig*, 74.
17 Cited in ibid.
18 Senses include "to become pregnant," "to have sexual intercourse," and "to
cheat (a person) of money, to 'fleece'" (OED). The satiric meaning is evident in *The
Trimming of Thomas Nashe* (1597), in which Gabriel Harvey calls himself the "Bar-
ber-chirurgeon" who will "cut more parts of him than are necessarie" (*Works*, 3:43).
19 Suzanne Hull takes the qualified view that addresses to female readers and patrons, especially in prefaces, constitute evidence that a given text is "for" women
(*Chaste*, 127–44). This argument has been challenged by other scholars, including

Fig. 11. From *The Brideling, Sadling and Ryding of a rich Churle in Hampshire*
(1595). Reproduced by permission of The Huntington Library, San Marino, California.

the mirrour and mappe of all cosonage and deceit, whereat all modest
women may blush and everie true meaning maid may smile at the follie
of the world. Pardon my penne, you modest Dames and grave Patrons, it
shall in no way impaire your honorable sexe, but truly imblazen to the
world, the cosoning devices of a shamelesse woman. (sigs. A2v–A3)

Lori Newcomb, who argues that writers and printers constructed a degraded female
reading public for many purposes, including allowing men to enjoy a "frisson" of fri-
volity and class transgressiveness by reading popular works addressed to women
(*Reading Popular Romance*, 45). In the case of the Philips pamphlets, I believe that
printers and writers did not rule out men as readers; yet they actively recruited
women as "publishers" of the scandal, customers, and audiences, in spite of the antifeminist satire displayed in the texts. Like plays touting their own antitheatrical-
ism, the rhetorical attack complicates but fails to erase the spectacle's appeal.

This is a none-too-covert invitation to women readers to "smile at" and "imblazen to the world" these illicit but above all amusing devices, described so that the occult trappings contrast lugubriously with homely details. In both narratives the setting is home and yard, with emphasis placed on the stealing of household stuff—linens, candlesticks, silver. Whether as servants or wives, women were guardians of such goods, and kept strict watch over their yards. The tripe wife was traduced within her home, where all events were supposedly under her control, and the churl and his wife groveled on their bellies for hours in their own garden, perilously close to the view of their neighbors. The text, like the woodcut, provides a window through the hedge for the neighbors who did not see the event, catching the coney once again:

> but when the poore foole sawe the time expired, and his expected
> woman did not return, he got him up and cast off his saddle and bridle,
> being halfe-dead with colde . . . when he entered his chamber, and saw
> both his linnen and his gold convaide away, fel into such a perplexity of
> mind, as though he had been distraight of his wits: one while greeving
> for the losse of his foureteen pounds, another while, for the abuse of his
> own good name, likewise for the penance and disgrace she put him and
> his wife unto, the base and rediculous manner of his sadling, his cold
> lodging and weary time spent under the tree, to his bitter infamy and
> shame. And lastly, the losse of his pure and fine linnen, but yet he dis-
> sembled his grief in such order, that his neighbors had no suspition
> thereof. (sig. Bv)

The narrative supplies a great amount of detail about the coneys compared to the very brief mention of Philips's capture and punishment. Despite the damning phrases, the reader is left with the impression that Philips is fascinating and her coneys absurd, a point of view supported by the contemptuous title and the title woodcut, with its telling details of money bag and fallen hat. *Brideling* manages to laugh at the stupidly supine wealth of both the tripe wife and the merchant, in contrast with the mobile, clever, interest-bearing alchemy of Philips and her confederates.[20] While Philips is a criminal capable of arousing horror and fear, she is drawn as far cleverer than her victims.

Theorizing why narratives should glamorize the rogue is nothing new

20 Agnew explores relationships among liquidity, roguery, and alchemy in *Worlds
Apart*, 71–73.

in Renaissance studies,[21] but most writers consider only the male jester, rogue, or court Machiavel.[22] When scholars turn their attention to female tricksters, they usually stress their sexual chicanery rather than their theatrical brilliance or mental agility.[23] Yet the deeds of Judith Philips, like those of Heywood's Wise Woman of Hogsdon, Shakespeare's Cleopatra, and Middleton and Dekker's Moll Cutpurse, are put into play by other kinds of desires and pleasures—namely, voyeurism, a taste for carnival excess, fantasies of wealth and power, and the love of witty invention and spectacular self-display.

The chief bait Philips offers is her friendship with the fairy queen. In the 1590s belief in fairies was still strong, especially in the countryside,[24] but a growing skepticism was fed by detection tracts—including Reginald Scot's massive *Discoverie of Witchcraft*, which called cunning women mere cozeners—and coney-catching tales that exposed faked occultism. To some people the notion of fairy gold was becoming ludicrous, like the gulls who believed it. There is an unmistakable tone of playful scorn for the credulous in both Philips pamphlets. In *A Quest of Enquirie*, the female judges ask the tripe wife's stepdaughter whether

---

21 See Kinney's comments in *Rogues*, esp. 11, 55; and Agnew on the "romanticization" of the rogue and the genre's "numerous hints of mock-heroic rascality" that show its ties to popular trickster tales (*Worlds Apart*, 66). Woodbridge reads rogue tales as directing hostile laughter at, and criminalizing, the destitute under this genial veneer (*Vagrancy*, esp. 54–55). Feinberg discusses attractive rogues in comic depictions of beggary in "Representations of the Poor," 156–57.

22 An exception is Richard Levin, who credits Philips with "spectacular exhibitions of her complete mastery of the situation and of her victims' complete gullibility, and therefore demonstrates much of the same kind of comic inventiveness that we attribute to Subtle, Face, and Doll, and to their creator." Despite this applause, he argues that no new light is shed on Jonson's play by linking it to the Philips texts ("Another 'Source,'" 219, 227).

23 The existence of the pícara and the English female rogue contradict Mahadev Apte's generalization that there are no female tricksters or clowns in the prose narrative of any culture (*Humour*, 70–71). See Kalter, *Pícara*. On fabliau trickster Dame Sirith, see Hines, *Fabliau*, 43–70. Ingram surveys sexual rogues and trickster bawds in plays in *Posture of a Whore*.

24 In Keith Thomas's view, some people took fairy stories and sightings literally, but "by the Elizabethan age fairy lore was primarily a store of mythology rather than a corpus of living beliefs" (*Religion*, 726). Robert Weimann, on the other hand, agrees with Katharine Briggs (*Anatomy*, 1–6), that fairies "retained much of their imaginative vitality. Growing skepticism . . . did not stand in their way," but paradoxically "made their playfully imaginative treatment in the public theater possible" (*Shakespeare and the Popular Tradition*, 192–93). Mary Ellen Lamb is more pessimistic: *Midsummer Night's Dream*, for example, defangs fairy lore while excluding mothers, "female caregivers, and the common culture that produced" tales about changelings, Robin Goodfellow, and fairy gold ("Taken by the Fairies," 311).

the tripe-wife sent "a Capon and Turkie" to the fairy queen and king, as Philips demanded. The witness answers, "I am not able to say: but I am sure our maide caried them with her, and delivered them to the woman, ere they came half way to the King of Fayries house, for they say his dwelling is at Paddington, and the maide dischargeth of her burthen in High Holbourne" (sig. B3v).

Some of the satire trades on the readily understood allure, and the links between, the forbidden knowledges of occultism and papistry. *Brideling* directs laughter at the Hampshire couple for believing Philips's boast that she had "come new from the Pope, and knowe[s] more of his mind than any woman born" (sig. B), which makes her specially qualified to enrich them and enhances the allure of her friendship with the fairy queen. To her victims, Rome and Faerie may have seemed plausibly contiguous realms. In *Daemonologie* (1597), James associated Rome and fairyland, complaining that many Scots still believed in a fairy king and queen who went riding and feasting, exacting from humans "a teynd [tithe] & dutie, as it were, of all goods." James sternly dismissed these beliefs as "the sortes of illusiones that was rifest in the reign of Papistrie, [but] ought not to be beleeved by Christians."[25]

Tales about the elf queen were old in English culture long before Spenser, who based his dream meeting of Arthur and the Queene of Faerie on Chaucer's comic "Tale of Sir Thopas." While specific links between these texts and the 1595 pamphlets are hard to prove, as is the extent of street knowledge of *The Faerie Queene*, they do share some uncanny resemblances.[26] The rich churl and Spenser's Arthur are humbled by unfulfilled fairy queen fantasies while lying on the cold ground. The churl dreams of his riches, rising only when he realizes "the ridiculous manner of his sadling." Like Arthur, who endures Una's teasing about his dream, the churl opens himself to mockery; like the bumbling Sir Thopas, he immediately jumps on his horse to give chase, shifting comically from ridden to rider.

In casting Elizabeth as Gloriana, his fairy queen and literary judge, and

25 James I, *Daemonologie*, 73–74.
26 Among more learned references to Spenser in 1595 is one from a popular jest book. In his preface to *Wits Fittes and Fancies*, Copley calls himself no university man, asking "*Spencer*, & other of the prime poets of our time, to pardon it" (sig. A3). According to Maley, books I–III of *The Faerie Queene* were entered in the Stationers' Register in December 1589 and published in December 1590, but copies had been circulating for several years (*Spenser Chronology*, 53–55). On the fairy queen's provenance see Spenser, *Faerie Queene*, 121.

mingling "big" and "little" traditions in his epic, Spenser aligned himself with the traditions of royal spectacle. At Woodstock in 1575 Elizabeth first confronted an actor dressed as "The Queen of Fairy," who was joined at Elvetham by the "King of Fairy." During the royal progress of 1591, Elizabeth received a chaplet from "the Fairy Queene," a gift to her from "Auberon, the Fairy King."[27] By the 1590s, the association of fairy queen, female judge, and actual queen was a commonplace. In the mid-1590s, while the presses turned out pamphlets and ballads about Philips and her coneys, Shakespeare's company performed a play close to the tripe wife's neighborhood that combined fairy queens, queenly judges, disguisings, and humiliation: *A Midsummer Night's Dream* presents a Titania who is herself humiliated by magic means and "love-ridden" by an ass, a Bottom bridled by fairies ("Tie up my lover's tongue" [3.2.201]), and a Queen Hippolyta who scoffs at a ridiculous performance. For several years, remarkably similar plots continued to reverberate in the public theaters and in ballads and tales of roguery.[28] In 1597, *The Merry Wives of Windsor's* Mistress Quickly, disguised as the queen of fairies, humiliates a horned Falstaff. Like the rich churl, the "bottom" is transformed into a beast and lies on his face (5.5.49).[29]

This is not to imply, post hoc propter hoc, that the Philips texts led to *Midsummer Night's Dream* or were derived from *Merry Wives* or *The Faerie Queene*. Rather, I suggest plausible common ideations in narratives of both the small and local and the lofty and royal. The spectacle of a woman on top of the nation, who called herself a Protestant prince while being apotheosized as a pagan goddess, spurred many plots featuring a divine female who combined awesome powers of judgment and disturbing forms of erotic glamour. Playwrights from Lyly and Peele to Marston and Jonson incorporated Elizabeth into plays as goddess, arbitrator, and pattern of virtue. As Leah Marcus and others have shown, adulatory invocations were often tempered with criticism and satire.

27 Butler, "Private and Occasional Drama," 133.
28 A similar scheme appeared in a ballad titled *The severall Notorious and lewd Cousnages of John West, and Alice West,* (1613). Predating *The Alchemist* by only two years, it mentions Philips, showing the longevity of her fame. The Wests were pilloried, not executed, because "claims of special favours from the Fairy Queen were tried as cozenages rather than witchcraft" (Briggs, *Anatomy of Puck,* 103). For more on these and other frauds and petty crimes playing on belief in fairy royals, see Thomas, *Religion,* 612–14, and Purkiss, *Troublesome,* 187–90.
29 Foley argues that the Philips pamphlets had a strong influence on *Merry Wives,* especially in Falstaff's abasement before Mistress Quickly as fairy queen ("Falstaff," 238–41).

Superstitious fears concerning the queen's Amazonian and Circean aspects and rumors of her reliance on necromancy help explain the doubling and displacement at work in such fictions as Shakespeare's warrior-witch Joan La Pucelle and his bloody Queen Margaret.[30] Given this environment, the association of Philips with the trio of fairy queen, papistry, and witchcraft raises the specter of Elizabeth as supreme trickster, the female Machiavel so feared by Knox and others. With so many similarly configured cultural markers in the Philips pamphlets, it seems possible that at least some of the fascination surrounding her arose from just such a structure of feeling.

More striking than the echoes in *Midsummer* and *Merry Wives* are those in Jonson's *The Alchemist* (1610), staged fifteen years after Philips was whipped through London. The idea that Jonson took details from the pamphlet has found scholarly support.[31] Dol Common's dramatics with the would-be gallant Dapper, like those of Doll Philips, involve claims of kinship with the Queen of Fairy; their trumperies both involve white clothes, clean linen, incantations, lit candles, and a bound coney waiting for the queen in humiliating postures—the rich churl on his belly, bridled and saddled for three hours, and poor Dapper blindfolded and gagged in a stinking privy for two. In both, the credulous greed of coneys is the prime laughing matter.

A more difficult, but I believe plausible, case can be made that the female rogue pamphlet plays a key role in charging the circuits of parody, political satire, and topical allusion in Jonson's play. Most important are the role and fate of the leading female character. Learned, theatrically gifted, warlike, seductive, a good marriage prospect, a flexible whore, a fairy queen, an accomplice, and an equal sharer, Dol Common is compared more than once to the philosopher's stone. Guesses at her original generally focus on her guise as the Queen of Fairy. Because Subtle is widely identified with John Dee, these speculations focus on Dee's kin and associates; Dol has sometimes been identified as Dee's wife.[32] A closer parallel with the Dapper con is a contemporary scandal involving a silly young heir named Thomas Rogers who was rooked by

30 Marcus, *Puzzling Shakespeare*, 51–105, esp. 68, 76, 81–82, 94. Also see Strong, *Cult of Elizabeth*.

31 Kay discusses the rogue literature and crimes (including the Philips case) that may have contributed to Jonson's play (*Ben Jonson*, 111). Levin uses the texts about Philips to focus his attack on all source-hunting ("Another 'Source.'").

32 Kay, *Ben Jonson*, 111.

two gentlemen who promised to marry him to the fairy queen (without, however, producing her in person).[33]

Dol, however, is much more than an accomplice. She is, I believe, an amalgam of all the rumors and slanders leveled against the polyglot, powerful, sexually anomalous Elizabeth. Dapper's dream of sexual union with an all-powerful woman on top is just the sort of "shaping fantasy" famously described by Louis Montrose, and the details in Jonson's *Alchemist* bear an uncanny resemblance to Simon Forman's famous erotic dream about kissing Elizabeth.[34] Gail Kern Paster calls the fairy queen/Dapper material "a satirical rendering of the Bottom-Titania relationship," with Dapper's privy ordeal making explicit the anal-erotic disciplines that are muted but present in the older text.[35] That the satire is directed not merely at Titania and Shakespeare but at the dead Elizabeth and Spenser seems more than likely. Jonson's most important reader and spectator was no admirer of Spenser. In the late 1590s James I threatened to retaliate against Spenser for painting his mother as Duessa, who plots to overthrow Elizabeth/Mercilla in *The Faerie Queene*.[36] Jonson professed both reverence and contempt for Spenser as a fellow poet, and his notorious bark of dismissal ("he wrote no language") could be applied to all the dark conceits uttered throughout the play.[37]

The Alchemist achieves its effects of spoken bedlam through an intricate patterning of speeches based on alchemical and theological treatises. Some of these printed texts are richly illustrated. Dol's most elaborate and difficult role, that of a lord's mad sister, calls on her skill in memorizing turgid passages from Hugh Broughton's *Concent of Scripture* (1590). She must keep spewing out Broughton nonstop as Subtle,

33 Rogers (a relative of Donne's father-in-law) was conned by Sir Anthony Ashley and two colleagues; the case was presented in Chancery between November 1609 and February 1610 (Jonson, *Ben Jonson*, 10:46–48.

34 Montrose, "*Midsummer Night's Dream*," 65–70.

35 Paster, *Body Embarrassed*, 143.

36 Before Elizabeth's death, James spoke of wanting to bring Spenser to trial and punish him. When he became king, James "did not censure *The Faerie Queene*, [but] it is intriguing to speculate what Spenser's fate would have been if he had lived into the new reign" (Waller, *Edmund Spenser*, 38).

37 *Discoveries*, in Jonson, *Ben Jonsen*, 1124. Riddell and Stewart argue (contra Frances Yates and David Norbrook, among others) that Jonson "claimed" and admired Spenser; that Jonson's cutting remarks about Spenser have been taken out of context; and that the parody of the fairy queen in *The Alchemist* is not satire: "he is attacking the dunces who fail to *understand* the poet" (*Jonson's Spenser*, 21).

Face, and Mammon talk over her. The combination of Rome, evil magic, and a fantastic mounted woman, which is presented in the Judith Philips pamphlet with no supporting explanation, also appears in the woodcut of the Whore of Babylon in the Broughton text that Jonson used. The marked resemblance between the woodcut of Philips astride the rich churl and the Whore astride the seven-headed beast invites speculation: it seems entirely possible that the *Brideling* engraver modeled his Philips-on-top on the well-known apocalyptic iconography of the day, down to the money bag held aloft at the same angle at which the Whore holds the Cup of Abominations.[38] If there is religious allegory in the fact that Dol is a whore who brilliantly babbles on, it might be found in Dekker's *Whore of Babylon* (1605), a national/apocalyptic drama featuring the good Protestant church—the British Titania—versus the bedizened church—the old Roman whore. Possibly the pamphlet's association between female roguery and papistry heightened its appeal for Jonson, displaying the heretical audacity of a woman who bragged she "came new from the Pope, and knew more of his mind than any woman born."

Jonson's use of rogue and coney-catching tales has been acknowledged by many scholars.[39] A genre about unorthodox performances, rogue literature invites such heterodox readings and uses. With its combination of the carnivalesque, moralizing warnings, jests, and the picaresque, rogue literature is formed of "a complexity of interlocking traditions that invalidates any overall definition of such material; and it invites reflection on the plurality of the readings it authorized, ranging from a belief in the veracity of the descriptions to a grasp of fiction as fiction."[40] Like Jonson's play, the *Brideling* pamphlet authorizes pleasure in mocking, judging, and manipulating others, a pleasure that is not confined to men.

The Joys of Tripe-Slinging

Soon after *Brideling* was printed, *A Quest of Enquirie* reached the stalls. This text portrays a fictionalized but still locatable urban do-

---

38 Gasper discusses the much-reproduced imagery of cup, woman, and beast in *Dragon*, 64–68.
39 Kay, *Ben Jonson*, 111.
40 Chartier, *Cultural Uses of Print*, 346.

main. The real name of the gulled widow is not mentioned (she is only called "Anne Tripe-wife"), and she is given a husband, "Nick Trickes"; but all the place names of actual locations and neighborhoods remain, including the tripe wife's home address "behind St. Nicholas shambles," a London slaughtering area and butchers' market.

A Quest is itself a playlet, with a fictive cast of characters gathered to judge and mock the tripe wife. Much as women were likely doing in the street, neighborhood women in the pamphlet review and add to the evidence against the tripe wife. Meanwhile Anne Tripe-wife and Nick Trickes, her invented husband, lament being made a target of "those that doe our fortunes hate / Jesting at us with ballads and with Jigs" (sig. Av). A Quest opens with a letter from Oliver Oat-meale to Nick Trickes, who has been running madly around London trying to tear down all the ballads he can find. That's not all Oliver says he has been working hard to help his friend: he has gained access to the all-women jury that has assembled to "try" his wife for foolishness; and he has commissioned a ballad-writer, Jeffrey Kexon, to pen a ballad in support of the beleaguered couple.[41] Oliver calls the verses both a "ballad" and a "jigge"; at the time, the two were often identical in meaning.[42] A jigge for the Ballad-mongers to sing fresh and fasting, printed in full in A Quest, is a rare example of a complete jig text, showing the close relation between the jig and satiric popular songs. Many ballads were enacted as jigs on stage as well as sung in the streets, and personal mockery and local scandal were often their subjects.[43] In this jig one of the tripe wife's neighbors extends mock sympathy:

> O Neighbor Tripewife,
> my heart is full of woe,
> That cousning Doll the Jugler,
> should jumble with you so.

41 I have found no trace of Kexon.

42 Jig referred to "brief farces written in ballad-measure, sung and danced on the stage to ballad-tunes, and published under the title and in the form of ballads" (Rollins, "Black-Letter," 298).

43 Baskervill, Elizabethan Jig, 73. Intriguingly, a possible echo of A jigge for the Ballad-mongers occurs in Chapman, Jonson, and Marston's Eastward Ho (1605), when Security sings "O Master Touchstone / My heart is full of woe! / Alas, I am a Cuckold: / And why should it be so?" The second line of the tripe wife ballad is identical, but it may indicate a common (lost) ballad tune rather than a direct connection.

I that am your poor neighbor,
had rather spent a crowne:
then have ye thus defamed
by boyes about the towne.

Abroad in everie corner,
the Ballads do report:
That you were trimd unwomanly,
and in most shameful sort:

By standing on a Trivet,
to heare what she could say:
She lopt off a lovers locke,
and carried it away.

Alas you were so simple,
to suffer such a thing:
Your owne maids sit and mocke ye,
and everie where doth ring,
The trimming of the Tripe wife:
it makes me in a rage
And doubt least that the players
will sing it on the Stage.[44]

The neighbor continues by faulting Nick Trickes, mocking him for his agonized regrets about marrying her for her money. By the last stanzas the sympathetic pose toward "neighbour Tripe-wife" evaporates:

A number do imagine,
that he repents his marriage,
And gladly to the shambles,
would send you with your carriage. . . .

If gold brings such a hart-breake,
Ile none I thanke ye I:
Tis shame it should be spoken,

44 According to Baskervill "a good deal of such personal satire as was sung about the streets was of a sort to hit the humor of the playhouse public in the form of jigs" (*Elizabethan Jig*, 73). A jig ridiculing a rural constable in 1616 asks "Would not this yield matter to make a stage playe, / For a ripe witt good neighbours" (quoted in Fox, "Ballads, Libels," 80).

> and if it be a lie.
> But would he be advisde by me,
> if it be true or no:
> I would turn her to her Tripes againe
> and let all matters go. (sigs. C2r–v)

This song probably predated *A Quest,* appearing first as a broadside ballad and perhaps as a stage jig. Its popularity may have prompted the pamphlet itself. Sought-after ballads and jigs led publishers to rush chapbooks on their topics into print; they could sometimes serve as advertisements for longer works, including plays. Like ballad-singing, jigging was not confined to male professionals: women participated in the world of the jig as spectators, creators, and performers. From 1550 to 1700, women and men performed jigs "in the streets, in tavern gatherings and feasts, in games, at fairs, and at entertainments of various sorts."[45] Jigs played a prominent role in shaming rituals such as skimmingtons, the broadcasting of rhyming libels, and horn fairs. None of this behavior is polite or tending to public peace; but it is exactly this sort of performance that *A Quest*'s jig invites, with the narrator providing explicit directions for peak effectiveness, even hinting that some tripe-slinging might result:

> I would not have ye mistake my meaning in the Song, that ye should goe about the streetes singing it, or chaunt it at her doore, ere she be up in a morning. No, God forbid, that would but breede domesticall disquietenesse, and if man and wife should happen to fall out about it, I (not knowing how neere the Tripe tub stands) might bring him in more immediate danger. (sig. C2v)

That these texts prominently feature ballads strongly suggests they were trying to attract the attention of women, acknowledged as avid ballad consumers and singers. Women who could not afford to buy a penny sheet could listen for free; borrow or "overlook" a neighbor's copy; or read parts of it on a post, an alehouse wall, or a church door. Visually, ballads altered and textualized the city scene: "What with ballad singers, cleft sticks, and posts and walls covered with broadsides, therefore, the Londoner, go where he would, found the ballad staring him in the

---

45 Baskervill, *Elizabethan Jig,* 35; on women jigging, see 11, 13, 19, 33, 41, 110, 124.

face."[46] Even young girls seem to have had access to this ubiquitous medium. In Henry Glapthorpe's *The Ladies Privilege* (1640), one character mentions "girls" among the chroniclers of criminals who were "sure / Ere they be scarce cold, to be chronicled / In excellent new ballads ... sung / In the streets 'mong boys and girls, colliers and carmen."[47]

Many writers described the powerful satiric potential of the ballad and the shame of being balladed. Despair over the proliferation of printed texts was far surpassed by horror at hearing one's name in every mouth. Descriptions of the ballad public were doubly marked as "low" by frequent mention of marketwomen and prostitutes. In his poem on a "ballad-singer's auditory," one poet hostilely depicts the crowd collecting around a ballad seller:

> First stands a porter; then an oyster-wife
> Doth stint her cry, and stay her steps to hear him;
> Then comes a cut-purse ready with a knife,
> And then a country client passes near him;
> There stands the constable, there stands the whore,
> And, listening to the song, heed not each other.[48]

In a similar vein, Thomas Nabbes's *The Bride* (1640) decries "wide-mouthed oyster-wives" who act as a "jury" as they listen eagerly to a ballad singer who "opened tunably the merry case."[49] The idea of a popular female court judging a "merry case" is central to *A Quest of Enquirie*, of course. The conceit of a women's court, which has roots in medieval and Tudor jest, fable, festive play, and love debate,[50] also alludes to more serious but no less familiar staging areas, the courtrooms

---

46 Rollins, "Black-Letter," 327; elsewhere he quotes from *The Return from Parnassus:* "Who makes a ballad for an ale-house door, / Shall live in future times for evermore" (302). Also see Smith, *Acoustic World*, chap. 7.

47 Quoted in Rollins, "Black-Letter," 277.

48 Sir John Davies, *Epigram* 38, cited in ibid., 309.

49 Ibid., 310.

50 Popular precedents include *gospelles of dystaves,* a translation of *Les evangiles des quenouilles,* in which women meet secretly and lay down their own laws, and the early Tudor poem *The Talk of Ten Wives on Their Husbands Ware,* in which wives act as a jury judging their husbands' penises. In the seventeenth century, examples include *Swetnam the Woman Hater Arraigned by Women* (1620) and a spate of royalist satires on Roundhead wives and husbands, such as *A Parliament of Ladies* (1640) and *The Parliament of Women* (1647). In France, May customs included the convening of "women's courts" that issued mock decrees (Davis, *Society and Culture,* 141).

where women complained, sued, and defended themselves. These particular jurors are Londoners; and women in the city dominated litigation as nowhere else, especially in matters of defamation.[51]

In *A Quest* the main charge against the tripe wife is that she allowed
herself to be preyed upon, opening herself to insults that she is everything from a drunken whore to a fool. The mock-solemn subtitle parodies well-known legal procedures: "A Quest of enquirie of twelve good,
honest, and substantiall women, upon examination of certaine persons,
whether the Tripe wife were trimde or no." The word *quest* may be a
reference to the special wardmote inquest held each Christmas, which
issued summons to offenders, usually in response to complaints by
neighbors, and held the power to order offenders out of the ward.[52] But
it is more likely that, given the salacious details of the pubic trimming,
the women's inquest summoned up a "jury of matrons," one of the pan-
els of women appointed to inspect other women's "privities" for signs
of witchcraft, virginity, pregnancy, sexual activity, or rape.[53] A ballad
called *The Norfolk Lass: or, the Maid that was Blown with Child* has a
crude woodcut showing a jury of matrons stripping a young woman
who claims she is not pregnant (see fig. 12). Her huge belly betrays her,
and she tries to claim the baby was "blown up into" her. The ballad
treats her desperation as a jolly laughing matter, but the woodcut leaves
a disturbing impression of violent invasion by the "good Wives of the
Town," who seize and mock the single woman.[54]

The tripe wife does not get a sympathetic hearing at her inquest either. The matron judges call two women to testify—the tripe wife's
sluttish stepdaughter and a vicious old neighbor and false friend,
Mother Messingham—and both give highly damaging (and funny) testi-
mony. Finally, the inquest decides to absolve the tripe wife on account
of her "simplicity." Knowing this will sound far too lenient to the outside world, the group punishes her with the label *Ignoramus* and orders
her to go to London Bridge to be married to whichever of her former
suitors will take her.[55] This turns out to be Nick Trickes, who also
proves to be an ignoramus and quickly comes to regret his choice.

---

51 Gowing, "Language," 28.
52 Archer, *Pursuit*, 78.
53 Sharpe, "Women, witchcraft," 112–13. Also see Oldham, "On Pleading the
Belly."
54 *Roxburghe Ballads*, 2:366.
55 In actual courts, "ignoramus" was a grand jury's finding of no case (Kermode
and Walker, *Women, Crime*, 192).

Fig. 12. A jury of matrons at work in *The Norfolk Lass,* from *The Roxburghe Ballads.* Reproduced by permission of the British Library.

Despite all the anxious textual fencings marked "male"—the males spying on the women's court, the commissioning of a ballad from a male writer, the male friends collaborating to contain the scandal—the men are unable to combat the voices resounding within the vastly energetic playing space of yard and street. As the tripe wife herself tells Trickes during the conjugal quarrel that opens the book,

> Run bootles madding, raving up and downe:
> All helplessly gainst jygging rymes complaine,
> Let everie Ballad-singer beare thee downe.

The pamphlet describes streets full of "the Tripe-wives effigies," which Trickes and his friends attempt to pull down or deface, and of

counter-ballads in her support, some written by the tripe wife herself.
The idea is not impossible. As Adam Fox has shown, some women did
compose mocking rhymes and songs; if the woman could not write, she
dictated to someone else. Many handwritten songs and libels were
posted in just this way, and a few songs eventually reached print as
broadside ballads.[56]

All this activity only brings on more shame for Trickes. As "D.D.,"
the author of the preface, puts it, scoffing at Trickes: "Now which way
in your opinion is best to prevent the writing or publishing of any odd
toy? shall he reconcile himselfe, and give good words . . . because his
widow hath been notoriously ridiculous? Or shall he run up and down
the town, with ricks and heighs, and follips, and trickes, accompanied
by some such wiseacres as himself?" (sig. A). Trickes proves to be a
milksop husband, ineffectual and outmaneuvered by his wife. She
grows angry and defiant and longs to return to her happy days of tripe
selling and making money. The depiction of the tripe wife as shrewish
and Trickes as uxorious (he futilely attempts to placate her with spices
and candies) marks him out for special savagery, and a large portion of
the pamphlet mocks him for wooing her in the first place. Moreover,
the text repeatedly exploits the symbols and props of rough music.
Trickes's friends try to pull down all the tripe wife's "effigies," either
pictures or stuffed figures meant for beating or burning; Anne Tripewife
is ordered by the tribunal of women to offer herself for marriage publicly at London Bridge, which would entail a shaming procession, and a
long list of bawdy and near-obscene libels appears as an addendum to
the book.[57] Most obviously, the ballad-jig's title directs "balladmon-
gers" to harass the tripe wife and her husband by singing it at their door
before dawn: *A jigge for the Ballad-mongers to sing fresh and fasting,
next their hearts every morning, insted of a new hunts-up, to give a
good morrow to the Tripe-wife.*

Women often took part in various shaming performances, most famously the skimmington, directed frequently but not exclusively
against weak or cuckolded husbands and shrewish wives. While the
skimmington riding itself was always uncommon in London, references
to the spectacle circulated throughout popular literature; and indeed, it

56 Fox, "Ballads, Libels," 58–59.
57 For the intriguing suggestion that one of these libels on the tripe wife led to a
stage jig and the play *Keep the Widow Waking,* see Foley, "Falstaff," 240.

could be argued that a sort of print skimmington evolved in the city with the rough music of urban ballading substituting for the rough ridings in town and village. That the tripe wife pamphlets and ballads quickly invented a weak husband to mock (none being mentioned in the crime pamphlet of a year earlier) may mean that the "news" was written to conform to this comic expectation and to gratify a specific audience that explicitly included women.

Verdict of the Smock

It seems safe to say, then, that non-elite women were an audience for at least some of the jesting texts and performances spurred by Judith Philips and her coneys. But this leaves an important question: why did London erupt in such a rich efflorescence of spite against the tripe wife and the rich churl?

By reading the texts as fragments of a larger symbolic structure rooted in social and economic history rather than as simple reportage or personal libel, we may produce the outlines of an answer. This approach emphasizes the texts' satiric targets rather than the rogue on top. The fact that Philips's victims are from inner London and a rural county holds out the old moral found in medieval estates satire (fools are ubiquitous); the motif of the woman rider is also reminiscent of woodcuts, jests, and songs about the shrew who beat the devil and rode him to hell and may also echo popular medieval drama, with Philips taking the part of the vaunting Vice who generally exited on the back of the devil.

But each of the locations named in the pamphlets also held particular meanings in the mid-1590s. These coneys are not random victims. The idea of rich churls in Hampshire and wealthy tripe wives in St. Nicholas Shambles aligns closely with prevalent suspicions and popular targets during "the crisis of the 1590s," a decade marked by apprentice riots, skyrocketing prices, fears of dearth, and food riots in London.[58] A yeoman farmer getting fat on selling overpriced corn would have attracted suspicion at this time. The well-off farmer in Hampshire may have been a "rich churle" indeed to city dwellers who felt cheated

58 Archer, *Pursuit*, 9–14. The decade was "the worst Londoners had known" in centuries in terms of falling income, riots, real and perceived dearth, and rising prices (13).

by bread prices, even before he was shown up as a fool. The pamphlet la-
bels him as "covetous" and "a myzer."[59] The tripe wife (tellingly depicted as rich yet working in "a stinking stall") has two counts against
her: she is a widow, and she has enough capital to run a business without a man.[60] As attempts to regulate London markets in the period at-
test, such a woman was the focus of major governmental anxiety and
local suspicions, both for being independent of male control and for operating as a small retailer with accusations of "regrating, forestalling,
and engrossing" dogging her steps from inspectors and informants.[61] A
woman in either position excited institutional distrust and community
gossip and envy. This is suggested in the "eglogue," when the newly
married tripe wife complains that she has had to give up her "past joy-
thriving trade" when she married Trickes:

> Accurst was I to leave the Butchers fees,
> How base so ere, they brought the golden gaine,
> The mistres Tripe-wives name by thee I leese:
> That losse, their lacke, I ceaseless do complaine.

The tripe wife's position was anomalous because, unlike the walking
basketwomen or street hucksters, she occupied a permanent stall in the
"Butchers fees" within the shambles, where free and foreign butchers
were confined by law. The selling of meat products, unlike fish and veg-
etables, was one trade in which women had some leeway to set up shop,
avoiding the fines and prison sentences meted out increasingly to fishwives, herbwives, and alewives in the 1590s. Thus, she may have been a
target of envy among other women, who were feeling the pinch of laws
aimed specifically at them.[62]

The suggestion that her status as privileged trader has been exaggerated for the purposes of satire appears on the last page of the pamphlet,

59 *Brideling*, sigs. A3v–Br.
60 Another rich tripe wife appears in Taylor, *Bull, Beare and Horse, Cuts, Curtols,
and Longtailes:* "Sowce-wives grow plump and fat, and 'tis because / Their sale is
quick for Muggets Paunches, Mawes, / Tripes, Reads, Neatfeet, Cowheel, and Chitt-
lerings" (*Works Not Included in the Folio Volume,* 14).
61 Archer et al., *Hugh Alley's Caveat,* 10.
62 The regulations of 1546 confined free and foreign butchers to St. Nicholas
Shambles, the Stocks, Eastcheap, and Leadenhall but confirmed that "women and
victuallers" might still sell "veale, pork, bacon, sowse and such other lyke things"
unmolested. ("Sowse," or cooked tripe, was one of the tripe wife's wares.) Fishwives,
in contrast, were prime targets of market regulators in the 1590s (ibid., 10).

where the anonymous narrator responds to Oliver Oat-meale, who has reported on the women's court, and attacks him for being biased in his account. In a final twist, the narrator accuses Oliver of secretly courting the tripe wife for her money, like Trickes before him. "[I]n the sowce-wives time of retailing, thou wert not verie familiar," rants the narrator, "but since Tripes have been ingrost thou hast been her sweet harts Secretarie. Shall I be plaine with thee? I mislike the partialitie of thy jurie" (sig. D3v).

This mention of retailing and engrossing bring up one of the most damaging and widespread charges against merchants at the time—that is, price fixing by cornering a market and driving up prices. The issue of food markets and prices was of keen importance to poorer women, who did much of the selling, buying, and cooking and could be both targets of riots (as sellers) and instigators and participants (as customers).[63] Although the word "riot" connotes chaotic violence, these were more often controlled displays of force. For example, a trader would be confronted and ordered to sell at a lower price than he (or she) demanded; if refused, the crowd seized and distributed the goods. The concept of fair price was thus expressed and understood in common, a display of what E. P. Thompson famously called "the moral economy of the crowd."[64]

In the early 1590s, at least one parodic but still identifiable example of controlled riot made its way into the rogue literature. Intriguingly, it also features a female jury as *posse comitatus*. Robert Greene's *A Notable Discovery of Cozenage* (1591), exposes the ruses of cheating colliers known as "legers," market rogues with many methods for short weighting customers. He provides two merry tales of "the cheater cheated." The first describes how a flaxwife got free coals and her money back by threatening a leger with an oven spit and the pillory.

---

63 The riots in 1595 were the work of apprentices, who took over the selling of butter in Southwark and forcibly lowered the price; they also chased down fishwives who were found to have had bought up all the mackerel in Billingsgate market. The fishwives were forced to sell at prices set by the lord mayor (Archer, *Pursuit*, 6). For examples of women's leading roles in food riots, see Houlbrooke, "Women's Social Life," 176–81.

64 Thompson, *Customs*, 184–258. Archer characterizes similar riots in the 1590s as "disciplined crowds operating according to values shared by the elite in actions designed to remind the magistrates of their duties" (*Pursuit*, 6). This is a far more guarded view than Thompson's, who held that, because of the crowd's "passionately held" notions of the common weal, "the authorities were, in some measure, the prisoners of the people" (188–89).

The second tale "How a flaxwife and her neighbors used a cozening Collier," features an angry female crowd. When a woman learns that a collier has just sold her short-weight sacks, she uses a ruse to trap him in a locked room full of her neighbors, all of whom have cudgels under their aprons.

There the "jolly dame" appointed as chief judge announces: "know that we are all assembled here as a grand Jury, to determine of thy villainies, for selling us false sacks of coals, and know that thou are here indicted upon cozenage." The collier scoffs and promptly receives a few whacks from the women, who "bade him speak more reverently to their Principal."

> The collier, feeling it smart, was afraid, and thought mirth and courtesy would be the best means to make amends for his villainy. And therefore he said he would be tried by the verdict of the smock. Upon this they paneled a jury and the flax-wife gave evidence, and because this unaccustomed jury required evidence, she measured the coals before the collier's face, upon which he was found guilty [and sentenced to] "as many bastinadoes as thy bones will bear, and then to be turned out of doors without sacks or money." . . . The women so crushed him that that he was not able to lift hands to his head, and so with a broken pate or two he was paid, and like Jack Drum, fair and orderly thrust out of doors.[65]

The antipathy visited against the coneys in the Philips pamphlets and ballads is not of this order, of course, yet the tensions that could produce such a snowballing series of works might well be related to the issue of fair price and anti-merchant sentiment. The food trade links both victims; and the common denominator of their shaming points to an underlying cause of rancor that hones the satiric edge of the coney pamphlet, a genre that often criticizes gulls who "are so naive they deserve their punishment" or who are themselves greedy and "cozeners at heart."[66]

Not least among the injuries visited on both the collier and the tripe wife is the laughter of women who have taken the law into their own

---

65 Quoted in Kinney, *Rogues*, 185–86.
66 Ibid., 159.

hands.[67] Note that these judgments are couched in merry tales and coney-catching books. Godly types were not amused. Daniel Rogers admonished his readers that such jesting jibes must be thoroughly rejected:

> Canst thou relish a bargaine, a game at cardes and dice, any base talke
> of the world, (though never so long) any idle tale, or gigge of a geering,
> jibing wit, or any merry conceit and discourse, or matters of the belly,
> backe, purse and commodity?[68]

Some women clearly could. Can their judging laughter have existed without a high degree of practical skepticism? The pamphlets about Philips and the tripe wife, like the flaxwife tales, resound with the scornful and pleasurable laughter of women who see through foolish credulity and theatrical trickery, revealing doubts about the power of pubic-hair charms, on the one hand, and the honesty of merchants and their adherence to the ideal of fair market price, on the other. Reading these pamphlets against the grain of their antifeminist satire provides a rich and intriguing—though fragmentary and highly mediated—sketch of early modern women who saw themselves as judges and mockers, not the mocked.

67 In the eighteenth century, most spontaneous crowd confrontations over unfair pricing—pelting a dealer with his own potatoes, fighting colliers with blows—were initiated by women, who "appear to have belonged to some pre-history of their sex before its Fall, and to have been unaware that they should have waited two hundred years for their liberation" (Thompson, *Customs*, 234). Women played major roles in food riots and other protests in the sixteenth and seventeenth centuries, as well; see Davis and Farge, *History of Women*, 489–506.

68 Daniel Rogers, *Nauman the Syrian His Disease and Cure* (London, 1642), quoted in Baskervill, *Elizabethan Jig*, 76.

6   Griselda the Fool

Before I proceed any further in this wonderfull discovery, I
am sure two things will bee objected against mee: first, the
impossibility of the story, secondly, the absurdity of the
example.

The Ancient, True and Admirable
History of Patient Grisel

A marquis weds a poor girl on the condition that she obey him utterly
and never complain. On her wedding day he has her stripped naked and
then dressed in rich robes. Griselda keeps her word so well that the
marquis decides he must test her. When a son and a daughter are born,
he lies to her, telling her they must be killed because his people resent
them as base. She asks only that they be decently buried. He hides the
children and has them raised far away. Years go by. He pretends to divorce her, sending her home to her father's hut. As she leaves, he again
strips her of her clothes, and she begs for a smock to hide her naked-
ness. Still unsatisfied, he soon brings her back to the palace to wait on
his new bride during his wedding feast. The bride is his own daughter,
now grown. Griselda complies, asking only that he treat his new wife
more gently than he has her. At the last moment, the marquis relents.
Reunited with her children, Griselda swoons, then revives. Dressed
again in her rich robes, she embraces her loving husband. Her fame
brings her eternal hosannas.[1]

But not from everyone. The name of Griselda has also been used as a

---

[1] This summary is based on Petrarch's exemplum "A Fable of Wifely Obedience
and Devotion" (circa 1373), a radical reworking of Boccaccio's final tale in the *Decameron* (circa 1348). (Chaucer, *Canterbury Tales*, ed. V.A. Kolve and Glending
Olson, 378–88.)

shorthand for female submissiveness so close to stupidity as to be indistinguishable from it. "The Wise Government of a Gentlewoman" from Painter's *Palace of Pleasure* (1566), a tale loosely based on a story by Marguerite de Navarre, turns sardonic laughter against the patient wife. When a gentlewoman's home is threatened with ruin because of her husband's nightly trysts with a maidservant, the wife chooses to go on the offensive. When her attempts to shame him don't work, she lights a fire in the maid's room and smokes him out in the middle of the night. The narrator urges wives in a similar fix to take action: "For what Griselde could suffer her wedded husband, assembled in bedde, in depth of sleep, to rise and runne a straie like a wylde horse, neying after the straied female kind of that sort?"[2]

This is not to deny that Griselda's story was potent and ubiquitous. On the contrary: her fable spawned a multitude of jests and tales that do not even name her. Some stories that draw on Griselda do, however, question the idea of total wifely submission. As if acknowledging the dangers of the tale as masculinist fantasy, some jests warn husbands not to try acting like the marquis at home:

> A young man lately married to a wife thought it was good policy to get the mastery of her in the beginning, and came to her when the pot was seething. . . . [H]e suddenly commanded her to take the pot from the fire which [she] answered and said that the meat was not ready to eat. And he said again: "I will have it taken off for my pleasure."
>
> This good woman, loath yet to offend him, set the pot beside the fire as he bad. And, anon after he commanded her to set the pot behind the door. And she said thereto again: "Ye be not wise therein."
>
> But he precisely said it should be so as he bad, and she genteely again did his commandement. This man yet not satisifed, commanded her to set the pot ahigh on the hen roost. "What!" quod the wife again, "I trow ye be mad."
>
> And he fiercely then commanded her to set it there or else, he said, she should repent. She somewhat afraid to move his patience, took a ladder and set it to the roost, and went herself up the ladder, and took

2 Painter, *Palace of Pleasure*, tale 63, a revision of novella 37 of Marguerite de Navarre's *Heptaméron*. For an argument that Boccaccio's Patient Griselda is the unstated intertext for a second *Heptaméron* novella, in which another lady with an unfaithful husband plays tit for tat and then dies unhappily, see Cholakian, "Heroic Infidelity," 62–76.

the pot in her hand—praying her husband then to hold the ladder fast
for sliding, which he so did.

And when the husband looked up and saw the pot stand there on
high, he said thus: "Lo, now standeth the pot there as I would have it."
The wife, hearing that, suddenly poured the hot pottage on his head and
said thus: "And now been the pottage there as I would have them."

By this tale men may see it is no wisdom for a man to attempt a
meek woman's patience too far, lest it turn to his own hurt and dam-
age.[3]

Refracted and diffused through thousands of popular texts and performances, the legend of patient Griselda is specially marked as an irritant
to women. As Wiltenburg points out in her study of the street literature
of England and Germany, "Authors of both countries noted that this
story annoyed real-life women, who had no intention of following
Griselda's example; but it was recommended to them nevertheless."[4]
Yet according to Peter Burke, popular imagery beat into everyone's head
the dictum that

> women had to know their place, as is clear not only from the popular
> (masculine) images of the woman as villain, such as the shrew, but even
> from the images of the heroine. For women, martyrdom was virtually
> the only way to sanctity. . . . equally passive were two heroines who
> often took the place of saints in Protestant countries: chaste Su-
> sanna . . . and patient Griselda, who were celebrated in German plays,
> in English puppet-plays, in Swedish ballads, and Danish chapbooks. . . .
> Judith slaying the tyrant Holofernes seems to have been an exception
> among heroines.[5]

Taking Wiltenburg's matter-of-fact comment about Griselda's annoy-
ingness as my guide, I want to discompose the overly static picture
painted by Burke. First, it is necessary to peel away some of the layers of
indignation and interpretation she has evoked since appearing on the
literary scene. Her story's power to shock and disturb women in particular has only intensified over time, according to Judith Bronfman, who
has studied its interpretive history from its beginnings in fourteenth-
century Italy to the present day. English reception of the legend begins

---

3 Zall, *Hundred Merry Tales*, 123–24.
4 Wiltenburg, *Disorderly Women*, 93.
5 Burke, *Popular Culture*, 164.

with Chaucer, whose Clerk of Oxenford presents the story of "paciente Grisildis" to his Canterbury pilgrims. His "may be the most disliked of all the *Canterbury Tales,*" but it is Griselda, not her husband, who arouses the most distaste today—suggesting that our age despises a passive victim even more than a dynamic sadist.[6] To many feminist scholars, Griselda furnishes a crux for analyses of gender ideology and functions as a paradigm of the violent subjugation and silencing of early modern women.[7] Reactions to her story can be highly charged; Lisa Jardine finds that "her resignation is terrifying."[8]

The fear and outrage Griselda provokes may have kept us from realizing there were cracks in her myth during the early modern period. Scholars have seldom noted signs of mocking criticism toward Griselda in tales and plays that seem engineered to praise her. When Griselda is divested of her rich robes of literariness and her alluring aura of religious and psychic enigma, she strikes more than a few observers as foolish. To the jesting women who mock her, she is not the Christly Fool of Saint Paul, the witty Folly of Erasmus, or the keen jester of *Lear* but the garden-variety fool whose deeds are dismissed as silly. To writers, Griselda's patience was shopworn and ripe for parody. Printers tried to dress up the old tale, familiar from ballads, puppet shows, and sermons, by stressing her glamorous social mobility. By 1619, Griselda was being used as a lesson in how to marry a millionaire: one pamphlet touted itself as "*shewing how Maides, By Her Example, In Their Good Behavior May Marrie Rich Husbands; and Likewise Wives By Their Patience and Obedience May Gaine Much Glorie.*"[9]

Didactically tooled and rhetorically productive, Griselda continues to be a conversation piece.[10] She may have begun her literary life in En-

---

6 Bronfman, *Chaucer's Clerk's Tale,* 3. She cites a passage in Lynn Sharon Schwartz's *Disturbances in the Field,* in which Columbia graduate students in the late fifties decide that "Walter was unspeakable, but it was Griselda who mortified us"; one student writes a parody in which Griselda castrates and kills Walter, to their delight (3).

7 For example, see Jardine, *Still Harping,* 182–93; Hull, *Chaste,* 82–83, 119, 143; and McLuskie, *Dekker and Heywood,* 97–105. Woodbridge does characterize the story this way but stresses elsewhere that audiences and authors could show skepticism toward such fictions (*Women,* 125–26, 133–34, 212–17).

8 Jardine, *Still Harping,* 183.

9 Title page, *The Ancient, True and Admirable History of Patient Grisel* (1619), which was reprinted roughly every twenty years until 1800.

10 For an excellent discussion of the "persuasive fiction" of the obediently eloquent wife whose speech was used to transfer "credit" between men, see Hutson, *Usurer's Daughter.*

gland as a secular saint; but by the sixteenth century, she had become a household word idealized in sermons and conduct books but treated by jests as an impossibility, like "the silent woman," a close relative. The nineteenth century, in contrast, tended to read Griselda as a slave, the twentieth as an abused wife.[11] But these are only broad outlines in the long and turbulent history of a tenacious ideological artifact. Griselda's fortunes take an especially interesting turn in the early modern world, when she became a cliche that so many found so troubling. "It is always possible to interrogate the dominant definitions," as Catherine Belsey points out,

> especially when these are themselves full of uncertainties, even though no coherent alternative may emerge from the process. . . . [S]tereotypes are inevitably subject to internal contradictions and so are perpetually precarious. This is the case with the type of the faithful, forgiving and silent woman, which probably finds its purest formulation in this period in the figure of patient Griselda.[12]

Because the fractured trajectories of the Griselda myth militate against a linear narrative, this analysis will examine moments in popular culture when counter-Griseldas ignore her example, when she is derided through proverbial argumentation, when her didactic value is mocked, and when her value as an exemplar of the new nuclear household is questioned.

Ur-Griseldas

If any character in English popular culture stands for the sheep, it is Griselda. Her chief detractor is, not surprisingly, the shrew. In Robert Snawsel's *A Looking Glass for Married Folks*, Eulalie preaches the Griselda gospel to Xanthippe and Margery, urging them to bear their husbands' blows and drunkenness with meek loving kindness. This is too much for Margery: "Are you a woman, and make them such dish-

---

11 Morse, "Exemplary Griselda." Charlotte Morse's praise for Chaucer's Griseldis is revealing: she is Christlike because she "achieves sovereignty over herself," managing to be a woman who is simultaneously and "miraculously the Stoic wise man" (85). Without meaning to, Morse puts her finger on the masculinist fantasy at the core of the myth.

12 Belsey, *Subject of Tragedy*, 165.

clouts and slaves to their husbands? Came you of a woman, that you should give them no prerogative, but make them altogether underlings?"[13]

Margery's scornful reference to slavery goes to the dark heart of the Griselda myth. Folklorists have argued about the ancestry of the famous tale for more than a century. William Edwin Bettridge and Francis Lee Utley have made a strong case that Griselda owes her features to a folktale from medieval Smyrna called "the Patience of the Princess." A prince buys a poor girl from her father and lays a wager with her that she will not be able to submit to all his demands with utter composure. The prince shuts her in a tower alone and tests her for twenty years, repeatedly impregnating her and then taking away her newborn infants, telling her that he is going to kill them. She builds a mother doll out of clay to talk to and cry to but never loses her patience, and in this way she wins the bet.[14] The tale, which matches the European narrative more closely than any other yet found, throws into stark relief the specter of female sexual slavery that haunts Griselda's story. The most striking variance between them is that the girl from Smyrna is sold into involuntary servitude by her father, whereas Griselda has a choice and agrees to voluntary and total obedience.

Passing into European culture, the story came to Boccaccio. In reworking it for the *Decameron* he reclothed it in local garb, fashioning his novella partly in terms of Italian wedding and dowry customs that were sharply weighted against brides and wives.[15] Boccaccio thought Griselda's story significant enough to give it pride of place as the last tale on the book's final day of storytelling. Petrarch read the novella and converted it to an exemplum in Latin for male scholars. Griselda entered English culture through Chaucer's "Clerk's Tale," which is largely based on Petrarch's version.[16] Plays, ballads, and pamphlets on Griselda issued forth on the continent and in England throughout the

13 Quoted in Dolan, *Taming,* 190. I thank her for suggesting that I read Snawsel with Griselda in mind.

14 Bettridge and Utley, "New Light." For variants of the tale, see Thompson, *Motif-Index,* H461, H1553, H1557. "Le Fresne," a twelfth-century lai by Marie de France, possibly contains a Griselda motif (although no child murders are involved) that may have been picked up in later versions. See text and commentary in *The Lais of Marie de France,* 73–91, esp. 88.

15 Klapisch-Zuber, "Griselda Complex: dowry and marriage gifts in the quattrocento," 228, 230.

16 Chaucer based his tale on Petrarch's Latin text and two French translations of Petrarch; see Baugh's note in *Chaucer's Major Poetry,* 421.

early modern period, with a cluster of publications and performances in the mid- to late sixteenth century.[17]

Arguably the most radical change between versions occurred when Petrarch reworked Boccaccio. The *Decameron*'s final tale is told by the satirist Dioneo, a crucial choice by Boccaccio. Refusing to let the happy ending stay happy, Dioneo spells out the political import of the story and caps it off with a horn joke against the marquis:

> Everyone was very happy with the way everything had turned out. . . . Gualtieri was judged to be the wisest of men (although the tests to which he had subjected his wife were regarded as harsh and intolerable), and Griselda the wisest of them all. . . . What more can be said here, except that godlike spirits do sometimes rain down from heaven into poor homes, just as those more suited to governing pigs than to ruling over men make their appearances in royal palaces? Who besides Griselda could have endured the severe and unheard-of trials that Gualtieri imposed upon her and remained with a not only tearless but happy face? It might have served Gualtieri right if he had run into the kind of woman who, once driven out of her home in nothing but a shift, would have allowed another man to shake her fur to the point of getting herself a nice-looking dress out of the affair![18]

Scholars often downplay Dioneo's bitter words about pig-tending and his final putdown of Gualtieri, attributing it to his cynicism; but their

17 The earliest recorded dramatization was *Le mystère de Griseldis*, performed in Paris in 1395. The first in England came 150 years later, with the Latin grammar school play *De patientia Grisilidis* (now lost), devised by Ralph Radcliff and performed circa 1556, followed by John Phillip's moral interlude *The Comodye of pacient and meeke Grissill* (circa 1559) and Dekker, Chettle, and Haughton's *The pleasant Comodie of Patient Grissill* (1599). Ballads include *a ballet intituled the sonnge of pacyente Gressell unto hyr make* (1565), *Danderly Dyscaffe* (1565), and *A most pleasant Ballad of Patient Grissell* (circa 1600). A Griselda ballad was included in Thomas Deloney's *The Garland of Good will* in an edition extant in 1593. A chapbook, *The Ancient, True and Admirable History of Patient Grisel* (1619), was almost certainly based on a lost mid-sixteenth-century original. See Hoy, *Introductions*, 1:131–33. In the mid- to late seventeenth century, Griselda starred in puppet shows and drolls (Reay, *Popular Culture*, 41). She has also been portrayed in dozens of operas, in novels (such as Maria Edgworth's *The Modern Griselda*), and at least one contemporary play (Caryl Churchill's *Top Girls*).

18 From the final sentences of the final tale (Boccaccio, *Il Decamerone*, 674):

> Che si potrà dir qui, se non che anche nelle povere case piovano dal cielo de' divini spiriti, come nelle reali de quegli che arien più degni di guardar porci che d'avere sopra uomini signoria? . . . Al quale non sarebbe forse stato male investito d'essersi abbattuto ad una che, quando fuor di casa l'avesse in camiscia cacciata, s'avesse sì ad uno altro fatto scuotere il pilliccione, che riuscito ne fosse una bella roba.

labors to match the tale's disturbing sadism with an uplifting exemplary meaning are less than persuasive. The passage is much more than a glib throwaway, as Edward Pechter points out: "the climax angrily repudiates theological allegory and exemplum."[19] Certainly, it seems fitting that the last lines of the last tale in the *Decameron* should recapitulate the Boccaccian theme of cuckoldry as female revenge. Dioneo's parting shot about "the shaking of the fur" is also an invitation to his listeners and the book's readers to come up with better interpretations than do the silly sheeplike courtiers of the tale, who judge "Walter wise and Griselda the wisest of all." Furthermore, it is a jest that asks for scornful laughter, especially from listeners who have grutched throughout the tale at Walter's arrogance, egotism, and sadism.[20]

Petrarch told Boccaccio that the story so fascinated him that he decided to spread the tale to scholars abroad. So "snatching up my pen, I attacked this story of yours."[21] The angle of Petrarch's attack on the novella (which he termed "a little too free at times") becomes manifest at the cuckoldry-free conclusion of "A Fable of Wifely Obedience and Devotion," in which he erases Boccaccio's satire and his bawdy call for female revenge:

> This story it has seemed good to me to weave anew, in another tongue, not so much that it might stir the matrons of our times to imitate the patience of this wife—who seems to me scarcely imitable—as that it might stir all those who read it to imitate the woman's steadfastness, at least; so that they may have the resolution to perform for God what this woman performed for her husband. . . . Therefore I would assuredly enter on the list of steadfast men the name of anyone who endured for his God, without a murmur, what this obscure peasant woman endured for her mortal husband.[22]

Petrarch's straight-faced version has none of Dioneo's political satire or irony. He is writing in Latin to male scholars, not in vernacular Italian to women and men, as Boccaccio had done. Nonetheless, it is Pe-

---

19 Pechter, "Patient Grissil," 103.

20 The mention of laughter within a Boccaccian novella is not always related to the comic but can signal a range of moods, including harsh opprobrium, or serve to structure a tale, as Elisabeth Arend points out in "Laughter and Humor," her study of patterns of represented female laughter in the *Decameron*. I would like to thank her for allowing me to read her paper before publication.

21 From Petrarch's letter to Boccaccio (1373), also used as the preface to Petrarch's translation (see Chaucer, *Canterbury Tales*, 389).

22 Quoted in ibid., 388.

trarch that Chaucer credits by name in the vernacular, mixed-audience "Clerk's Tale," although he departs from Petrarch in crucial ways. The Clerk does follow his source in insisting that his moral applies not to wives but to all humankind:

> This storie is seyd, nat for that wyves sholde
> Folwen Grisilde as in humilytee,
> For it were inportable, though they wolde;
> But for every wight, in his degree,
> Should be constant in adversitee
> As was Grisilde. . . .
>
> (1142–47)[23]

Chaucer actually intensifies Petrarch's warning that wives should not try to imitate Griselda, calling her example "inportable," or unbearable.[24] (The Merchant, whose turn comes next, blatantly ignores this caveat, complaining "Ther is a long and large difference / Bitwix Grisildis grete pacience / And my wyf the passyng crueltee."[25]) Still, scholarly attempts to align Chaucer's Walter with God do not work because Walter is described as "tempting" his wife, a word almost always associated with sin and vice. In another departure from Petrarch, Chaucer's Clerk breaks in several times to condemn the marquis. After Walter first decides to try his wife, the Clerk interjects hotly

> what neded it
> Hir for to tempte, and alwey moore and moore,
> Thogh som men preyse it for a subtill wit?
> But as for me, I seye that yvele it sit
> T'assaye a wyf whan that it is no nede,
> And putten hire in angwysshe and in drede.
>
> (457–62)

Chaucer's version subtly calls Grisildis's ovine quality into question. The lamb of God is Christ, of course, and Grisildis' meekness when her daughter is taken away resembles his suffering: "Grisildis moot al suffre and al consente, / And as a lambe she sitteth meke and stille"

---

23 Chaucer, *Chaucer's Major Poetry*, 438. Unless otherwise noted, all subsequent Chaucer citations are from this edition.
24 Cooper, *Oxford Guide*, 190.
25 "The Merchant's Prologue," ll. 1223–25.

(537–38). But "moot" she? Within English popular culture, sheep and lambs do sometimes stand for the positive values of resignation and endurance—for example, in emblems on patience.[26] But there is no doubt that sheep generally connote passivity, cowardice, and stupidity.[27] In terms of sheer frequency, the negative secular connotation overwhelms the positive religious one. A related complicating effect is the criticism leveled at "the unsad" (that is, fickle and sheeplike) people of the realm, who at first deplore Walter's acts but change their minds when they see the pretty new queen (actually his daughter), leading "sadde folk" to exclaim: "O stormy people! unsad and evere untrewe!"[28]

As the Clerk finishes his tale, he shows that he is fully aware that not all his listeners will appreciate Griselda's virtues. With teasing wit he acknowledges the Wife of Bath, who has been called the tale's motivating force and dialogic counterpart.[29] Just before the comic envoy he promises "for the Wyves love of Bathe" to gladden her "and al hire secte" with a song urging them to ignore Grisildis and revel in shrewdom (1169–74). By shifting the Clerk's role from that of the preacher of a pious exemplum to a merry jester-singer, Chaucer undercuts his clerkly authority and blurs the moral legibility of his tale, already obscured by Griselda's lack of moral agency and her husband's viciousness.

Nonetheless, Griselda quickly proved alluring to husbands, and she retained that allure despite proving highly problematic as a pattern for wives. Like the new husband in the jest about the pottage, men who wanted very much to promote Griselda as a model found her too hot to handle. In the training manual he prepared for his young wife in the 1390s, the Ménagier de Paris offers a confused and troubled account of why he wants her to learn about Griselda. He rushes to assure his wife that he'll never torment her "beyond reason" as the "foolish, arrogant" Walter does Griselda, nor does he expect such obedience:

26 For example, see Wither, Collection of Emblemes, 2:63, which includes the lines "Rage by Opposition gathers Might . . . when er'e I suffer, let me be, the while / As the silent Lambe before the Shearer." The pre-Walter Griselda is often pictured with her sheep, an apt association given the focus on the "shearing" and stripping she repeatedly endures. For examples and a nuanced study of the motif of Griselda's clothing, see Jones and Stallybrass, Materials, chap. 9, esp. fig. 47.

27 For example, "Why doost thinke thy audience like a flock of sheepe, that one cannot leape over a hedge, but all the rest will follow?" (Wilson, Oxford Dictionary, S309).

28 "The Clerk's Tale," ll. 995–96.

29 From Marion Wynne-Davis' commentary in Chaucer, Tales of the Clerk, 15–18.

I have set down this story here only in order to instruct you, not to apply it directly to you, and not because I wish such obedience from you. I am in no way worthy of it. I am not a marquis, nor have I taken in you a shepherdess as my wife. Nor am I so foolish, arrogant, or immature in judgment as not to know that I may not properly assault or assay you thus, nor in any such fashion. God keep me from testing you in this way or any other, under color of lies or dissimulations. . . . I apologize if this story deals with too great cruelty—cruelty, in my view, beyond reason. Do not credit it as having really happened; but the story has it so, and I ought not to change it nor invent another, since someone wiser than I composed it and set it down. Because other people have seen it, I want you to see it too, so that you may be able to talk about everything just as they do.[30]

What he really wants, it seems, is for his wife to be *au courant*. Griselda had "much currency off the page as a talking point in the late fourteenth century" and was "a subject about which wives might be expected to have an opinion."[31] Codified as a way to get women talking (instead of shutting them up), the narrative about testing is itself a means of testing a woman's opinions and conduct. Is Griselda sick or stoic? Enslaved or free? Is hers a saint's tale, with Walter an abstract tool in the central mystery of her endurance, or is it as much a story about Walter and his court? Is he a cruel tyrant or a stern but loving husband with every right to test his wife? Is Walter God and Griselda a female Christ or Abraham or Job? All these positions have been argued during the six centuries of the debate.[32] Some recent readers still find Griselda admirable and even question whether she should be regarded as a passive victim. Harriet Hawkins has argued that Chaucer's tale should be read as a criticism of unquestioning obedience to authority, even divine authority, while Lars Engle hears "an implicit voice of sane moral protest" in Grisildis's mild objections to her husband.[33] Such strained attempts at recuperation show that Griselda disturbs more than she edifies, raising but failing to answer questions about the limits of obedience in the face of tyranny and the conflict between Christian duty and wifely subjection.

30 Quoted in Chaucer, *Canterbury Tales*, 391–92.
31 Johnson, "Reincarnations," 195.
32 For a summary of these positions, see Bliss, "Renaissance Griselda."
33 Hawkins, "Victim's Side"; and Engle, "Chaucer."

Crimes of Submission

Early modern readers may have sensed they should treat Griselda's story as a wonderful fable rather than a practical model for reasons not often mentioned by later commentators: her approval of tyranny, her complicity in infanticide, and her latent heresy. In most modern analyses the political allegory in the story takes a back seat to its homiletic and marital aspects. Yet in the literary original by Boccaccio, the narrator Dioneo focuses insistently on the public humiliation of Griselda and the inadequate reactions of the court, making his tale a parable about the limits of rule and the responsibility of subordinates to oppose tyranny. With his barb about "those more suited to governing pigs than to ruling men," Dioneo chastises not only Gualtieri for ruling badly but his subjects for behaving like dumb beasts. After all, his counselors did nothing to stop the supposed murder of the legitimate heirs, nor did they protest when Griselda was illegally divorced and sent back to her father in her shift. Boccaccio also pays particular attention to the responses of the gentlewomen at court. The only help they offer is weak and ineffectual: they urge Walter to give her clothing at various moments of crisis and they shed tears at her treatment; but no one confronts the marquis or urges others to disobey his murderous orders. They offer sympathy but not mutual aid. In short, they behave not like neighbors but like the sheep in Aesopian lore that see the shepherd kill one after another of their flock and do nothing to stop it until all are gone.[34]

Dioneo's story provokes great debate among his women listeners, with "some taking one side and some taking the other, some criticizing one thing about it and some praising another."[35] It is highly significant that the final tale in the *Decameron* leads not to laughter but to controversy, and not about women in general but *among* specific women. The political and moral crime of infanticide, and Griselda's complicity in it, form the ugly and irreducible nub of the story. This crime demands special attention from women listeners whose political role and moral identity were inextricably bound to their sexual and reproductive lives.

34 For an acute analysis of this fable as an allegory about tyranny and the need for the weak to protect their own, see Patterson, *Fables of Power*, chap. 1.
35 Boccaccio, *Decameron*, 682.

By the late sixteenth century, the plays of the saints had been banned, but the sufferings of secular martyrs such as Lucrece and Griselda had replaced them as moral spectacles.[36] Making Griselda a model for English wives meant that the political valences of the story rose in prominence. The connection between domestic and political tyranny would not have been lost on an audience hammered with the analogy between the ordered family and the ordered state. The killing of children had provided a spectacular dramatic correlative for barbarism and tyranny ever since the medieval plays enacting Herod's massacre of the innocents. These were so familiar that early modern audiences would not have missed the resemblance between Herod of the pageants and Griselda's Walter. In both narratives, the slaughter is politically motivated. Herod has heard that a rival king will be born among the Jews; and the massacre is intended to stave off a political threat, just as Walter's fabricated reason for killing his children is political necessity. Confronted with the tableaux of Griselda giving up her children, audiences would not have forgotten the mothers of the pageants who fought the soldiers come to slaughter their babies. In the "N-Town" *Massacre of the Innocents,* three mothers enter, trying to hush their crying babies. Ordered to surrender them, the women stand and fight. Verbal shaming is the tactic of the first mother:

> [*Soldier*] We must full-fyl Erodis commandement,
> Elis be we asse trayturs and cast all in care.

> [*I. Woman.*] Sir knyghtis, of your curtessee,
> Thys dey schame not your chevaldre,
> But on my chyld have pytte
> For my sake in this styde;
> For a sympull sclaghtur yt were to sloo
> Or to wyrke soche a chylde woo,
> That can noder speyke nor goo,
> Nor even harme did.[37]

36 As a ballad heroine, Griselda strongly resembles Saint Ita, an abused countess turned saint, because "she attains ultimate honor and vindication through passivity, taking no action whatever in her own defense, but submitting wholly to the power of her husband as the saint submits to both her husband and to God" (Wiltenburg, *Disorderly Women,* 93).

37 From *The Pageant of the Shearmen and Taylors* in Manly, *Specimens,* 1:49. All subsequent quotations from this play are from this source.

The second woman, seeing this take no effect, vows to kill anyone who harms her child. Her courage is riveting, considering that she has no sword and her arms are full:

> He that sleyis my chyld in syght,
> Yff that my strokis on hym ma lyght,
> Be he skwar or knyght,
> I hold hym but lost.
> Se, thow fals losyngere,
> A stroke schalt thow beyre me here
> And spare for no cost.

This taunt spurs on the third woman, who does have a weapon, albeit a weak and homely one. In this women's war, the women lose but not without inflicting their curses and guilt on the soldiers. At their moment of defeat, the traditional weapon and speech of the shrew boil to the surface:

> Sytt he neyver so hy in the saddull
> But I schall make his braynis addull,
> And here with my pot-ladull
> With hym woll I fyght.
> I schall ley on hym as though I wode were,
> With thys same womanly geyre;
> There schall noo man steyre,
> Wheddur thatt he be kyng or knyght.

The women put up a furious fight. In stark contrast, the pageant of the Passion shows another exemplary mother, the Virgin Mary, watch her only child die. Her eyes are full of tears, but her sobs are quiet, her hands empty. The *mater dolorosa* is enshrined by her abjection at the foot of the cross, not bloodied in her resistance.

On the early modern stage these diametrically opposed positions were often combined within a single work. The split loyalties demanded of women—that they be vigilant neighbors and protective mothers yet always obey husbands, fathers, and kings—produce such pairings as the nurse and Grissill in John Phillip's moral interlude, *The Comodye of Pacient and Meeke Grissill* (circa 1565), the passive queen and angry mother in Preston's *Cambyses*, and Hermione and Paulina in *The Winter's Tale*. The counter-Griseldas, all women of lower status

than the Griselda types, reject the "natural" (and horrifying) nobility
exhibited by the supremely unnatural Griselda of myth yet come to the
aid of mistresses under her thrall. While some critics interpret the social inferior as speaking for the silenced sufferer, with angry words that
function as a safety valve, a high degree of tension and conflict exists
between the two stances.[38]

The vocal and gestural grit of the three mothers in the *Massacre of
the Innocents* recurs in the nurse in Phillip's *The Comodye of Pacient
and Meeke Grissill.* The marquis Guatier falls under the sway of a com-
ical Vice, Politick Persuasion, thus losing any claim to moral superiority or godlikeness. Often contradictory in its effort to teach the duties
of the new Protestant family, the interlude offers lessons for children as
well as wives. Phillip stresses the revolutionary principle that every
Christian must uphold "divine edict over obedience to earthly superi-
ors."[39] Only Grissill's nurse acts as a true Christian and challenges
Guatier's demands that the children be killed. Confronting the marquis's courtier Dilligence, the nurse invokes the sixth commandment,
to no avail. Her protest dims the glory of Griselda's submission. Touching on a point on which most commentators are silent—the complicity
of Griselda in child killing—Lee Bliss argues:

> In the recasting the fourteenth-century tale in part to teach sixteenth-
> century domestic ideals, he increases its internal criticism of the mar-
> quis as father, husband, and ruler. Moreover, if we were to follow out
> the implications of the nurse's remarks . . . we would even question the
> very virtue for which Griselda stands, since she too believes the chil-
> dren are to be killed.[40]

As if to solder the ideological gaps in his text, Phillip makes the nurse
a substitute for Grissill as a mother and a model for Grissill as a Christian. In the second child snatching, the nurse is blatantly a stand-in for
her mistress because the baby is wrested out of her arms after she sings

38 Marilyn L. Williamson argues that angry women "speak for" the silenced
("Doubling"). Charlotte Spivack asserts that Jacobean writers were able to portray
transgressive women with "sympathy and admiration" by couching them within an
inversionary "anti-structure" pairing them with pure but weaker women ("Woman,"
177). I see a far greater hostility between types than Spivack and Williamson do: Uxor
does not speak for the martyr but in opposition to her.
39 Bliss, "Renaissance Griselda," 310, n. 18.
40 Ibid., 310.

a lullaby, a famous tableau in which Griselda had always starred. The nurse offers to go into exile and rear the child herself; and when she is refused, she angrily denounces Guatier's "tirannie" and unnaturalness and scolds Dilligence that he should "knowe it is better to please God, than anie mortall man."[41] Erasmus had expanded on precisely that Christian precept in his advice to wives in *Institutio matrimonii christiani* (1526). Instead of obeying her husband unthinkingly, a wife must exercise her conscience: "If he orders you to do something that is contrary to faith or good manners, gently refuse to obey him; but if he persists in wishing to be obeyed, remember that it is better to obey God than men."[42] Grissill's strange acquiescence troubles the nurse. At the end of a remarkable tirade against the marquis, the nurse finally turns her thoughts to Grissill, whose patience deeply puzzles her:

> O cruell father, o most intollerable case,
> In the brest of this Marquis Nature hath no place,
> Neyther canst thou before God, thy selfe excuse,
> That seemeth such tirannie to thy flesh to use. . . .
> But thou to thy owne flesh art father unkynde,
> To crye out against thee, poor Nurse I do mynde. . . .
> I mourne thee poore Grissill, thy hap I lament,
> *But thou in this case are marvellous pacient:*
> To court I will haste mee, to comfort thee all
> that maye bee,
> But to crye out on the Marquis I will not delaye mee.
>   (1448–71 [emphasis added])

Later playwrights went beyond compliance and protest as possible responses for women faced with sadistic demands and male violence. Plays as different in kind as Preston's *Cambyses* and Elizabeth Cary's *Tragedy of Mariam* offer up multiple portraits of women who react with silent and noble suffering, backtalk, furious grief, and armed defiance. Cary's *Mariam* is a veritable patchwork of attitudes matched to characters: the mouthy and confused Mariam, who can't contain her ire; the rejected queen Doris, whose fury falls on Mariam; the vengeful mother Alexandra, whose son has been slain—all impotently speechify-

---

41 *Comodye of pacient and meeke Grissill*, sig. Fiiii. There is no record of performance, and it may have been intended principally for women (Woodbridge, *Women and the English Renaissance*, 268, n. 1).

42 Erasmus quoted in Jordan, *Renaissance Feminism*, 62.

ing under the disapproving eyes of a Griselda-preaching chorus.[43] There
is no moral challenger like the nurse, nor is there any group female action. On the contrary, the play is almost an allegory about the dangers
of female divisiveness. The true Griselda figure is the slave Graphina,
who is clearly on the way up via her liaison with an aristocrat who finds
her utter ductility supremely attractive. Only the shrewd and ambitious
Salome expresses anti-Griselda sentiments, with her prescient argument for divorce.

In *Cambyses,* a play with evident debts to pageant drama, Noah Uxor
is reborn in the redoubtable Madge May-Be-Good, who cudgels the Vice
who has set her husband to fighting with a neighbor. They provide
knockabout farce that forms a radical contrast to the spectacular sufferings of two elite women: a Griselda-like queen whom Cambyses forces
into an incestuous marriage and then murders, and a courtier's wife
whose child he slaughters onstage. Enraged at a courtier who criticizes
him, Cambyses orders him to bring out his son and then shoots an
arrow at the boy, killing him. Still not satisfied, he orders a knight to
cut out the child's heart. The mother rushes in to find the tableau.
Holding the mutilated child, she cries

> With velvet pap I gave thee suck,
>   with issue from my breast:
> And daunced thee upon my knee,
>   to bring thee unto rest.
> Is this the joy of thee I reep (o king) of tigers brood?
> O tigers whelp had thou the heart to see
>   this childs hart blood.
> Nature enforceth me alas, in this wise to deplore;
> To wring my hands O welaway, that I should
>   see this houre.[44]

Nature never "enforces" the Chaucerian Griselda to deplore or even to
weep. In stark contrast to these women, Griselda hands over her chil-

---

43 The chorus nags Mariam continuously, at one point intoning, "When [wives] to
their Husbands they themselves do bind, / Do they not wholly give themselves
away?" (Cary, *Tragedy of Mariam,* 3:233–34). After Mariam goes defiantly to her
death, the chorus declares: "The fairest action of our human life, / Is scorning to revenge an injury" (4:629–30), which is, of course, Griselda's specialty.

44 Johnson, *Critical Edition of Thomas Preston's Cambises,* 80–81, ll. 591–96.

dren, asking only that her husband grant her wish to have the bodies buried so they are not eaten by wild animals, eerily evoking the real-world practice of infanticide by abandonment.[45] She remains alone in her spotlight of pain, refusing allies or counsel, arguing for her husband's right to do with her as he pleases. The obvious flaw in this perfect circle of abjection is that Griselda is a Christian who is responsible to God's law first and then to her husband—the same criticism implied by the nurse in the Phillip interlude. Her story equates Christian submission with ignorance of divine law, and for a Protestant reader her failure to place the Word of God over an earthly authority must give pause.

Impatient Grizels

Shakespeare may have used Phillip's moral interlude in writing *The Winter's Tale*, which invokes and interrogates the Griselda legend. Anna Baldwin argues that Phillip's nurse is the direct ancestor of Paulina, whose loud and fierce protests over the threatened infant Perdita throw into relief the proud reserve of the innocent Hermione, who cannot prevent her son from dying of grief.[46] When first accused, Hermione's reaction imitates the famously tearless Griselda: "I must be patient . . . Good my Lords, / I am not prone to weeping (as our sex / Commonly are" (2.1.131–32).[47] At the trial, however, her initial words are challenging and un-Griseldine. She refuses to say she is not guilty and demands the respect due to her as queen, "a great Kings daughter," and the mother of a prince (3.2.41–42). In contrast, the Griselda of Chaucer and Petrarch is low-born and always insists on her lowliness and abjection. When her behavior in court has no effect, Hermione changes course, explicitly invoking the powerful image of Griselda the martyr by declaring herself willing to "lay down" her life to the level of her husband's "dream" (3.2. 85–87) and saying that she counts her "life nothing without his love" (3.2.101–2).

45 Frances Dolan calls child abandonment "a widespread practice of deferred, dis-placed violence" in which fathers, "in practice as well as in fairy tales, may often have taken the initiative" (*Dangerous Familiars*, 124).

46 Baldwin, "From the *Clerk's Tale* to *The Winter's Tale*," 208.

47 The tearlessness of the medieval Griselda is taken as miraculous evidence of her conformity to Walter's demand that she never show the least sign of objecting to his orders.

Her tactic does not work. Hermione's solemn eloquence emerges as
the losing approach in a world of bewhoring, tyranny, and child murder.
In a proleptic example of appropriating and rewriting the fairy tale,
Paulina translates the slander from the judicial sphere to the realm of
marvels, dreams, and fairy tales.[48] Such symbolic structures inform the
noxious political ideogram that must be untaught, so Paulina hijacks
the Griselda plot of the abject mother and refits it. By playing the railing satirist, Pygmalion, marriage counselor, mother confessor, and im-
presario, she undoes the Griselda story by staging it as utterly fake, an
old wives' tale best for winter and a ridiculous, credulous, and unde-
serving king. Indeed, the final recognition scene can be read as an extended joke about Leontes' vision, which is so poor that he ogles his
own daughter and takes his wife for a statue. If his madness weren't so
murderous, it would be funny:

> *Leontes.* Come follow us,
>   We are to speake in publique; for this businesse
>   Will raise us all.
> *Antig.* To laughter, as I take it,
>   If the good truth, were knowne.
>   (2.1.232–36)

Griselda haunts the play particularly in the denouement, but she
does not dictate its meaning. A lost daughter returns, after the same gap
of time as in the daughter does in Chaucer and Petrarch. The king then
casts a lustful eye on her, echoing the incest motif in the old versions,
in which the marquis brings back his own daughter as his new bride.
More important than these resemblances are the departures from the
story. The shunned wife is reactivated as queen by a female ally, not her
tyrant husband. Not all of what is lost is found: Mamilius is in his
grave, and Hermione has been separated from her daughter for sixteen
years that can never be recovered. Griselda suffers too, but unlike
Hermione, she chooses her husband over her children, and regains all.
    The strongest anti-Griselda motif of *The Winter's Tale*, and one di-
rectly linked to jesting tradition, is the fact that throughout those sixteen years Paulina continues to scold the king, who urges her to do so.
The marquis of Chaucer and Petrarch suffers only a few moments of re-

48 On feminist appropriations and revisions of fairy tales, see MacLean, "Oppositional Practices."

morse and never hears a word of complaint. Paulina's performative power and her railing words—which she calls "as medicinall, as true; / (Honest, as either)" (2.3.46)—stem from a tradition of privileged speech that has been called sanctioned shrewishness but that is more justly termed female satire.[49] Given its scathing moral tone, Paulina's satire should be compared to certain speeches and deeds of women characters in mysteries, saints' plays, and later morality-based dramas, which are invested with moralizing power and draw some of their strength from medieval complaint and invective.[50]

Such correctives are not always comic, but they are satiric. Like the speeches of the three mothers in the *Massacre of the Innocents* or the railing curses of Queen Margaret in *Richard III*, Paulina's long speech of accusation before Leontes (3.2.190–230) intends to stir shame, not laughter. After her excoriation, structured as a long string of sardonic rhetorical questions, Leontes promptly denounces her as a shrew, whore, and witch and threatens to have her burnt. In dramatic terms he is ineffective: she survives. In linguistic terms he has been shown to be hurling slanders, not truth statements. Although Paulina apologizes (strategically) for exceeding the bounds of speech, it does not follow that she is a "justified shrew" in the eyes of all watching. Effective satire is always provocative and often draws ad hominem response; so satirists assume masks, or feint between thrusts, for self-protection. For a woman in a shrew-baiting world, the danger was greater than for a man; yet the satiric mode is a staple of women writers and not a few female characters. Like most satirists, Paulina uses hyperbolic "crisis rhetoric"—the queen is not quite dead—but unlike many, she succeeds in producing political change.[51]

---

49 Woodbridge, *Women*, 51, 86–87, 98; Jardine, *Still Harping*, 117–19.

50 Satiric detraction and religious intent were joined in the complaint tradition, often marked by extreme danger to the speaker. Religious drama also presented spectacles of female defiance. In one saint's play, Saint Margaret is tortured for her preaching by having her tongue cut out; she spits it at her torturer, who is blinded by it. For satiric religious writing by women, see the works of Margery Kempe, Anne Askew, and Sor Juana Inès de la Cruz, who excelled in the artful mockery of benighted tormentors. Later writers who employ the stance of the female satirist for more secular purposes and laughter include Rachel Speght, Isabella Whitney, Mary Wroth, Margaret Cavendish, and Aphra Behn.

51 Satirists seek out moments of high crisis and, when the time is right, use "the rhetoric of autocracy (the iron fist)," "the rhetoric of tirade (the Jeremiad)," and "the rhetoric of resignation (stoic retreat)" (Seidel, "Crisis Rhetoric," 169). Picking her moment, Paulina uses all of these styles in her satiric performance.

"News of a most amazing woman"

Griselda's foreignness has not drawn much critical notice, partly because of the universalizing trend in allegorical and psychoanalytic readings, partly because she has become so thoroughly assimilated into English popular culture. Chaucer, however, makes a point of her exoticism. At the start of his envoy, the Clerk warns his listeners not to try to imitate Grisildis because she is a fabulously rare bird from far away, and one not just endangered but extinct: "Grisilde is deed, and eek her patience, / And both atones buryed in Italie" (1176–77). By invoking Italy at this crucial juncture, Chaucer sets up an implicit comparison. England fancied itself a "paradise of women" compared to Italy, where women were assumed to live in terror of their jealous husbands, renowned for imprisoning, abusing, beating, and killing wives on the smallest pretext.

By the seventeenth century, Griselda's status as a marvelous luxury import had certainly decayed as her story penetrated every corner of Europe; but enough of her oddness lingered to spur at least one sustained parody. *News of a most amazing woman whom a merchant recently brought over by sea from India* (1620), a German example of the early comic strip, depicts the patient wife as a freak whose self-abnegation makes her absurdly "other." The comic strip pokes fun at both her slavishness and the boorishness of her husband (see fig. 13). This wonder woman from India out-doormats Griselda. In a dozen scenes this "most amazing woman" gives her husband money to gamble, cleans up his vomit after he spends all night in the tavern, and feeds him dainties while he flirts with other women. She even holds a candle for him as he dances with a sexy young thing, "fearing he might knock himself against a wall. Afterward, she lit his way home without any sign of impatience." Finally she offers to hold classes in her home to teach other wives how to please their husbands; but they roundly rebuff her, "saying they had already been to school. . . . these other women would not listen, which is why she remains a strange woman, unique of her kind in the whole wide world."[52] According to historian David Kunzle, "A strip such as this helps to balance the one-sided impression left by so much misogynistic satire" because it paints the Griselda-like foreigner

52 Kunzle, *Early Comic Strip*, 239.

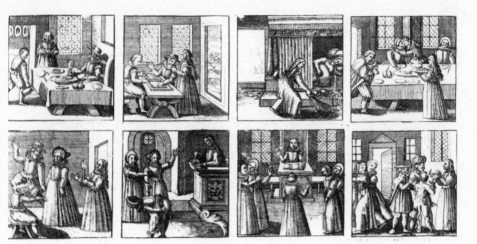

Fig. 13. Patient wife as tame fool. Detail from an early German comic strip *News of a most amazing woman whom a merchant recently brought over by sea from India* (circa 1620). This caption is based on David Kunzle's translation of the German original. A merchant's new Indian bride feeds him and gives him money, urging him to try to win back what he has lost the night before (1). He loses everything, but she arrives with more cash (2). After losing that, too, he gets so drunk that she has to help him home; of course, she is only too glad to clean up his vomit (3). The next day, the merchant goes out with some "merry ladies" and his wife comes by with a tray of food (4). That night he dances with a lovely young girl, and his wife holds out her arms lest he fall and hurt himself (5). The wonderful woman decides to teach other women her virtues; but her new students all balk (6 and 7). She could have converted Jew, Turk, and the devil himself; but the other wives she cannot teach (8). Reproduced by permission of the Herzog Anton Ulrich-Museums Braunschweig.

as a witless marvel of masochism, while strongly satirizing "the domineering, slothful, lecherous husband, who expects his wife to pander to all his vices."[53]

Some jesting texts from the same era call Griselda laughably quaint and out of date. As a sign that the trial of the patient wife was becoming hackneyed in theatergoers' eyes, Jasper in *Knight of the Burning Pestle* decides to threaten his love with murder so that "the world and memory / May sing to aftertimes her constancy" (3.1.74–75). In *Westward for Smelts* (1620) a fishwife regales her friends with the tale of a slandered gentlewoman whom her lover tries to have killed. She escapes by

53 Ibid., 236.

taking a boy's disguise, winning the protection of a king and exposing her slanderer. Throughout her ordeal she is forgiving and patient. Some have argued that the tale was published earlier and is a source for *Cymbeline*, and the heroine certainly bears a striking resemblance to Imogen and to her prototype, Griselda.[54] After the fishwife ends her tale, she asks, "How like you of this woman?" Most of her listeners praise her "extraordinarily," but she doesn't please the arch-shrew among them, who carps: "I like her as a garment out of fashion; shee shewed well in that innocent time, when women had not the wit to know their own libertie: but if she lived now, she would shew as vild as a paire of Yorkeshire sleeves in a Goldsmithes shop."[55]

Just as a rogue is more interesting than a law-abiding citizen, the shrew was generally more engaging onstage than the patient wife—in part because the shrew springs straight out of festivity and jest, unfazed by the iron laws of conduct books, sermons, and antifeminist texts. Griselda types are insipid in comparison, with no natural constituency among women; even married men often shun them. While Griselda is often listed among "legends of good women" in the formal controversy, defenders of women never managed to make her any more appealing. If anything, their formulaic citations tended to flatten what had once seemed mysterious, accomplishing "little more than to proffer a stereotype of the good woman to complement the attack's stereotype of the bad," remarks Woodbridge, adding, "I rather prefer the bad. I would rather be Semiramis than Patient Grissill any day of the week."[56]

When Shrews Debate Sheep

Some dramatists leavened the Griselda lesson by offering what may be described as a double bill, playing the shrew off the sheep. *How to Choose a Good Wife from a Bad*; Dekker, Chettle, and Haughton's *Patient Grissill*; and Shakespeare's *Comedy of Errors* capitalized on a common obsession of controversy literature and advice manuals: the attempt to define wifely virtue by contrasting it with an amusing exhibition of shrewish misrule. The shrew is not always the weaker rhetori-

54 See Klein, "Introduction" in *Westward for Smelts*, 6–7.
55 *Westward for Smelts*, sig. C4v.
56 Woodbridge, *Women and the English Renaissance*, 133.

cian, however. When these characters talk together onstage, elements of the jest tradition often complicate didactic effects and offer a different way of reading and judging the debaters. The competing strains give rise to a dialectic that questions the wisdom of the model wife and reconsiders the assumed foolishness of shrews.

Pragmatism is a fairly constant element in the jesting tradition: people do not trouble themselves with striving after virtue but with ways to gain pleasure, status, power, and revenge. It is also alluring as argument, no matter how much it flies in the face of doctrine. Adriana's reasoning in the *Coniugium*-like exchange in *Comedy of Errors* is a case in point. When Adriana's husband does not come home for dinner, she argues with her sister Luciana about the attitude a wise wife should take:

> *Luc.* O, know he is the bridle of your will.
> *Adr.* There's none but asses will be bridled so.
> *Luc.* Why, headstrong liberty is lash'd with woe. . . .
>   The beasts, the fishes, and the winged fowls
>   Are their males' subjects and their controls:
>   Man, more divine, the master of all these . . .
>   Are masters to their females, and their lords:
>   Then let your will attend on their accords.
> *Adr.* This servitude makes you to keep unwed.
> *Luc.* Not this, but troubles of the marriage-bed.
> *Adr.* But were you married, you would bear some sway.
> *Luc.* Till I learn love, I'll practice to obey.
> *Adr.* How if your husband start some other where?
> *Luc.* Till he come home again, I would forbear.
> *Adr.* Patience unmov'd! no marvel though she pause—
>   They can be meek that have no other cause.
>   (1.2.12–33)

Such volleys between shrews and Griseldas seesaw unevenly between jest and earnest, praxis and doctrine. On the whole, the jesting side tends to offer much more workable advice for women whose husbands "start some other where." The motif of the lecherous husband is treated very differently in two major sources of sententiae: training manuals and sermons, on the one hand, and jests, proverbs, and merry tales, on the other.[57] While law courts held almost no possibility for redress and advice manuals and sermons counseled Griseldine patience for wives whose husbands were unfaithful (after all, Griselda does not complain when she is replaced by a younger woman), the jest tradition offered spectacles of husbandly comeuppance through wifely acumen.[58] In merry tales, the wife who suspects her husband's fidelity may be shrewish, but she is rarely mistaken; and she is always intent on stopping his affair. One novella-derived jest recounts how "an esquires wife [who] was too much a scold" suspected that her husband was dallying with the gardener's wife. The husband arranges to have a servant carry his paramour to him, disguised in a basket covered with "hearbs and sallets." On the morning of the tryst,

> The Master of the house got up early to keep his appointment: so was the Mistress, to dogge her husband, as mistrusting his early rising: and in this way meets this fellow with his basket, the bottom of which, by reason of the weight of the woman, was quite broken, and her legs and feet hung down below his knees: which shee perceiving, call'd the fellow unto her, and asked him what hee had in his basket? Sallets Mistresse, saith hee: Sallets, and nothing else. Nothing Mistresse, saies he, but hearbs and sallets. Well saith shee, carry them to your Master, and tell him from mee, this is a fish day, and bid him beware what flesh he tasteth with those sallets. The fellow nothing perceiving all this while, makes way to the lodge, and delivers his burthen; the Gentlewoman followes, and before her Husbande discovers the woman. The cause was bitterly debated between them; but all the choler being vented, they fell to a more mild atonement: in which it was concluded, he would ever after forsake his lust, so long as shee would forbeare her *lecture.*[59]

While the jest faults the wife for her scolding, it also rewards her for her cleverness by turning laughter onto her husband, who comes to terms with her. Her foresight and her dramatic intervention have their own strong appeal as modus vivendi. Had this woman followed Luciana's

---

57 Parten explores the dramatic and conduct-book debates on a wife's proper response to male infidelity in "Masculine Adultery."
58 While wives could "in theory" sue husbands for adultery in the church courts, they "hardly ever did so. In practice, it was women's and not men's adultery that was culpable" (Gowing, *Language,* 34).
59 Heywood, *Curtaine lecture,* 227.

counsel, the result would have been more salad-hauling—and a zero gain in marital harmony.

Although Grissill is the title character in Dekker, Chettle, and Haughton's *The Pleasant Comodie of Patient Grissill* (1599), she and the marquis share the stage with a fiery Welsh shrew Gwenthian and her browbeaten husband Sir Owen. Grissill's trials inspire contempt in Walter's sister Julia, insubordination in the king's servant Furio, japes and mockery in the clown Babulo, crocodile tears in the voyeuristic and schizoid marquis, rebellion in her scholar-brother Laureo, resignation in her father, and sycophancy in the court. The reactions of Gwenthian and Sir Owen provide the chief comic matter—not comic relief but a running counterpoint and commentary. Gwenthian explodes in fury when her husband recommends that she follow Grissill's example:

> *Sir Owen.* Pray Gwenthian be patient, as her cozen Grissill is.
> *Gwenthian.* Grissill owe? owe? Grissil? no, no, no, no, no, her shall not, ag Gwenthian such ninny pobbie foole as Grissill.[60]

Sir Owen comes to agree with her and to realize that the Grissill-Walter spectacle is undermining his own peace of mind by making Gwenthian far more angry and shrewish. Exasperated, he urges Walter to desist, twice telling him bluntly that Grissill is a fool:

> *Sir Owen.* Gwenthian is worse and worse, out of awl cry, shee's fear'd to be made fool as Grissil is, and as God udge me, her mag fine pobbie foole of Sir Owen. (3.2.139–41)

> *Sir Owen.* . . . cozen [marquis,] because Grissill is made foole and turne away, Gwenthian mag foole of sir Owen: is good? ha, is good? (4.3.135–36)

The marquis's unmarried sister Julia displays disgusted impatience with the choice of shrewdom versus sheepdom. The cruelty of Walter and the sheeplike behavior of Grissil nauseate her, and the farces perpetrated by Gwenthian and Owen exhaust her. Painted as the sanest voice of the bunch, Julia rejects her suitor with these words: "Not I, would you have mee pitie you and punish my selfe? . . . *Gwenthians* peevishnes and

---

60 Dekker, Chettle, and Haughton, *Pleasant Comodie of Patient Grissill*, in Dekker, *Dramatic Works*.

Grissils patience, make me heere to defie that Ape Cupid" (4.3.204–5, 216–18). Julia's defiance upsets the rush to symmetry at the close, when the marquis tries to announce that his beloved wife is restored, Sir Owen is reconciled to Gwenthian, and all's well that ends well. Julia cannot let this pass, and she interrupts him with a direct appeal to an audience that has seen marriage painted as a continual torment for both sexes:

> Nay brother your pardon awhile: besides our selves there bee a number heere, that have behelde Grissils patience, your own tryals, and Sir Owens sufferance, Gwenthians frowardnes. . . . amongst this company I trust there are some mayde batchelers, and virgin maydens, those that live in freedom and love it, those that know the war of marriage and hate it, set their hands to my bill, which is rather to die a mayde and lead Apes in hell, then to live a wife and be continually in hell. (5.2.275–83)

Although this speech begins by distributing pity and blame with an even hand, it turns into a mocking gibe directed chiefly against the title character—for who has shown more willingness to be punished, unfree, and "continually in hell" than she? Griselda's fictive patience is an irritant to both men and women, but the women find her most exasperating by far. In Snawsel's *A Looking Glass for Married Folks*, the shrew Margery has finally had enough of Eulalie's Griselda talk and threatens to call in her neighborhood gossips: "Here are fetters for the legs, and yokes for the necks of women! Must they crouch in this manner to their currish and swinish husbands? . . . I will be sworn, if there were but three or four more here, if they were of my mind, we would teach you how to defame and shame us in this manner."[61] This externalization of conflict and interdependence between women—one Griselda can ruin it for everyone—is more important to drama than fictions of interiority. One man's ideal may well be her neighbor's "tame fool."[62]

Profitable Shrews

The disjunction between the lived real, on the one hand, and the ideal mouthed by innumerable champions of the patient wife, on the other, produced other fissures in the realm of stereotype. Choosing a Griselda

---

61 Quoted in Dolan, *Taming*, 190–91.
62 For an astute essay on the play and the varying interpreters of the myth, see Pechter, "Patient Grissil."

as a mate could have economic drawbacks as implied by two financial variations on the shrew/sheep proverb: *it is an olde saying, one shrew is worth two sheepe,* and *a shrew profitable may serve a man reasonable.*[63] By the early modern period, "a Griselda" meant "the shrew's opposite," so by the logic of the proverb, Griseldas are equated with sheep. The trouble is that proverbial sheep rarely evoke the Christly associations heard in Chaucer and Petrarch. Applied to wives, the epithet connoted a slow-wittedness that is unwanted, obnoxious, and deadly boring: "It is better to marry a Shrew than a sheep: for though silence be the dumb Orator of Beauty, . . . yet a Phlegmatic dull Wife is fulsome and fastidious."[64]

From a householder's point of view, the demands of running a household meant that wifely cleverness, initiative, and outspokenness were to be preferred to passivity despite all sermons to the contrary. (As one Wiltshire man stated in court in 1621, "an honest woman may have some froward qualities."[65]) On this score, the "wisdom literature" of the time (the riddles, proverbs, jokes, and exempla that pepper popular advice manuals, dialogues, and almanacs) presents a more nuanced picture of quotidian concerns than do polemics or tracts.[66] This body of old saws and jesty maxims contains an ample share of misogyny and shrew baiting, but it also reveals a countercurrent expressing a more pragmatic attitude.

A brief glimpse of "how a shrew profitable may serve a man reasonable" appears in a tale about a vintner's wife who was

> very famous in the place where shee lived for making of dainty Marrow-bone Puddings, at which shee had scarce her fellow in the City; and they two betwixt them had got a very faire estate. [The vintner,] being in very earnest discourse with a neighbor of his, they fell into talke about their meanes that God had blest them with : saith this neighbour to him, you by your industry have got a faire and competent estate, hee answered him agayne, yes indeed I have, and whatsoever I posesse, is come unto mee by the grace of God : which his wife com-

---

63 *One shrew is worth two sheepe* (1575), in Wilson, *Oxford Dictionary,* S412;. "shrew profitable" (1557, 1616) (S414). A later version (1662) reads: *A Profitable Shrew may well content a reasonable man, the Poets feigning Juno chaste and thrifty, qualities which commonly attend a shrewd nature* (S414).

64 From a letter (circa 1645), quoted in ibid., S412.

65 Ingram, "Scolding Women," 68.

66 On the various kinds of mediation in such sources and why none can provide direct access to *mentalité,* see Burke, "Oblique Approaches."

ming by, and hearing, made replie, come, come saith shee, you talke
that what you have got came by the grace of God, but I know what I
know, I am sure it came by my making of Puddings.[67]

This jest is a prime example of one whose wit lies in the ear of the
hearer. Both wife and husband are less than perfect—he is platitudi-
nous; she takes credit away from God and contradicts her husband. Yet
she does get the crucial last word. Her quip gets the laugh, undercutting
her husband's self-satisfied piety.[68] Neither his response nor an authorial rebuke is recorded, leaving open the space for female laughter.

Surprisingly enough, proverbs about the profitability of shrews (and
by implication the undesirability of Griseldas) issue regularly from
male mouths in household manuals. Some contain dialogues in which
a misogynist bachelor resists getting married and another man urges
him to reconsider. In these manuals the connotations of *shrew* are far
closer to "shrewd" or "savvy" than to "scold."[69] According to Martin
Ingram, "strong, active, able wives were often prized (as an economic
asset for example)—despite the fact that the behavior of such wives was
unlikely to conform to the stereotype of female virtue."[70] In dairy,
farm, brewhouse, or factory, women's tasks "could not be carried out by
a passive woman," notes Amussen, while a "meek woman would be unable to bargain effectively at the market. . . . wives could not fulfill
their obligations if they were excessively demure. Women thus received
contradictory messages: in the market they should be assertive, at
home obedient. The transition between the two could not have been
easy; it certainly was a source of tension in the household manuals."[71]

Thomas Tusser's much reprinted *A hundred good points of husbandrie* (1577) contains a lugubrious debate between two bachelors about
the pros and cons of marrying. The misogynist bachelor quotes an old

67 Chamberlain, *New Booke of Mistakes*, 39.
68 Marriage treatises acknowledging that a wife could be more capable than a husband only redoubled their calls for husbandly vigilance. In Stefano Guazzo's *Civile
Conversazione* (1567), Annibale observes that "some women have the right art to
order things so wel, that the husbandes should be content amisse, if they should dis-
pose them otherwise"; but he hastens to add that strong wives are "restife jades" and
that husbands who follow wives instead of ruling them are fools. Michael Schoen-
feldt quotes and discusses this contradictory passage in Turner, *Sexuality and Gender*, 317.
69 Jardine does not explore this connotation in her chapter on the unruly female
tongue, "Shrewd or Shrewish?" in *Still Harping*, 103–40.
70 Ingram, "Ridings," 176.
71 Amussen, *Ordered Society*, 119.

saw to the effect that it's best for young men to wait, for old men to forgo marriage, and in short for all men not to marry at all. The other counters that one must choose carefully. A lazy wife is a drone, but a shrewd wife "helps a man to thrive" through her market acumen, her thrift, and her constant labor, especially her spinning and sewing: "Upon hir distaffe she will spin, / And with a needle she will win, / If such ye hap to wive."[72]

The anti-marriage spokesman curtly dismisses this idea (no "pricking on a clout / can make a man to thrive"), saying that if forced to choose, he'd much prefer a mute and unaggressive wife: "Now be she lambe or be she ewe, / Give me the sheepe, take thou the shrew." Though he harps on about this phobia, his opponent wins:

> *Objection.*
> So hard a thing I spie it is,
> the good to chuse, the shrew to mis,
> that feareth me to wive.

> *Affirmation.*
> She may in something seeme a shrew,
> Yet such a huswife as but few,
> To helpe thee for to thrive. . . .
> Although the sorce be very small,
> Yet will shee helpe thee thrive:
> Lay thou to save as well as she,
> And then thou shalt enriched be,
> When such thou hapst to wive.[73]

When the fearful bachelor objects that his neighbors will mock him for letting his wife wear the breeches, the reasonable man counsels him to ig-

---

72 Tusser, *Hundreth good points of husbandrie*, sigs. Hiii–iiij. First published in 1577, the work went through twenty-three editions.

73 At the close of this section appears "The Wedded Man's Judgment" (ibid., sig. Hiiijv):

> In jest and in earnest here argued we find,
> That husband and huswife together must dwell,
> And thereto the judgement of wedded mans mind,
> That husbandrie otherwise speedeth not well:
> So somewhat more now I intend for to tell,
> Of huswiferie like as of husbandrie told,
> How huswiferie huswife helps bring in the gold.

nore them. His prime goal should be to thrive—to wed whoever will best help "bring in the gold." The implication is clear enough. If the wife is the stronger partner, a wise man will not fight it but profit from it. One proverb ruefully acknowledged that, in many households, a shrew ruled because she was simply more talented: *the grey mare is the better horse.*[74]

Monogamy Capital: Griselda Retooled

These saws about horses, shrews, and sheep did not name Griselda, and they certainly did not finish her off. On the contrary, they point the way to a new incarnation of Griselda, one that argued for her economic and symbolic utility within a newly enclosed early modern household. From the middle of the sixteenth century onward, Griselda was pressed into service as a model for a new kind of wife, joined in partnership with her husband alone, turning over to him all the fruits of her womb, her labor, and her speech, independent of her neighbors and kin.

The idea that well-run households should not only maintain themselves but expand and create wealth completely apart from all neighbors and most kin is old news to us, but it was novel in 1577. The profound changes it wrought in "customs in common" are visible in the early modern transformation of the Griselda legend. Compared with those of Chaucer and Boccaccio, later versions show how the traditional demands of community began to clash with the new demands of monogamy capital—"the streamlining" of the patriarchal family "for more efficient property acquisition, social mobility, and preservation of the line."[75] The late medieval rise of capitalist modes of production relied on, yet downgraded, women's work in the household and began to exclude women from more and more kinds of work outside the home.[76] Domestic enclosure meant that neighbors were suddenly an issue, their

---

74 In *Local Origins*, David Rollinson argues that, like all proverbial culture, this proverb shows an "exclusively male-oriented view of marriage" (81); but proverbs cannot be limited to the uses or perspectives of one gender. The saying about the grey mare would also suit the purposes of proud, derisive, or complimentary female speakers as well. So would *beware, clubs are trumps,* which a Gloucestershire man called the warning cry of "caution for the maids to be gone for their mistresses anger hath armed her with a cudgell: or, to the silly husband to be packing, for his wife draweth toward her altitude" (80).

75 Davis, *Society, Culture,* 126.

76 See Cahn, *Industry of Devotion,* esp. 1–65; Prior, "Women"; and Clark, *Working Women.*

longstanding presence in others' households debatable. The newer versions of the Griselda story show a fascinated ambivalence toward the slowly evolving concept that married people might be able to shut out the world within a wealth-banking enclave called the private home.

As ideologeme, Griselda is supremely suited to this new formation because she places her role as wife above all others, including mother and neighbor. The strain between the isolated Griselda and the rule of neighborhood is spelled out in a pair of answer ballads, *Rock the Cradle, John* (1631) and *Rock the Baby, Jone* (1632). In the first ballad, a foolish young country boy woos a city girl who makes him promise to wait on her hand and foot if she agrees to marry him, although "her ship she knew was soundly man'd, her belly wondrous round." She gives birth to twins one month after the wedding, which causes much hilarity in the neighborhood:

> The same day month that they were wed,
>   the married man was fairly sped,
> His wife was safely brought to bed,
>   and had both sonne and daughter,
> Which by the Midwife in was brought,
>   quod she, "you have a strange thing wrought,
> Two children in a month begot!" and so took up a
>   laughter.
> *Rocke the Cradle, rocke the cradle, rocke the Cradle,*
>   *John;*
> There's many a man rockes the Cradle, when the child's
>   *none of his own.*[77]

The neighbors conceal the bride's predicament and the midwife plays a crucial role in turning the tide of scorn against John.[78] While the neighbors laugh, he is overjoyed at his good luck: " 'My wife is fruitful, now I see, and will some great increase bring mee!' / 'They are your own assuredly!' then said the Midwife mild."

The subterfuges of pregnant brides and the suspicion that midwives

---

77 *Roxburghe Ballads*, 7:162–64.

78 The feared power of the midwife to confirm or cast doubts on the legitimacy of a child is glanced at in Shakespeare's *Henry VIII*, in which the midwife is full of smiles after Elizabeth's birth, assuring the king that the child is his spitting image. After she receives what she considers to be a skimpy fee, she grumbles angrily: "I'll have more, or else unsay't" (5.1.175).

collude to conceal illegitimate births are, of course, satiric targets here;
but the main butt is John. Framed with warnings to country swains
about city ways, the ballad is also a satiric portrait of an urban community that protects one of its own and mocks an outsider. Although the
neighbor so protected is a shrew and a liar, her daring exorbitance
shows she is anything but a sheep.

The ballad was soon answered by *Rock the Baby, Jone*, ideologically
more ambitious than its predecessor because it stresses the economic
incentives for wifely self-sacrifice (from the husband's point of view)
and proposes a new kind of marriage that ignores the world's opinion.
The exaction that took the form of deprivation in the Griselda tale—
most famously, the two infants torn from their mother's breasts—gives
way to an exaction attendant on male reproductive excess. John brow-
beats Jone, who has just given birth, into ignoring neighborhood opinion and custom to comply with his outrageous demand that she nurse
and raise his bastard by another woman as well as her own baby. The
narrator is a neighbor who has heard all about the scandal:

> A young man in our Parish,
> His wife was somewhat currish,
> For she refused to nourish
> A child which he brought home:
> He got it on an other,
> And death had tane the mother,
> The truth he could not smother,
> all out at last did come. . . .
>
> The Parish him enforc'd
> To see the infant nursed.
> He being but lightly pursed,
> desir'd to save that charge:
> He brought it to his own wife,
> Whom he loved as his own life,
> To her the cause was known rife,
> he told her all at large. . . .
> *Suckle the Baby,*
> *Huggle the Baby,*
> *Rocke the Baby Jone.*[79]

79 *Pepys Ballads*, 2:214–18. All quotations from this ballad are from this source.

Jone furiously denounces John and threatens to leave him. He brushes aside her anger at his lechery by assuring her "the wench is dead" and then appeals to her pity by saying the child will die if she doesn't take care of it. Besides, he says shrewdly, if she doesn't feed the child " 'twould be charge double, / If every month a Noble, / I pay for milk and bread." She comes back with her strongest argument yet: the rule of neighborhood.

> Twould be to my discredit,
> Should I both board and bed it,
> For never woman did it
> To a bastard of this kind. . . .
> My neighbors will deride me,
> And none that dwell beside me
> Will evermore abide me
> For such a President. . . .
> *I scorn to suckle the Baby,*
> *Unlesse it were mine owne.*

The husband is ready with his rebuttal, which is that Jone should reject their opinions and set a new pattern for all wives through her saintly patience:

> No Jone thou art mistaken,
> Twill other wives awaken,
> Then let some course be taken
> for the childs nourishment. . . .
> Let patient *Grissels* storie,
> Be still in thy memorie,
> Who wonne a lasting glory,
> through patience in like sort.

Jone's resistance vanishes at the magic words "patient *Grissels* storie," which tames her "currish" anger:

> Well John thy intercession
> Hath changed my disposition,
> And now upon condition
> thou'lt goe no more astray:
> Ile entertaine thy Baby,

And love it well as may be. . . .
Weele suckle the Baby,
And huggle the Baby.
Gramercy honest Jone.
O John Ile rock thy Baby,
As well as 'twere mine owne.

The antagonism between neighborhood values and the ideology of wifely obedience appears in stark relief. In fact, the dubious lesson here is not only that a wife must comply with her husband's most offensive demands, but that she must ignore "all that dwell beside," somehow turning their derision into admiration by this odd behavior.[80] Reactions to such a message were in all likelihood mixed. Those who had chafed at the anti-masculinism of *Rock the Baby, John,* may have been gratified by the answer ballad's putdown of female collusion, to say nothing of wifely will. As for those who agreed with Jone that such compliance would be ridiculous and unseemly, set a bad precedent, and fly in the face of convention, her about-face may well have been met with scorn and disbelief. The sudden conversion of a woman who has just given birth and who has held fast through nine stanzas of refusal, constantly invoking the pressure of her friends on her behavior ("I doubt I shall be forced, / From thee to be divorced") is comically quick. Her cave-in before this icon may have led some female listeners to scoff at the idea of aping "patient *Grissels* storie."

Hostility to community opinion and denial of its jurisdiction are sharply expressed in *A most pleasant Ballad of patient Grissell* (in print by 1565). Walter is no tyrant; in fact he is wise and kind, but he is greatly vexed by his snobbish and gossipy court, which refuses to accept his low-born wife. To prove her worth he must reluctantly try her, with many sighs and tears. After they are reunited he chastises the court: "And you that have envied her estate, / Whom now I have made my loving mate, / now blush for shame."[81] Remaking "Grissells storie" into an allegory about malicious gossip certainly takes the sting out of any animus against Walter. The sympathetic bystanders of the earlier ver-

---

80 The powerful threat of neighborly ridicule was not lost on preachers such as Gouge, who inveighed in *Domesticall Duties* that "a masterly wife is as much despised and derided for taking rule over her husband as he for yeelding to her" (sig. Cv).

81 Bronfman, "Griselda," 219. Unfortunately she appears to agree that pater knows best: "His testing and her response allow the marriage to be permanent, peaceful, and happy, immune to outside disturbance."

sions have been replaced by obnoxious snobs in the interests of promoting a husband's right to stage such psychodramas as he sees fit in order to consolidate his property and legitimate his rise.

This is, of course, the message of *The Taming of the Shrew*, a Griseldine parable that applauds the flouting of a community's right to limit the powers of an outsider. Petruchio virtually abducts Kate, forcing her to leave family and friends at the moment of their greatest claims, and later makes her deny both the testament of her senses and the outer world's claims on her. The idea that a shrew could be rendered ovine was not new, as is obvious from Lyly's reversal of the old saw in *Euphues:* "Whereby they noted that although the virgin were somewhat shrewish at first, yet in time she might become a sheep."[82] The difference is that Kate comes to embody not merely "a second Grissel" as predicted but a curiously revamped one whose cutaway wedding presents "the permanent enigma of the new-style conjugal household to bewildered neighbors, kin and friends," in the words of Lorna Hutson.

> Petruchio has created for himself a mobile and histrionic oikonomia, a conceptual household over which he rules, and in which he may innovate at will, unimpeded by old customs perpetuated by neighborhood. As two sets of husbands and wives—Hortensio and his widow, Lucentio and Bianca—settle comfortably into the same-sex alliances that are the traditional repositories of survival techniques in the conjugal struggle, a third set—Katherina and Petruchio—express an entirely new alignment of the resources of cultural production in the sustaining of the marriage contract.[83]

According to Natasha Korda, the realignment of Kate entails both her conversion to a domestic commodity and the domestication of the emergent commodity form itself, symbolized by the special "cates" that are bought outside the home.[84] While this new product's name is Kate, its brand name is indelibly yet invisibly *Griselda*. Petruchio parades his new "cates" in the final wager scene, in which Kate leaves the company of women and comes quietly to her husband, in distinction to the grousing but neighborly foot dragging of her sister and the widow.

82 Tilley, *Elizabethan Proverb Lore*, 2:273.
83 Hutson, *Usurer's Daughter*, 222–23.
84 Korda, "Domesticating Commodities," 109, 131. Korda's theory underlies my contention that Griselda came to England as a luxury import, not a native product.

Jardine chafes at the surreal wrongness of Kate's convertite Griselda act and in particular at the assertion that wives owe all to their husbands. When Petruchio tells Kate to throw off her cap and she complies and then stamps on it, Bianca bursts out in a line expressing many observers' probable reaction: "Fie! what a foolish duty call you this?" (5.2.125) Jardine objects in roughly the same vein:

> Duty is an abstract; it never correlates with the unreasonable demands of petulant (or bloody-minded) husbands. And it is by no means the case that Kate is obliged in Christian humility to serve her breadwinner husband: he is a fortune-hunting rascal, supported by her fine dowry. If obedience correlates with financial support, then it is Petruchio who should kneel to Kate.[85]

Jardine's rhetoric is vexed, colloquial, satiric, and lucid, rooted in material realities and appealing to a sense of equity. As I have shown, anti-Griselda expostulations not so very different in tone are scattered among jesting women in the popular literature of a much earlier time. In the most reprinted Griselda pamphlet of the seventeenth century, *The Ancient, True, and Admirable History of Patient Grisel* (1619), a comically hysterical narrator chastises his women readers in a way that makes clear he expects no less. At the highest crisis in the story, just after the marquis tells Griselda that her second child must be killed, the narrator breaks out in fury:

> Now you ladies and dames of these time, that stand upon tearms of spirit and greatnesse of heart (some will have it courage and magnanimity of mind). . . . I speake not of strumpets, or of such as are willing to brand themselves with the impurity of uncleannesse, and dare out of impudency or cunning, tel their husbands to their faces they will go where they list, and do what they please, but of such that under that impregnable target of honestie are yet so impatient at every distemperature, that they dare answer taunt for taunt: yea, like viragoes indeed, offer the first blow, though a horrible confusion follow; what would you have answered this lord? or with what fire-works would you have made your approaches unto him? I will not tarry for your answere, lest I pull the old house in peeces, and so, though I scape the timber, I may be crushed with the rubbish; but I will now anticipate (or prevent) all objections by telling you

85 Jardine, *Still Harping*, 60.

what faire Grisel said: and if there be hope of reformation, insert it as a caution to divert you from your natural fierceness.[86]

Griselda keeps producing fierce discourse. Her tale appears to beg a frame lest she stands exposed as stark naked, a slave, or an idiot before our unwilling eyes. Chaucer tried to purge the air with pathos at the climax of his tale, with Griselda falling into a swoon, her children pinned in her arms, and tears all around. Then, in an odd swerve away from piety, "The Clerk's Tale" culminates with a rant, a funny monster, and laughter, offering up a comic envoy that disturbs the solemn political and religious allegory that has just ended.[87] However ironic Chaucer intended his lines to be, exhorting women to ignore Griselda's example and defy and beat their husbands, his envoy also seems crafted to placate those women angered by the tale, readers far closer in temperament to the Wife of Bath "and all hire secte" than to Griselda:

> O noble wyves, ful of heigh prudence,
> Lat noon humilitee your tonge naille,
> Ne lat no clerk have cause or diligence
> To wryte of yow a storie of swich mervaille
> As of Grisildis, pacient and kinde,
> Lest Chichevache yow swelwe in hire entraille!
> (1183–88)

Chichevache is a giant cow who feeds only on patient wives; but the old joke is that there are no more Griseldas, so the monster is always hungry. There are scattered references to Chichevache and her twin, Bicorne, the fat beast who feeds on patient husbands, in English and French texts and woodcuts from the fourteenth century on. Lydgate wrote a comic dialogue entitled *Bycorne and Chychevache*, but the beasts are Englished to Pinch Belly and Fill Gut in a popular print (see fig. 14).

How did the skinny monster look to wives who were instructed that husbands had the absolute right to do them any harm, including strip-

---

86 *Ancient, True and Admirable History of Patient Grisel*, 3:23.
87 McClellan calls the envoy "the counter-argument to the dominating Petrarchan allegoresis" in his essay "Lars Engle."

Fig. 14. Chichevache, doom of patient wives. Detail from *Fill Gut, & Pinch Belly: One being Fat with eating good Men, the other Leane for want of good Women* (1620). Reproduced by permission of the Society of Antiquaries of London.

ping them naked, killing their children, and replacing them with anyone they desired, including their own daughters?[88] More to the point, how much sympathy did they feel for the patient wife suspended in her hungry jaws? To the antifeminist writers who referred to her, Chichevache was always lean because wives were always wicked. But to the wives whose patience was sorely tried by priests and husbands invoking Griselda, Chichevache was kept lean in part by their efforts to ridicule a narrative that rewarded abjection, complicit infanticide, and sexual slavery with fame and riches. Chichevache is a reminder of the power of popular culture to create fabulous referents for the pain and rage created by myths of gender, in this case a folktale about an enslaved woman's resistance that was converted to a sermon about a "free" woman's voluntary subjection.

88 Cramer analyzes the sadomasochistic erotics of the tale in "Lordship."

Griselda still walks among us, named or nameless. Like the Timex watch, she takes a licking and keeps on ticking. In Caryl Churchill's play, *Top Girls*, Griselda comes in for the largest share of satire, straining the nerves of the other top girls of history who are having tea together. They keep peppering her with questions about her motives and her inexplicable inaction. When they turn to her husband's cruelties, she concedes he was a bit harsh: "I do think—I do wonder—it would have been nicer if Walter hadn't had to." Asked if it hadn't been *terribly* difficult to give up not only one but two babies, she doesn't miss a beat: "It was always easy because I always knew I would do what he said."[89] Some women still believe that brutal and capricious husbands are sent by God, that suffering will be rewarded, and that submission is easier than resistance. Worse, some husbands still believe that Griselda is the perfect wife. That is why it is still necessary to keep Chichevache lean.

89 Churchill, *Plays*, 77, 81.

Epilogue
The Problem of Fun

> That we are more witty which comes by nature it cannot
> better be proved then that by our answers, men are often
> driven to a *Non plus,* & if their talk be of worldly affaires,
> with our resolutions they must either rest satisfied, or
> prove themselves fooles in the end.
>
> *Jane Anger, her Protection for Women*

Finding jesting women in early popular culture has not been difficult—more like combing through a bulging midden than re-creating a
vanished city. Framing them in right relation to historical and dramatic
discourses about gender has been a harder task. Many jesting texts are
found in works by men, making them suspicious to gynocritics, while
the genre's incontinent bawdiness has made women's participation
sound improbable. Even more damning is the fact that almost any
single jesting performance, text, or image can be labeled antifeminist
satire. The genre's frequent sojourns into what Roland Barthes has
called "the nauseating realm of the stereotype" has made jests as un-
palatable to some scholars as "idle bookes & riffe raffes" were to
Thomas Bodley when he banned them from his library.[1] As documents,
jests seem both frivolous and fragmentary, like confetti; the feminists
whose insights created the field in which I work tend to choose graver
genres for their analyses of gender ideology.

The understandable desire of literary scholars to be taken seriously,
and that of historians to amass sober records about work, property and
death, militates against the study of an elusive quality in culture: what
might be called (with proper seriousness) "the problem of fun." Yet as

---

1 Quoted in Hackel, " 'Rowme' of Its Own," 121.

Robert Weimann warns, "any criticism, and especially a politically committed criticism, would condemn itself to a grim kind of puritanism if the sheer element of fun, release, reckless enjoyment were ever minimized, or . . . theoretically ostracized."[2] Some minimizing does occur because of the wish to avoid the killing charge of "romantic nostalgia" or "celebratory feminism" that might be triggered by efforts to reconstruct the pleasures and desires of early modern women rather than their silencing and oppression. Certainly, jesting seems the idlest of pastimes, bearing only a tenuous relation to the conditions of unending work, continuous child bearing, and doctrinal subjection that defined most women's lives. Joan Kelly's famous question—"Did women have a Renaissance?"—has evoked many narratives of loss, silencing, and defeat; yet it is surely worth noticing that some stories registered women's amusement at, or stubborn indifference to, the admonitions raining down on them.[3]

Despite strenuous disciplinary efforts by clerics, husbands, and conduct book writers, some women continued to enjoy the trivial pursuits they were warned to shun, buying and singing ballads, going to plays, reading "small merry books." These texts sometimes show women getting the laugh on those they were supposed to obey. Not paying attention is a form of resistance, as any teacher knows; so is the act of making fun. In the words of Susan Purdie, the seemingly trivial act of joking "can—and sometimes does—confirm relationship and identity beyond the miserable limits of patriarchy." A woman who controls laughter becomes an agent, while those who laugh can deny a target his "discursive potency"—defined as "the power to construct and define *us.*"[4] But could these crude forms in any sense represent women to themselves?

No representation can provide a transparent window into *mentalité.* All forms of culture that scholars study are subject to mediation—by authors, performers, ballad sellers, printers, transcribers, and scholars themselves.[5] My own readings of jests are undoubtedly conditioned by my desire to find what I seek and by my perspective as a feminist aca-

2 "The Problem of Fun" is a poem by my friend, the late Casey Finch, in *Harming Others*, 36–37. The Weimann quotation is from "Towards a Literary Theory" in Howard and O'Connor, *Shakespeare Reproduced*, 272.

3 Kelly, *Women, History, and Theory*, 19–50.

4 Purdie, *Comedy*, 148. For a very different take on Purdie, see Holcomb, *Mirth Making*, 130. I disagree with his reading, which implies that culture always denies discursive potency to jesting women, negating their claims to mastery.

5 Burke, "Oblique Approaches," esp. 73–74, 77.

demic working on literary and subliterary texts. Although it comes to
us through layer upon layer of such filters, early modern jesting culture
does at least suggest the needs and pleasures of those who participated
in it. I remain confident that the phrases, songs, and fictions of ridicule
and comedy formed an important part of the vocabulary of common
culture available to women. To make this claim, I have had the privilege of being able to build on the groundbreaking work of historians of
early modern women, especially those who study the family and neighborhood; women's working lives; popular festivity and ritual; and slander, violence, and crime. Surprisingly often, details carefully documented by historians mirror passages in the far less creditable pages of
jest. Sometimes, however, the picture developed from lowly popular
sources complicates and deepens, or even challenges, judgments based
primarily on documents about doctrine, property, and law. As I discussed in chapter 2, many historians who study the world of the alehouse call it a male-dominated space off-putting to "respectable"
women.[6] Yet the gossips' literature and jest books show all kinds of
women gathering in the alehouse, with special emphasis on the alewife
and gossip as central actors in the dramas of everyday life, including the
control of neighbors through mockery and gossip. Drawing attention to
the jesting alewife and the alehouse also serves to focus much-needed
attention on working women, the participation of women in print culture, and women's presence in the public sphere long before the rise of
the coffeehouse and salon.

My second example concerns wife beating. The law permitted it as
long as death did not result, while the church attempted to discourage
husbands from using violence to correct their wives. Despite the controversy, official culture told women that their lot was to obey and suffer, like the perfectly patient wife, Griselda. At the same time, a number of plays, ballads, and jests presented images of wives losing patience
and tricking or beating drunken and violent husbands or banding together to cuckold or confound violent husbands. Some even mock
Griselda as a fool. All this is encoded as merry entertainment, yet it
also serves serious social functions: to represent the powerful force of
neighborhood, to rehearse "the powers of the weak," and to warn husbands against abusing their wives—long before the state promulgated
laws against wife beating. As Lena Orlin has observed, disparities be-

6 Clark, English Alehouse, 131–32.

tween literary texts and historical documents must not mean that one type is ignored and the other validated. Both should be combined to produce better questions about, and more nuanced visions of, the worlds of early modern women.[7] If my book has contributed to this important ongoing enterprise in feminist scholarship, it will have achieved its purpose.

I also harbor the hope that this book will persuade readers that antimasculinist satire is absolutely necessary to women today, just as it was to women four hundred years ago. Women still stand in sore need of quick answers whenever male "wits" labor to top each other's antifeminist quips. In the early modern period, a typical vehicle for such jesting was the extended comparison: the object held to resemble or surpass a woman could be a horse, a pipe of tobacco, or even a chandelier. Castiglione advised caution to all those "who take pleasure in comparing men and women to horses, does, birds, and often to chests, wagons, chandeliers, which is sometimes to the point and sometimes falls very flat."[8] Jest forms are peculiarly long-lived and highly adaptable: Castiglione's example survives today on frat-boy T-shirts listing "one hundred reasons why beer is better than a woman." What did not survive so vigorously was the way in which women gave mock for mock, countering and shaping the antifeminist position—note that Castiglione says that *men* were subjected to the game, too.[9] In the early modern period, women's laughter and jesting cast shame on some and rewarded others, altering perception and behavior, functioning as a means of social control. At times women's jesting called upon a sense of female community: groups of women mocking a wife beater or a bad play had a tiny but real measure of social power.

Because this power was not supposed to exist, jesting women are often painted as unruly shrews; but even satires on women's comic misrule may contain the stubborn seeds of counter-hegemonic thought. The most important effect of low genres such as gossips' literature may lie not in their contemporary transgressiveness but in their proleptic

7 Orlin, "Women on the Threshold."
8 Castiglione, *Book of the Courtier*, 207.
9 According to Huizinga, ancient slanging matches between men and women may have been the source of poetry itself and later of antifeminist satire: "at the feasts of Demeter and Apollo, men and women chanted songs of mutual derision, which may have given rise to the literary theme of the diatribe against womankind" (*Homo Ludens*, 68).

sketching of a world in which women seek and enjoy power—and to a degree dreamed of only by the most rabid shrews in their secret conventicles. In our rush to avoid any statement that smacks of teleology, we may be overlooking the ways in which familiar culture could serve as a staging area where topsy-turvy ideas became templates for action over the long haul and where some women could find weapons against the everyday reality of oppression. The worm may turn at last or, as one proverb had it, *a sheep may kill a butcher.*[10] Over time, and after a huge struggle, the shrew's pipe dream stopped being a joke. Women preach, vote, serve on juries, and attend universities; they become judges, professors, lawyers, and priests; they make laws, criticize books and plays, gloss the Bible, and sit in Congress and Parliament. Some wives demand that husbands share housework and child care, while others obtain divorces or send abusive husbands to jail. These "rights" of women were not generated entirely by Enlightenment thinkers or later movements to enfranchise and liberate women. They first appeared in the jesting literature as contemptible images of a world gone mad.

Some women may have laughed with a difference. After all, just as *no man is born master,* no woman is born a tame fool.

10 Stevenson, *Home Book of Proverbs,* 2087. On the usefulness of play and performance as means to project alternative futures, see Turner, *Anthropology of Performance,* 24.

Bibliography

Primary Sources

The Academy of Pleasure. . . . Teaching all sorts of men, Maids, Widows, &c. to Speak and Write wittily, and to bear themselves gracefully, for the attaining of their desired Ends. London, 1665.

Aldington, Richard, ed. *A Book of Characters.* London: Routledge, 1924.

Alfonso, Pedro. *The Scholar's Guide. A Translation of the Twelfth-Century Disciplina Clericalis of Pedor Alfonso,* translated by J.R. Jones and J.E. Keller. Toronto: Pontifical Institute of Medieval Studies, 1969.

The Ancient, True and Admirable History of Patient Grisel. [1611]. In *Early English Poetry, Ballads, and Popular Literature of the Middle Ages,* vol. 3. London: Percy Society, 1891.

Armin, Robert. *A Nest of Ninnies.* [1608]. In Zall (1970), 15–72.

Ashton, John, ed. *Chapbooks of the Eighteenth Century.* London: Chatto and Windus, 1882.

The Bachelors Banquet. [1603], edited by Faith Guildenhuys. Binghamton, N.Y.: Medieval and Renaissance Texts and Studies, 1993.

Bacon, Francis. *Apophthegmes new and Old.* London, 1626.

A Banquet of Jests New and Old. London, 1657.

A Banquet of Jests. Or Change of Cheare. London, 1639.

Basse, William. *A Helpe to Discourse. Or A Miscellany of Seriousnesse with Merriment.* London, 1627.

Bayly, Thomas. *Witty Apophthegms delivered at Severall Times, and upon Severall Occasions, by King James, King Charles, the Marquess of Worcester, Francis Lord Bacon, and Sir Thomas Moore.* London, 1658.

Beaumont, Francis. *The Knight of the Burning Pestle*, edited by Sheldon P. Zitner. Manchester, U.K.: Manchester University Press, 1984.

Boccaccio, Giovanni. *Il Decamerone*. Milano: Ulrico Hoepli, 1951.

——. *The Decameron*, translated by Mark Musa and Peter Bondanella. New York: Penguin, 1982.

Bowen, Barbara C., ed. *One Hundred Renaissance Jokes: An Anthology*. Birmingham, U.K.: Summa, 1988.

Bracciolini, Poggio. *The Facetiae or Jocose Tales of Poggio*. [1470]. Paris: Lisieux, 1879.

Brathwait, Richard. *Ar't Asleep Husband? A Boulster Lecture*. London, 1640.

——. *The English Gentlewoman*. London, 1631.

——. *Essaies upon the five senses*. London, 1619.

——. *Whimzies: or a new cast of characters*. London, 1631.

Breton, Nicholas. *A Poste with a Packet of mad Letters*. London, 1607.

Brewer, Derek, ed. *Medieval Comic Tales*, translated by Peter Rickard, Alan Deyermond, Derek Brewer, David Blamiris, Peter King, and Michael Lupridge. Cambridge, U.K.: Brewer, 1972.

The Brideling, Sadling and Ryding, of a rich Churle in Hampshire, by the subtill practice of one Judith Philips. London, 1595.

Bulwer, John. *Chirologia, or the Naturall Language of the Hand*. London: Thomas Harper for Henry Twyford, 1644.

——. *Chironomia, Or, the Art of Manuall Rhetoricke*. London, 1644.

Captain Cox, his Ballads and Books; or, Robert Laneham's Letter, edited by Frederick Furnivall. Hertford, U.K.: Austin, 1891.

Cary, Elizabeth. *The Tragedy of Mariam, the fair queen of jewry*, edited by Barry Weller and Margaret W. Ferguson. Berkeley: University of California Press, 1994.

Castiglione, Baldassare. *The Book of the Courtier*. Garden City, N.Y.: Anchor, 1959.

——. *The Courtyer of Count Baldassar Castiglio: Divided into Foure Bookes: Very Necessary and Profitable for Younge Gentlemen and Gentlewomen. . . . done into Englyshe by Thomas Hoby*. London, 1561.

Cavendish, Margaret. *Convent of Pleasure and Other Plays*, edited by Anne Shaver. Baltimore: Johns Hopkins University Press, 1999.

Caxton, William. *The Fables of Alfonce and Poge*. [1484]. In Zall (1963), 12–56.

——. *Here begynneth the book of the subtyl historyes and Fables of Esope*. London, 1484.

Certayne Conceyts and Jests. [1639]. In Hazlitt 3: 3–18.

Chamberlain, Robert. *Conceits, clinches, flashes, and whimzies*. London, 1639.

——. *A new Booke of Mistakes, Or, Bulls with Tales, and Buls without Tales. But no lyes by any meanes*. London, 1637.

Chapman, George, Ben Jonson, and John Marston. *Eastward Ho*. In *Elizabethan Plays*, edited by Hazleton Spencer. 473–516. Boston: Little, Brown, 1940.

Characterismi, or Lenton's Leasures. London, 1631.

Chaucer, Geoffrey. *The Canterbury Tales: Nine Tales and the General Prologue,* edited by V. A. Kolve and Glending Olson. New York: Norton, 1989.

———. *Chaucer's Major Poetry,* edited by Albert C. Baugh. New York: Appleton-Century-Crofts, 1963.

———. *The Tales of the Clerk and the Wife of Bath,* edited by Marion Wynne-Davies. London: Routledge, 1992.

The Chester Mystery Cycle, edited by R. M. Lumiansky and David Mills. London: Early English Text Society–Oxford University Press, 1974.

Chettle, Henry. *Kind-Hartes Dream,* edited by G. B. Harrison. New York: Barnes and Noble, 1962.

A Choice banquet of Witty Jests, rare fancies, and pleasant Novels. London, 1660.

Choice, Chance and Change: Or, Conceits in their Colours. London, 1606.

Churchill, Caryl. *Top Girls.* In *Plays: Two.* London: Methuen, 1990.

A C. Mery Talys. [1526]. In Zall (1963), 58–150.

The Cobler of Caunterburie and Tarltons Newes out of Purgatorie, edited by Geoffrey Creigh and Jane Belfield. Leiden, the Netherlands: Brill, 1987.

A Collection of Seventy-five Black-Letter Ballads and Broadsides Printed in the Reign of Elizabeth Between the Years 1559 and 1597. Detroit: Singing Tree Press, 1968.

Copley, Anthony. *Wits, Fits and Fancies: Or, a Generall and serious Collection, of the Sententious Speeches, Answers, Iests and Behauiours, of all sortes of Estates, From the Throane to the Cottage.* London, 1614.

Cornu-Copiae. Pasquils Nightcap: Or, Antidot for the Head-Ache. London, 1612.

Dekker, Thomas. *The Dramatic Works of Thomas Dekker,* edited by Fredson Bowers. 3 vols. Cambridge: Cambridge University Press, 1953.

Deloney, Thomas. *The Novels of Thomas Deloney,* edited by Merritt E. Lawlis. Bloomington: Indiana University Press, 1961.

Des Périers, Bonaventure. *The Mirrour of Mirth and Pleasant Conceits,* edited by James W. Hassell, Jr. Columbia: University of South Carolina Press, 1959.

A Disputation Betweene a Hee Conny-catcher, and a Shee Conny-catcher, whether a Theefe or a Whore, is most hurtful in Cousenage, to the Commonwealth. London, 1592.

DuVal, John, trans. *Fabliaux Fair and Foul.* Binghamton, N.Y.: Medieval and Renaissance Texts and Studies, 1992.

Earle, John. *Microcosmographie, or, a Peece of the World Discovered; in Essayes and Characters.* London, 1629.

Edmundson, Henry. *Comes facundus in via. The Fellow Traveller.* London, 1658.

The Euing Collection of English Broadside Ballads. Glasgow: University of Glasgow Publications, 1971.

The Female jester or, Wit for the Ladies. London, [?1778].

Finch, Casey. *Harming Others*. Athens: University of Georgia Press, 1993.

Fletcher, John. *A Critical Edition of John Fletcher's Comedy "The Wild-Goose Chase,"* edited by Rota Herzberg Lister. New York: Garland, 1980.

——. *The Dramatic Works in the Beaumont and Fletcher Canon*, edited by Fredson Bowers. 10 vols. London: Cambridge University Press, 1966–96.

——. *The Woman's Prize, or The Tamer Tamed*, edited by G. B. Ferguson. The Hague: Mouton, 1966.

Goddard, William. *A satyricall dialogue or sharply-invective conference, betweene Alexander the great, and that truely woman-hater Diogynes.* [?Dort, 1616].

The gospelles of dystaves. London, [?1510].

The Gossips Greeting: or, a new Discovery of such Females meeting. Wherein is plainely set forth the sundry sorts of those kinds of women, with their severall humors and Conditions. London, 1620.

Gratiae Ludentes. Jests, from the universitie, by H. L. Oxen. London, 1628.

Grosart, Alexander. *Grosart's Occasional Issues: Elizabethan England in Gentle and Simple Life.* Manchester, 1881.

Harrison, William. *The Description of England.* Washington, D.C.: Folger Shakespeare Library/Dover, 1994.

Harvey, Gabriel. *The Works of Gabriel Harvey*, edited by Alexander Grosart. 3 vols. 1885; reprint, New York: AMS Press, 1966.

Hazlitt, W. Carew. *Shakespeare Jest-Books.* 3 vols. New York: Franklin, 1864.

Heywood, Thomas. *A curtaine lecture: as it is read by a Country Farmers wife to her Good man. By a Countrey Gentlewoman or Lady to her Esquire or Knight. By a Souldiers wife to her Captain or Lieutenant. By a Citizens or Tradesmans wife to her Husband.* London, 1637.

——. *The Wise Woman of Hogsdon*, edited by A. Wilson Verity. London: Vizetelly, 1888.

Hickes, William. *Oxford Jests.* London, 1671.

Hobbes, Thomas. *Leviathan*, edited by Edwin Curley. Indianapolis: Hackett, 1994.

Hopkins, Cathy, and Alison Everitt. *Revenge of the Essex Girls.* London: Robson, 1992.

Howleglas. [?1528]. In Zall (1963), 151–238.

Huth, Henry, ed. *Ancient Ballads and Broadsides.* London, 1867.

I. C. [Cotgrave, John]. *Wits Interpreter, The English Parnassus.* London, 1658.

Jacke of Dover his Quest of Inquirie. [1604]. In Hazlitt 2: 312–54.

James VI and I. *Daemonologie.* Edinburgh, 1597.

Jestes to make you Merie: with the Conjuring up of Cock Watt. . . . London, 1607.

Jonson, Ben. *Ben Jonson*, edited by C. H. Herford, Percy Simpson, and Evelyn Simpson. 11 vols. Oxford: Clarendon, 1925–52.

Joubert, Laurent. *Treatise on Laughter* [1579], translated by Gregory de Rocher. University, Ala.: University of Alabama Press, 1980.

Jyl of Breyntford's Testament . . . The Wyll of the Devyll and his Last Testament, a Talk of Ten Wives on their Husbands Ware, edited by Frederick J. Furnivall. London: Taylor, 1871.

Laugh and Lie Down: or, The worlds folly. London, 1605.

Lenton, F. *Characterismus.* London, 1631.

Le Strange, Nicholas. *'Merry Passages and Jeasts': A Manuscript Jestbook of Sir Nicholas Le Strange (1603–1655).* Ed. H.F. Lippincott. Elizabethan & Renaissance Studies 29. Salzburg: Institut für Englische Sprache und Literatur, 1974.

The Life and Death of the merry Devill of Edmonton. London, 1631.

Long Meg of Westminster. London, 1635.

Manly, John, ed. *Specimens of the Pre-Shakespearean Drama.* 2 vols. New York: Dover, 1987.

Marguerite de Navarre. *The Heptaméron*, translated by P.A. Chilton. Harmondsworth, U.K.: Penguin, 1984.

——. *The Queene of Navarres Tales. Containing, Verie pleasant Discourses of fortunate Lovers.* London: V.S. for John Oxenbridge, 1597.

Marie de France. *The Lais of Marie de France*, translated by Robert Hanning and Joan Ferrante. Grand Rapids, Mich.: Baker, 1978.

Martone, Valerie, and Robert L. Martone, eds. and trans. *Renaissance Comic Tales of Love, Treachery, and Revenge.* New York: Italica, 1994.

Merie Tales of the Mad Men of Gotham. In Hazlitt 3: 4–26.

The Merry Jests and Witty Shifts of Scogin. London, 1626.

Middleton, Thomas, and Thomas Dekker. *The Roaring Girl*, edited by Havelock Ellis. London: Vizetelly, 1890.

A new Booke of Mistakes, Or, Bulls with Tales, and Buls without Tales. But no lyes by any meanes. London, 1637.

Painter, William. *The Palace of Pleasure.* [1566–67]. 4 vols. London: Cresset, 1929.

——. *The Palace of Pleasure. Beautified, adorned and well furnished, with Pleasaunt Histories and excellent novelles, selected out of divers good and commendable authors.* London, 1566.

A Parliament of Ladies. London, 1647.

The Parliament of Women, with the merry Lawes by them newly Enacted. To live in more Ease, Pompe, Pride and Wantonnness: but especially that they might have Superiority. London, 1640.

Pasquils Jests. With the merriments of Mother Bunch, Wittie, pleasant, and delightfull. London, 1629.

Pasquils Palinodia, and His progresse to the taverne, Where after the survey of the Sellar, you are presented with a pleasant pynte of poeticall Sherry. London, 1619.

Peacham, Henry. *The Compleat Gentleman*. London, 1622.

Peele, George. *Merrie Conceited Jests of George Peele*. London, [?1620].

——. *The Old Wive's Tale*. In *The Minor Elizabethan Drama*. Vol. 2. London: Dent, 1964.

The Pepys Ballads, edited by Hyder Edward Rollins. Cambridge: Harvard University Press, 1929.

Phillip, John. *The Comodye of Pacient and Meeke Grissill.* London: Malone Society Reprints/Chiswick, 1909.

Platter, Thomas. *Thomas Platter's Travels in England*, translated by Clare Williams. London: Cape, 1937.

Politeuphuia. Wits Commonwealth. London, 1598.

Porter, Henry. *The Pleasant Comedie of the Two Angrie women of Abington.* Oxford: Oxford University Press for the Malone Society, 1912.

Preston, Thomas. *A Critical Edition of Thomas Preston's "Cambises,"* edited by Robert Carl Johnson. Salzburg: Institut für Englische Sprache und Literatur, 1975.

Puttenham, George. *The Arte of English Poesie*, edited by G.D. Willcock and A. Walker. Cambridge: Cambridge University Press, 1936.

A Quest of Enquirie, by women to know, Whether the Tripe-wife were trimmed by Doll yea or no. London, 1595.

Ray, John. *A Collection of English Proverbs*. London, 1670.

Riche, Barnabe. *Riche His Farewell to Military Profession*. London, 1581.

Rowlands, Samuel. *The Complete Works of Samuel Rowlands*. Glasgow: Hunterian Club, 1880.

——. *Humors Ordinarie. Where a Man May be verie merrie, and exceedingly well used for his Sixe-pence*. London, 1607.

——. *Tis Merry When Gossips Meet*. London, 1602.

——. *A whole crew of kind Gossips, all met to be merry*. London, 1609.

The Roxburghe Ballads, edited by W. Chappell and J. Ebsworth. 9 vols. Hertford, U.K.: Austin, 1866–99.

The Sackfull of newes. London, 1653.

Salgado, Gamini, ed. *Cony-Catchers and Bawdy Baskets: An Anthology of Elizabethan Low Life*. New York: Penguin, 1972.

Samuel Pepys' Penny Merriments, edited by Roger Thompson. New York: Columbia University Press, 1977.

Scott, Sir Michael. *The Philosophers Banquet*. London, 1609.

——. *The Philosophers Banquet, newly furnished and decked forth*. London, 1614.

Shakespeare, William. *The Riverside Shakespeare*, edited by G. Blakemore Evans et al. Boston: Houghton Mifflin, 1974.

——. *The Taming of the Shrew: Texts and Contexts*, edited by Frances E. Dolan. New York: Bedford/St. Martin's, 1996.

Shepherd, Simon. *The Woman's Sharp Revenge: Five Women's Pamphlets from the Renaissance*. New York: St. Martin's, 1985.

Spenser, Edmund. *The Faerie Queene,* edited by A.C. Hamilton. London: Longman, 1977.

Stephens, John. *Satyricall essayes characters and others.* London, 1615.

Stow, John. *Survey of London.* New York: Dutton, 1956.

Tales and Quick Answers. [?1535]. In Zall (1963), 239–322.

Taming of a Shrew. In *Narrative and Dramatic Sources of Shakespeare,* edited by Geoffrey Bullough, 8 vols. I: 68–109. London: Routledge and Kegan Paul, 1957.

Tarlton's Jests. London, 1611.

Tarltons Newes out of Purgatorie. Onelye such a iest as his Iigge, for a Gentleman to laugh at in alehouse, &c. London, 1590.

Taylor, John. *All the Works of John Taylor, the Water Poet.* London, 1630.

——. *A Brown Dozen of Drunkards: (Ali-Ass Drink-hards) whipt, stript and shipt to the Isle of Gulls : with their abusing of Mr. Malt the bearded Sob, and Barley-broth the brainlesse daughter of Sir John Barley-corne.* London, 1648.

——. *A Juniper Lecture.* London, 1639.

——. *Works of John Taylor the Water Poet not Included in the Folio Volume of 1630.* Manchester, U.K.: Spenser Society, 1876.

Tom Tyler and His Wife. [London]: Chiswick Press for the Malone Society, 1910.

Tusser, Thomas. *A hundreth good points of husbandrie. Lately maried unto a hundreth good points of huswifry, newly corrected and amplified.* London, 1599.

Twyne, Thomas. *The schoolmaster, or teacher of table philosophie.* London, 1576.

Udall, Nicholas. *Ralph Roister Doister.* In *Medieval and Tudor Drama,* edited by John Gassner. 266–345. New York: Applause, 1987.

Vele, Abraham. *The deceyte of women, to the instruction and ensample of all men yonge and olde.* London, 1563.

Wardroper, John. *Jest Upon Jest.* London: Routledge, 1970.

Westward for Smelts, Or the Water-mans Fare of mad-merry Western wenches. [1620], edited by Holger M. Klein. Hildesheim, Germany: Gerstenberg Verlag, 1978.

Whately, William. *A Bride Bush.* London, 1616.

Wilson, Thomas. *Arte of Rhetoricke,* edited by Thomas J. Derrick. New York: Garland, 1982.

Wither, George. *A Collection of Emblemes.* [1635.] Aldershot, U.K.: Scolar, 1989.

Wits Recreations. Selected from the Finest Fancies of the Modern Muses. London, 1640.

The womens sharpe revenge . . . performed by Mary Tattle-well, and Joane Hit-Him-Home. London, 1640.

The York Cycle of Mystery Plays, edited by J.S. Purvis. London: SPCK, 1978.

Zall, P. M., ed. *A Hundred Merry Tales and Other English Jestbooks of the Fifteenth and Sixteenth Centuries.* Lincoln: University of Nebraska Press, 1963.
———. *A Nest of Ninnies and other English Jestbooks of the Seventeenth Century.* Lincoln: University of Nebraska Press, 1970.

Secondary Sources

Achinstein, Sharon. "'Women on Top' in the Revolution." *Women's Studies* 24, nos. 1–2 (1994): 131–64.
Aers, David. *Community, Gender and Individual Identity: English Writing, 1360–1430.* London: Routledge, 1988.
———, ed. *Culture and History, 1350–1600.* Detroit: Wayne State University Press, 1992.
Agnew, Jean-Christophe. *Worlds Apart: The Market and the Theatre in Anglo-American Thought, 1550–1750.* Cambridge: Cambridge University Press, 1986.
Alford, John A., ed. *From Page to Performance: Essays in Early English Drama.* East Lansing: Michigan State University Press, 1995.
Amussen, Susan Dwyer. "'Being Stirred to Much Unquietness': Violence and Domestic Violence in Early Modern England." *Journal of Women's History* 6, no. 2 (1994): 70–90.
———. "The Gendering of Popular Culture." In Harris, 48–68.
———. *An Ordered Society: Gender and Class in Early Modern England.* Oxford: Blackwell, 1988.
———. "Punishment, Discipline and Power: The Social Meanings of Violence in Early Modern England." *Journal of British Studies* 34, no. 1 (1995): 1–34.
Anderson, Patricia Anne. "Gossips, Ale-wives, Midwives, and Witches." Ph.D. diss., State University of New York at Buffalo, 1992.
Apte, Mahadev L. *Humour and Laughter: An Anthropological Approach.* Ithaca: Cornell University Press, 1985.
Archer, Ian. *The Pursuit of Stability: Social Relations in Elizabethan London.* Cambridge: Cambridge University Press, 1991.
Archer, Ian, Caroline Barron, and Vanessa Harding, eds. *Hugh Alley's Caveat: The Markets of London in 1598.* Washington, D.C.: Folger Shakespeare Library, 1988.
Arend, Elisabeth. "Laughter and Humor in Early Italian Literature and Especially Boccaccio's *Decameron*—Some Methodological Considerations." Unpublished paper, 1996.
Armstrong, Nancy, and Leonard Tennenhouse. *The Imaginary Puritan: Literature, Intellectual Labor, and the Origins of Personal Life.* Berkeley: University of California Press, 1992.

Ashton, John, ed. *Humour, Wit, and Satire of the Seventeenth Century.* New York: Bouton, 1884.

Bakhtin, Mikhail M. *The Dialogic Imagination: Four Essays,* translated by Caryl Emerson and Michael Holquist, edited by Michael Holquist. Austin: University of Texas Press, 1981.

———. *Rabelais and His World,* translated by Hélène Iswolsky. Bloomington: Indiana University Press, 1984.

Baldwin, Anna. "From the *Clerk's Tale* to *The Winter's Tale.*" In *Chaucer Traditions: Studies in Honour of Derek Brewer,* edited by Ruth Morse and Barry Windeatt. Cambridge: Cambridge University Press, 1990.

Bamber, Linda. *Comic Women, Tragic Men: A Study of Gender and Genre in Shakespeare.* Stanford: Stanford University Press, 1982.

Barber, C. L. *Shakespeare's Festive Comedy.* 1959; reprint, Princeton: Princeton University Press, 1972.

Barreca, Regina, ed. *Last Laughs: Perspectives on Women and Comedy.* New York: Gordon and Breach, 1988.

———. *Untamed and Unabashed: Essays on Women and Humor in British Literature.* Detroit: Wayne State University Press, 1994.

Barry, Jonathan. "Literacy and Literature in Popular Culture." In Harris, 69–94.

Barthes, Roland. *Mythologies,* translated by Annette Lavers. New York: Noonday, 1972.

Baskervill, Charles Read. *The Elizabethan Jig and Related Song Drama.* Chicago: University of Chicago Press, 1929.

Belsey, Catherine. *The Subject of Tragedy: Identity and Difference in Renaissance Drama.* London: Methuen, 1985.

Bennett, Judith. *Ale, Beer, and Brewsters in England: Women's Work in a Changing World, 1300–1600.* New York: Oxford University Press, 1996.

———. "Misogyny, Popular Culture, and Women's Work." *History Workshop Journal* 31 (1991): 166–88.

Bergson, Henri. "Laughter." In *Comedy: An Essay on Comedy,* edited by Wylie Sypher. Baltimore: Johns Hopkins University Press, 1980.

Bettridge, William Edwin, and Francis Lee Utley. "New Light on the Origin of the Griselda Story." *Texas Studies in Literature and Language* 13 (1971): 153–208.

Bigsby, C. W. E. *Approaches to Popular Culture.* Bowling Green, Ohio: Bowling Green University Press, 1976.

Billington, Sandra. *The Social History of the Fool.* Sussex, U.K.: Harvester, 1984.

Blagden, C. "Notes on the Ballad Market." *Studies in Bibliography* 6 (1954).

Blain, Virginia, et al. *The Feminist Companion to Literature in English.* New Haven: Yale University Press, 1990.

Bliss, Lee. "The Renaissance Griselda: A Woman for All Seasons." *Viator: Medieval and Renaissance Studies* 23 (1992): 301–43.

Bloch, R. Howard. "Medieval Misogyny." *Representations* 20 (Fall, 1987): 1–24.

——. *The Scandal of the Fabliaux.* Chicago: University of Chicago Press, 1986.

Bly, Mary. *Queer Virgins and Virgin Queans on the Early Modern Stage.* Oxford: Oxford University Press, 2000.

Blyth, Reginald. *Humor in English Literature.* 1959; reprint, Tokyo: n.p., 1970.

Boose, Lynda E. "The Priest, the Slanderer, the Historian, and the Feminist." *English Literary Renaissance* 25, no. 3 (Autumn 1995): 320–40.

——. "Scolding Brides and Bridling Scolds: Taming the Woman's Unruly Member." *Shakespeare Quarterly* 42 (Summer, 1991): 179–213.

Boulton, Jeremy. *Neighbourhood and Society: A London Suburb in the Seventeenth Century.* Cambridge: Cambridge University Press, 1987.

Bourdieu, Pierre. *Distinction: A Social Critique of the Judgement of Taste.* London: Routledge, 1979.

Bowen, Barbara C. "Renaissance Collections of *Facetiae,* 1344–1490: A New Listing." *Renaissance Quarterly* 39, no. 1 (1986): 1–15.

——. "Renaissance Collections of *Facetiae,* 1499–1528: A New Listing." *Renaissance Quarterly* 39, no. 2 (1986): 263–75.

Bradbrook, Muriel. "Dramatic Role as Social Image: A Study of *The Taming of the Shrew.*" *Shakespeare Jahrbuch* 94 (1958): 132–50.

Brand, John. *Observations on the Popular Antiquities of Great Britain.* 3 vols. London: Bell, 1875.

Brant, Clare, and Diane Purkiss. *Women, Texts and Histories, 1575–1760.* London: Routledge, 1992.

Breitenberg, Mark. *Anxious Masculinity in Early Modern England.* Cambridge: Cambridge University Press, 1996.

Bremmer, Jan, and Herman Roodenberg. *A Cultural History of Humour.* Cambridge, U.K.: Polity, 1997.

Brewer, Derek. "Elizabethan Merry Tales and *The Merry Wives of Windsor:* Shakespeare and Popular Literature." In *Chaucer to Shakespeare: Essays in honour of Shinsuke Ando,* 145–61. Cambridge, U.K.: D. S. Brewer, 1992.

——. "Prose Jest-Books Mainly in the Sixteenth to Eighteenth Centuries in England." In Bremmer and Roodenberg, 90–111.

Brewer, E. Cobham. *Dictionary of Phrase and Fable.* Philadelphia: Lippincott, 1903.

Bridenthal, Renate, and Claudia Koontz. *Becoming Visible: Women in European History.* Boston: Houghton Mifflin, 1977.

Briggs, Katharine. *The Anatomy of Puck: An Examination of Fairy Beliefs among Shakespeare's Contemporaries and Successors.* London: Routledge, 1959.

Briggs, Robin. *Witches and Neighbours: The Social and Cultural Context of European Witchcraft.* London: HarperCollins, 1996.

Bristol, Michael. *Carnival and Theater: Plebeian Culture and the Structure of Authority in Renaissance England.* London: Methuen, 1985.
——. "Shamelessness in Arden: Early Modern Theater and the Obsolescence of Popular Theatricality." In *Print, Manuscript, Performance: The Changing Relations of the Media in Early Modern England,* edited by Arthur F. Marotti and Michael D. Bristol, 279–306. Columbus: Ohio State University Press, 2000.
Bronfman, Judith. *Chaucer's "Clerk's Tale": The Griselda Story Received, Rewritten, Illustrated.* New York: Garland, 1994.
——. "Griselda, Renaissance Woman." In Haselkorn and Travitsky, 211–23.
Brown, Pamela Allen. "'Fie, what a foolish duty call you this?' *Taming of the Shrew,* Women's Jest, and the Divided Audience." In *The Blackwell Companion to Shakespeare: The Comedies,* edited by Jean E. Howard and Richard Dutton. Oxford: Blackwell. Forthcoming.
——. "*Othello* and Italophobia." In *Shakespeare and Intertextuality: The Transition of Cultures Between Italy and England in the Early Modern Period,* edited by Michele Marrapodi. 179–92. Rome: Bulzoni, 2000.
Brunvand, Jan Harold. *"The Taming of the Shrew": A Comparative Study of Oral and Literary Traditions.* New York: Garland, 1991.
Bruster, Douglas. *Drama and the Market in the Age of Shakespeare.* Cambridge: Cambridge University Press, 1992.
Burke, Peter. "Frontiers of the Comic in Early Modern Italy, c. 1350–1750." In Bremmer and Roodenberg, 61–75.
——. "Oblique Approaches to the History of Popular Culture." In *Approaches to Popular Culture,* edited by C. W. E. Bigsby, 69–84. Bowling Green, Ohio: Bowling Green University Press, 1976.
——. *Popular Culture in Early Modern Europe.* New York: Harper Torchbooks, 1978.
Burt, Richard, and John Michael Archer, eds. *Enclosure Acts: Sexuality, Property, and Culture in Early Modern England.* Ithaca: Cornell University Press, 1994.
Butler, Judith. *Gender Trouble: Feminism and the Subversion of Identity.* New York: Routledge, 1990.
——. "Performative Acts and Gender Constitution: An Essay on Phenomenology and Feminist Theory." In *Performing Gender: Feminist Critical Theory and Theatre,* edited by Sue-Ellen Case. 270–82. Baltimore: Johns Hopkins University Press, 1990.
Butler, Martin. "Private and Occasional Drama." In *The Cambridge Companion to English Renaissance Drama.* 127–60. Cambridge: Cambridge University Press, 1990.
——. *Theatre and Crisis, 1632–1642.* Cambridge: Cambridge University Press, 1984.
Cahn, Susan. *Industry of Devotion: The Transformation of Women's Work in England, 1500–1660.* New York: Columbia University Press, 1987.

Callaghan, Dympna, ed. *A Feminist Companion to Shakespeare*. Oxford: Blackwell, 2000.

Callaghan, Dympna, Lorraine Helms, and Jyotsna Singh. *The Weyward Sisters: Shakespeare and Feminist Politics*. Oxford: Blackwell, 1994.

Campbell, Mildred. *The English Yeoman Under Elizabeth and the Early Stuarts*. New Haven, Conn.: Yale University Press, 1942.

Capp, Bernard. "The Double Standard Revisited." *Past and Present* 162 (1999): 70–100.

———. "'Long Meg of Westminster': A Mystery Solved." *Notes and Queries* 45, no. 3 (1998): 302–5.

———. "Popular Literature." In Reay (1985), 198–243.

———. "Separate Domains? Women and Authority in Early Modern England." In Griffiths, Fox, and Hindle, 117–45.

———. *The World of John Taylor the Water Poet, 1578–1653*. Oxford: Clarendon, 1994.

Carroll, William C. *Fat King, Lean Beggar*. Ithaca: Cornell University Press, 1996.

Certeau, Michel de. "On the Oppositional Practices of Everyday Life," translated by Fredric Jameson and Carol Lovitt. *Social Text* 3 (1980): 3–43.

———. *The Practices of Everyday Life*, translated by Steven Rendall. Berkeley: University of California Press, 1984.

Chambers, E. K. *The Elizabethan Stage*. 4 vols. Oxford: Clarendon, 1923.

———. *The Mediaeval Stage*. 2 vols. Oxford: Clarendon, 1903.

Charles, Lindsey, and Lorna Duffin. *Women and Work in Pre-Industrial England*. London: Croom Helm, 1985.

Chartier, Roger. *The Cultural Uses of Print in Early Modern France*, translated by Lydia G. Cochrane. Princeton: Princeton University Press, 1987.

———. "Culture as Appropriation: Popular Cultural Use in Early Modern France." In Kaplan, 229–53.

———. "Leisure and Sociability: Reading Aloud in Early Modern Europe." In *Urban Life in the Renaissance*, edited by Susan Zimmerman and F. E. Weissman. 103–120. Newark: University of Delaware Press, 1989.

Cholakian, Patricia Francis. "Heroic Infidelity: Novella 15." In Polachek, 62–76.

Cixous, Hélène. "The Laugh of the Medusa." In *New French Feminisms: An Anthology*, edited by Elaine Marks and Isabelle de Courtivron. New York: Schocken, 1981.

Clanchy, M. T. *From Memory to Written Record: England, 1066–1307*. Cambridge: Harvard University Press, 1979.

Clark, Alice. *Working Life of Women in the Seventeenth Century*. 1919; reprint, London: Routledge, 1992.

Clark, Peter. *The English Alehouse: A Social History, 1200–1830*. Harlow, U.K.: Longman, 1983.

Clark, Sandra. "The Economics of Marriage in the Broadside Ballad." Unpublished paper.

——. *The Elizabethan Pamphleteers*. London: Athlone, 1983.

——. "'Wives may be merry and yet honest too': Women and Wit in *The Merry Wives of Windsor and Some Other Plays*." In *"Fanned and Winnowed Opinions": Shakespearean Essays Presented to Harold Jenkins*, edited by John Mahon and Thomas A. Pendleton. 249–67. London: Methuen, 1987.

Clement, Robert J. *Anatomy of the Novella: The European Tale Collection from Boccacio and Chaucer to Cervantes*. New York: NYU Press, 1977.

Cook, Ann Jennalie. "'Bargaines of Inconstancie': Bawdy Behavior at the Playhouses." *Shakespeare Studies* 10 (1977): 171–90.

——. *The Privileged Playgoers of Shakespeare's London*. Princeton: Princeton University Press, 1981.

Cooke, Thomas D., and Benjamin Honeycutt, eds. *The Humor of the Fabliaux*. Columbia: University of Missouri Press, 1974.

Cooper, Helen. *Oxford Guide to Chaucer*. Oxford: Oxford University Press, 1984.

Cramer, Patricia. "Lordship, Bondage, and the Erotic: The Psychological Bases of Chaucer's 'Clerk's Tale.'" *Journal of English and Germanic Philology* 89 (October 1990): 491–511.

Crandall, Coryl. *"Swetnam, the Woman Hater": The Controversy and the Play*. Lafayette, Ind.: Purdue University Studies, 1969.

Crane, Mary Thomas. *Framing Authority: Sayings, Self and Society in Sixteenth-Century England*. Princeton: Princeton University Press, 1993.

Crane, William G. *Wit and Rhetoric in the Renaissance: The Formal Basis of Elizabethan Prose Style*. Gloucester, Mass.: Smith, 1964.

Crawford, Patricia. *Women and Religion in England, 1500–1720*. London: Routledge, 1993.

Cressy, David. *Birth, Marriage and Death: Ritual, Religion and the Life-Cycle in Tudor and Stuart England*. New York: Oxford University Press, 1997.

——. *Literacy and the Social Order: Reading and Writing in Tudor and Stuart England*. Cambridge: Cambridge University Press, 1980.

Cunnington, B.H. "A Skimmington in 1618." *Folklore* 41 (1930): 287–90.

Curlee, Judith. "'One Said a Jealous Wife was Like': The Constructions of Wives and Husbands in Seventeenth-Century English Jests." In *Performing Gender and Comedy: Theories, Texts, and Context*, edited by Shannon Hengen, 35–46. Amsterdam: Gordon and Breach, 1998.

Curtius, E.R. *European Literature and the Latin Middle Ages*. New York: Harper and Row, 1953.

Davidson, Clifford. "Women and the Medieval Stage." *Women's Studies* 11, nos. 1–2 (1984): 99–113.

Daly, Peter M. *Literature in the Light of the Emblem*. Toronto: University of Toronto Press, 1979.

Daniels, Richard. *"Uxor* Noah: Raven or Dove?" *Chaucer Review* 14, no. 1 (1979). 23–32.

Darnton, Robert. *The Great Cat Massacre and Other Episodes in French Cultural History.* New York: Vintage, 1985.

Davis, Natalie Zemon. *Fiction in the Archives: Pardon Tales and their Tellers in Sixteenth Century France.* Cambridge: Polity, 1988.

———. *Society and Culture in Early Modern France: Eight Essays.* Stanford: Stanford University Press, 1975.

———. "Some Themes and Tasks in the Study of Popular Religion." In *The Pursuit of Holiness in Late Medieval and Renaissance Religion,* edited by C. Trinkhaus. Leiden: Brill, 1974.

Davis, Natalie Zemon, and Arlette Farge, eds. *A History of Women III: Renaissance and Enlightenment Paradoxes.* Cambridge: Belknap Press of Harvard University Press, 1993.

Derrick, Thomas J. "Merry Tales in *Much Ado about Nothing." Thalia* 8, no. 2 (1985): 21–26.

Desens, Marliss C. *The Bed-Trick in English Renaissance Drama.* Newark: University of Delaware Press, 1994.

Detmer, Emily. "Civilizing Subordination: Domestic Violence and *The Taming of the Shrew." Shakespeare Quarterly* 48 (Fall, 1997): 273–94.

DiGangi, Mario. *The Homoerotics of Early Modern Drama.* Cambridge, U.K.: Cambridge University Press, 1994.

Dolan, Frances E. *Dangerous Familiars: Representations of Domestic Crime in England, 1550–1700.* Ithaca: Cornell University Press, 1994.

———. "Household Chastisements: Gender, Authority, and 'Domestic Violence.'" In Fumerton and Hunt, 204–28.

Donaldson, Ian. *The World Upside-Down: Comedy from Jonson to Fielding.* Oxford: Clarendon, 1970.

Doniger, Wendy. *The Bedtrick: Tales of Sex and Masquerade.* Chicago: University of Chicago Press, 2000.

Douglas, Mary. *Implicit Meanings.* London: Routledge, 1975.

———. *Purity and Danger: An Analysis of the Concepts of Pollution and Taboo.* London: Routledge, 1966.

———, ed. *Rules and Meanings: The Anthropology of Everyday Knowledge.* Harmondsworth, U.K.: Penguin, 1971.

Dugaw, Dianne. *Warrior Women and Popular Balladry, 1650–1850.* Cambridge: Cambridge University Press, 1989.

Eagleton, Terry. *Walter Benjamin; or, Towards a Revolutionary Criticism.* London: Verso, 1981.

Easton, Susan, Alun Hawkins, Stuart Laing, Linda Merricks, and Helen Walker, eds. *Disorder and Discipline: Popular Culture from 1550 to the Present.* Aldershot, U.K.: Temple Smith, 1988.

Eisenstein, Elizabeth. *The Printing Press As an Agent of Change: Communi-*

cations and Cultural Trasformations in Early Modern Europe. Cambridge: Cambridge University Press, 1979.

Elias, Norbert. *The Civilizing Process,* translated by E. Jephcott. Oxford: Blackwell, 1994.

Elliot, Robert C. *The Power of Satire: Magic, Ritual, Art.* Princeton: Princeton University Press, 1960.

Elsky, Martin. *Authorizing Words: Speech, Writing and Print in the English Renaissance.* Ithaca: Cornell University Press, 1989.

Emmison, F.G. *Elizabethan Life: Disorder.* Chelmsford, U.K.: Essex County Council, 1970.

——. *Elizabethan Life: Morals and the Church Courts.* Chelmsford, U.K.: Essex County Council, 1970, 1973.

Engle, Lars. "Chaucer, Bakhtin and Griselda." *Exemplaria* 1, no. 2 (1989): 429–59.

English, James F. *Comic Transactions: Literature, Humor, and the Politics of Community in Twentieth-Century Britain.* Ithaca: Cornell University Press, 1994.

Erickson, Amy. *Women and Property in Early Modern England.* New York: Routledge, 1993.

Ezell, Margaret J.M. "The Myth of Judith Shakespeare." *New Literary History* 21, no. 3 (1990): 580–91.

——. *The Patriarch's Wife: Literary Evidence and the History of the Family.* Chapel Hill: University of North Carolina Press, 1987.

Feinberg, Anat. "Representations of the Poor in Elizabethan and Stuart Drama." *Literature and History* 12, no. 2 (1986): 152–63.

Ferguson, Margaret W. *Dido's Daughters: Literacy, Gender, and Empire in Early Modern France and England.* Chicago: University of Chicago Press. Forthcoming.

——. "Response: Attending to Literacy." In Travitsky and Seeff, 265–79.

Ferguson, Margaret W., Maureen Quilligan, and Nancy J. Vickers, eds. *Rewriting the Renaissance: The Discourses of Sexual Difference in Early Modern Europe.* Chicago: University of Chicago Press, 1986.

Findlay, Alison. *A Feminist Perspective on Renaissance Drama.* Oxford: Blackwell, 1999.

Finnegan, Ruth. *Literacy and Orality: Studies in the Technology of Communication.* Oxford: Blackwell, 1988.

——. *Oral Poetry: Its Nature, Significance, and Social Context.* Cambridge: Cambridge University Press, 1977.

Finucci, Valerie, and Regina Schwartz, eds. *Desire in the Renaissance: Psychoanalysis and Literature.* Princeton: Princeton University Press, 1994.

Fletcher, Anthony. *Gender, Sex and Subordination in England 1500-1800.* New Haven: Yale University Press, 1995.

Fletcher, Anthony, and John Stevenson, eds. *Order and Disorder in Early Modern England.* Cambridge: Cambridge University Press, 1985.

Foley, John Miles. *Oral Traditional Literature.* Columbus, Ohio: Slavica, 1980.

Foley, Stephen. "Falstaff in Love and Other Stories from Tudor England." *Exemplaria* 1, no. 2 (1989): 226–46.

Fox, Adam. "Ballads, Libels and Popular Ridicule in Jacobean England." *Past and Present* 145 (1994): 47–84.

——. *Oral and Literate Culture in England, 1500–1700.* Oxford: Clarendon, 2000.

Foyster, Elizabeth. "A Laughing Matter? Marital Discord and Gender Control in Seventeenth-Century England." *Rural History* 4, no. 1 (1993): 5–21.

——. "Male Honour, Social Control and Wife Beating in Late Stuart England." *Transactions of the Royal Historical Society,* 6th ser., no. 6 (1996), 215–24).

——. *Manhood in Early Modern England: Honour, Sex and Marriage.* London: Longman, 1999.

Frantz, David O. *Festum Voluptatis: A Study of Renaissance Erotica.* Columbus: Ohio State University Press, 1989.

Freud, Sigmund. *Jokes and Their Relation to the Unconscious,* translated and edited by James Strachey. New York: Norton, 1960.

Freud, Sigmund, and D. E. Oppenheim. *Dreams in Folklore.* New York: International Universities Press, 1958.

Frye, Susan, and Karen Robertson, eds. *Maids and Mistresses, Cousins and Queens: Women's Alliances in Early Modern England.* New York: Oxford University Press, 1999.

Fumerton, Patricia, and Simon Hunt, eds. *Renaissance Culture and the Everyday.* Philadelphia: University of Pennsylvania Press, 1999.

Furnivall, Frederick J. *Early English Meals and Manners.* London: Oxford University Press, 1868.

Gardiner, Harold C. *Mysteries' End: An Investigation of the Last Days of the Medieval Religious Stage.* New Haven: Yale University Press, 1946.

Garner, Shirley Nelson. "*The Taming of the Shrew:* Inside or Outside of the Joke?" In *"Bad" Shakespeare: Revaluations of the Shakespeare Canon,* edited by Maurice Charney. 105–19. Rutherford, N.J.: Fairleigh Dickinson University Press, 1988.

Gasper, Julia. *The Dragon and the Dove: The Plays of Thomas Dekker.* Oxford: Clarendon, 1990.

Gassner, John, ed. *Medieval and Tudor Drama.* New York: Applause, 1987.

Gay, Penny. *As She Likes It: Shakespeare's Unruly Women.* London: Routledge, 1994.

Geertz, Clifford. *The Interpretation of Cultures.* New York: Basic Books, 1973.

George, Margaret. *Women in the First Capitalist Society: Experiences of Seventeenth Century England.* Brighton, U.K.: Harvester, 1988.

Gillooly, Eileen. *Smile of Discontent: Humor, Gender and Nineteenth-Century British Fiction.* Chicago: University of Chicago Press, 1999.

Gowing, Laura. *Domestic Dangers: Women, Words, and Sex in Early Modern London*. Oxford: Clarendon, 1996.

——. "Language, Power, and the Law: Women's Slander Litigation in Early Modern London." In Kermode and Walker, 26–47.

——. "Women, Status and the Popular Culture of Dishonour." *Transactions of the Royal Historical Society*, 6th ser., no. 6 (1996): 225–34.

Gray, Douglas. "Rough Music: Some Early Invectives and Flytings." In *English Satire and the Satiric Tradition*, edited by Claude Rawson. 21–43. Oxford: Blackwell, 1984.

Gray, Frances. *Women and Laughter*. Charlottesville: University Press of Virginia, 1994.

Greenbaum, Andrea. "Women's Comic Voices: The Art and Craft of Female Humor." *American Studies* 38, no. 1 (1997): 117–38.

Griffiths, Paul, Adam Fox, and Steve Hindle, eds. *The Experience of Authority in Early Modern England*. New York: St. Martin's, 1996.

Grudin, Robert. "Renaissance Laughter: The Jests in Castiglione's *Il Cortegiano*." *Neophilologus* 58 (1974): 199–204.

Gurevitch, Aaron. *Medieval Popular Culture: Problems of Belief and Perception*. Cambridge: Cambridge University Press, 1988.

Gurr, Andrew. *Playgoing in Shakespeare's London*. Cambridge: Cambridge University Press, 1987.

Habermas, Jurgen. *The Structural Transformation of the Public Sphere: An Inquiry into a Category of Bourgeois Society*. Cambridge: MIT Press, 1989.

Hackel, Heidi Brayman. " 'Rowme' of Its Own: Printed Drama in Early Libraries." In *A New History of English Drama*, edited by John D. Cox and David Scott Kastan. 113–32. New York: Columbia University Press, 1997.

Hair, Paul. *Before the Bawdy Court: Selections from Church Court and Other Records Relating to the Correction of Moral Offences in England, Scotland and New England, 1300–1800*. New York: Harper and Row, 1972.

Hajzyk, Helena. "Some Little-Known Ladies of Lincolnshire, 1603–1640." *Lincolnshire History and Archeology* 13 (1978): 39–42.

Halasz, Alexandra. *The Marketplace of Print: Pamphlets and the Public Sphere in Early Modern England*. Cambridge: Cambridge University Press, 1997.

Hammerton, A. James. "The Targets of 'Rough Music': Respectability and Domestic Violence in Victorian England." *Gender and History* 3, no. 1 (1991): 23–45, 27.

Hanawalt, Barbara A. *"Of Good and Ill Repute": Gender and Social Control in Medieval England*. New York: Oxford University Press, 1998.

——, ed. *Women and Work in Preindustrial Europe*. Bloomington: Indiana University Press, 1986.

Harbage, Alfred. *Shakespeare's Audience*. New York: Columbia University Press, 1941.

Harris, Tim, ed. *Popular Culture in England, c. 1500–1800*. New York: St. Martin's, 1995.

Harvey, Elizabeth. *Ventriloquized Voices: Feminist Theory and English Renaissance Texts*. London: Routledge, 1992.

Haselkorn, Anne, and Betty Travitsky, eds. *The Renaissance Englishwomen in Print: Counterbalancing the Canon*. Amherst: University of Massachusetts Press, 1990.

Hawkins, Harriet. "The Victim's Side: Chaucer's *Clerk's Tale* and Webster's *Duchess of Malfi*." *Signs* 1 (1975): 339–62.

Haynes, Jonathan. *The Social Relations of Jonson's Theater*. Cambridge: Cambridge University Press, 1992.

Hazlitt, W. C. *Studies in Jocular Literature*. London, 1890.

Helgerson, Richard. *Self-Crowned Laureates: Spenser, Jonson, Milton and the Literary System*. Berkeley: University of California Press, 1983.

——. "The Women's World of Shakespeare's Windsor." In Fumerton and Hunt, 171–75.

Henderson, Katherine Usher, and Barbara F. McManus. *Half Humankind: Contexts and Texts of the Controversy about Women in England*. Urbana: University of Illinois Press, 1985.

Herman, Peter C. "Leaky Ladies and Droopy Dames: The Grotesque Realism of Skelton's *The Tunnynge of Elinor Rummynge*." In *Rethinking the Henrician Era: Essays on Early Tudor Texts and Contexts*, edited by Peter C. Herman, 145–67. Urbana: University of Illinois Press, 1994.

Herrup, Cynthia. *The Common Peace: Participation and the Criminal Law in Seventeenth Century England*. Cambridge: Cambridge University Press, 1987.

Hill, Carl. *The Soul of Wit: Joke Theory from Grimm to Freud*. Lincoln: University of Nebraska Press, 1993.

Hindle, Steve. "The Shaming of Margaret Knowsley: Gossip, Gender, and the Experience of Authority in Early Modern England." *Continuity and Change* 9, no. 3 (1994): 391–419.

Hines, John. *The Fabliau in English*. London: Longman, 1993.

Hohne, Karen, and Helen Wussow, eds. *A Dialogue of Voices: Feminist Literary Theory and Bakhtin*. Minneapolis: University of Minnesota Press, 1994.

Holcomb, Chris. *Mirth Making: The Rhetorical Discourse on Jesting in Early Modern England*. Columbia: University of South Carolina Press, 2001.

Holstun, James, ed. *Pamphlet Wars: Prose in the English Revolution*. London: Cass, 1992.

Houlbrooke, Ralph. *The English Family, 1450–1700*. London: Longman, 1984.

——. "Women's Social Life and Common Action in England from the Fifteenth Century to the Eve of the Civil War." *Continuity and Change* 1, no. 2 (1986): 171–89.

Howard, Jean E. *The Stage and Social Struggle in Early Modern England*. London: Routledge, 1994.

Howard, Jean E., and Marion F. O'Connor, eds. *Shakespeare Reproduced: The Text in History and Ideology.* London: Methuen, 1987.

Howell, Martha. *Women, Production and Patriarchy in Late Medieval Cities.* Chicago: University of Chicago Press, 1986.

Hoy, Cyrus. *Introductions, Notes, and Commentaries to Texts in "The Dramatic Works of Thomas Dekker."* 4 vols. Cambridge: Cambridge University Press, 1980.

Huizinga, Johan. *Homo Ludens: A Study of the Play Element in Culture.* Boston: Beacon, 1950.

Hull, Suzanne W. *Chaste, Silent and Obedient: English Books for Women, 1475–1640.* San Marino, Calif.: Huntington Library, 1982.

Hunt, Margaret. "Wife Beating, Domesticity and Women's Independence." *Gender and History* 4, no. 1 (1992): 10–33.

Hutson, Lorna. *The Usurer's Daughter: Male Friendship and Fictions of Women in Sixteenth-Century England.* London: Routledge, 1994.

Hutton, Ronald. *The Rise and Fall of Merry England: The Ritual Year 1400–1700.* Oxford: Oxford University Press, 1994.

Ingram, Angela. *In the Posture of a Whore: Changing Attitudes to "Bad" Women in Elizabethan and Jacobean Drama.* 2 vols. Salzburg: Institut für Anglistik und Amerikanistik, 1984.

Ingram, Martin. *Church Courts, Sex and Marriage in England, 1570–1640.* Cambridge: Cambridge University Press, 1987.

——. "The Reform of Popular Culture? Sex and Marriage in Early Modern England." In Reay (1985), 129–65.

——. "Ridings, Rough Music and Mocking Rhymes in Early Modern England." In Reay (1985), 166–97.

——. "'Scolding women cucked or washed': A Crisis in Gender Relations in Early Modern England?" In Kermode and Walker, 48–80.

Jardine, Lisa. *Still Harping on Daughters: Women and Drama in the Age of Shakespeare.* 2d ed. New York: Columbia University Press, 1989.

Johnson, Lesley. "Reincarnations of Griselda: Contexts for the *Clerk's Tale?*" In *Feminist Readings in Middle English Literature,* edited by Ruth Evans and Lesley Johnson. London: Routledge, 1994.

Jones, Ann Rosalind. "Counterattacks on 'the Bayter of Women': Three Pamphleteers of the Early Seventeenth Century." In Haselkorn and Travitsky, 45–62.

——. *Currency of Eros: Women's Love Lyric in Europe, 1540–1620.* Bloomington: Indiana University Press, 1990.

——. "Maidservants of London: Sisterhoods of Kinship and Labor." In Frye and Robertson. 21–32.

Jones, Ann Rosalind, and Peter Stallybrass. *Renaissance Clothing and the Materials of Memory.* Cambridge, U.K.: Cambridge University Press, 2000.

Jones, Emrys. "London in the Seventeenth Century: An Ecological Approach." *London Journal* 6 no. 2 (1980): 123–33.

Jordan, Constance. *Renaissance Feminism: Literary Texts and Political Models.* Ithaca: Cornell University Press, 1990.

——. "Renaissance Women and the Question of Class." In *Sexuality and Gender in Early Modern Europe: Institutions, Texts, Images,* edited by James Grantham Turner, 90–106. Cambridge: Cambridge University Press, 1993.

Jost, Jean E., ed. *Chaucer's Humor: Critical Essays.* New York: Garland, 1994.

Judges, A. V. *The Elizabethan Underworld.* 1930; reprint, New York: Octagon, 1965.

Kahn, Coppélia. *Man's Estate: Masculine Identity in Shakespeare.* Berkeley: University of California Press, 1981.

Kalter, Anne K. *The Pícara: From Hera to Fantasy Heroine.* Bowling Green, Ohio: Bowling Green State University Press, 1991.

Kaplan, M. Lindsay. *The Culture of Slander in Early Modern England.* Cambridge: Cambridge University Press, 1995.

Kaplan, Steven L., ed. *Understanding Popular Culture: Europe from the Middle Ages to the Nineteenth Century.* Berlin: Mouton, 1984.

Kastan, David Scott, and Peter Stallybrass, eds. *Staging the Renaissance: Reinterpretations of Elizabethan and Jacobean Drama.* New York: Routledge, 1991.

Kay, W. David. *Ben Jonson: A Literary Life.* New York: St. Martin's, 1995.

Kegl, Rosemary. "'The Adoption of Abominable Terms': The Insults that Shape Windsor's Middle Class." *English Literary History* 61 no. 2 (1994): 253–78.

Kelly, Joan. "Early Feminist Theory and the *Querelle des Femmes,* 1400–1789." *Signs* 8, no. 1 (1982): 4–28.

——. *Women, History, and Theory: The Essays of Joan Kelly.* Chicago: University of Chicago Press, 1984.

Kennedy, Gwynne. *Just Anger: Representing Women's Anger in Early Modern England.* Carbondale: Southern Illinois University Press, 2000.

Kermode, Jenny, and Garthine Walker, eds. *Women, Crime, and the Courts in Early Modern England.* Chapel Hill: University of North Carolina Press, 1994.

Kernan, Alvin. *The Cankered Muse: Satire of the English Renaissance.* New Haven: Yale University Press, 1959.

Kinney, Arthur. *Rogues, Vagabonds, and Sturdy Beggars.* Amherst: University of Massachusetts Press, 1990.

Klapisch-Zuber, Christiane. "The Griselda Complex: Dowry and Marriage Gifts in the Quattrocento." In *Women, Family, and Ritual in Renaissance Italy,* translated by Lydia Cochrane, 213–46. Chicago: University of Chicago Press, 1985.

Korda, Natasha. "Domesticating Commodities in *The Taming of the Shrew.*" *Shakespeare Quarterly* 47 (Summer 1996): 109–31.

Kunzle, David. *The Early Comic Strip: Narrative Strips and Picture Stories in the European Broadsheet from c. 1450 to 1825.* Berkeley: University of California Press, 1973.

Lamb, Mary Ellen, "Taken by the Fairies: Fairy Practices and the Production of Popular Culture." *Shakespeare Quarterly* 51 (Fall 2000): 277–312.

Laroque, Francois. *Shakespeare's Festive World: Elizabethan Seasonal Entertainment and the Professional Stage.* Cambridge: Cambridge University Press, 1993.

Laslett, Peter. *The World We Have Lost: England Before the Industrial Age.* 3d ed. New York: Scribner's, 1984.

Legman, Gershon. *The Horn Book: Studies in Erotic Folklore and Bibliography.* New Hyde Park, N.Y.: University Books, 1964.

Leinwand, Theodore. *The City Staged: Jacobean Comedy, 1603–1613.* Madison: University of Wisconsin Press, 1986.

Levin, Richard. "Another 'Source' for *The Alchemist* and Another Look at Source Studies." *English Literary Renaissance* 28 no. 2 (1998): 215.

——. "Women in the Renaissance Theatre Audience." *Shakespeare Quarterly* 40 (Summer 1989): 165–74.

Lipking, Joanna B. "Traditions of the *Facetiae* and Their Influence in Tudor England." Ph.D. diss., Columbia University, 1970.

Luborsky, Ruth. "Connections and Disconnections Between Images and Texts: The Case of the Secular Tudor Book Illustration." *Word and Image* 3 no. 1 (1987): 74–85.

Malcolmson, Robert W. *Popular Recreations in English Society, 1700–1850.* Cambridge: Cambridge University Press, 1973.

Maley, Willy. *A Spenser Chronology.* Lanham, Md.: Barnes and Noble, 1994.

Manley, Lawrence, ed. *London in the Age of Shakespeare.* University Park: Penn State University Press, 1986.

Marcus, Leah S. *The Politics of Mirth: Jonson, Herrick, Milton, Marvell, and the Defense of Old Holiday Pastimes.* Chicago: University of Chicago Press, 1986.

——. *Puzzling Shakespeare: Localization and Its Discontents.* Berkeley: University of California Press, 1988.

Marotti, Arthur F., and Michael D. Bristol, eds. *Print, Manuscript, Performance: The Changing Relations of the Media in Early Modern England.* Columbus: Ohio State University Press, 2000.

Marx, William G. "The Problem with Mrs. Noah: The Search for Performance Credibility in the Chester *Noah's Flood* Play." In Alford, 109–26.

Mason, John. *Gentlefolk in the Making: Studies in the History of English Courtesy Literature and Related Topics from 1531 to 1774.* New York: Octagon, 1971.

Maus, Katharine Eisaman. "Horns of Dilemma: Jealousy, Gender, and Spectatorship in English Renaissance Drama." *English Literary History* 54 (1987): 561–84.

McCarthy, Penny. "'Milksop Muses' or Why Not Mary?" *Studies in English Literature* 40, no. 1 (2000): 21–40.

McClellan, William. "Lars Engle—'Chaucer, Bakhtin, and Griselda': A Response." *Exemplaria* 1, no. 2 (1989). 499–506.

McGehee, Paul. "The Role of Laughter and Humor in Growing Up Female." In *On Becoming Female: Perspectives on Development,* edited by Claire B. Kopp. New York: Plenum, 1979.

McLean, Marie. "Oppositional Practices in Women's Traditional Narrative." *New Literary History* 19, no. 1 (1987): 37–50.

McLuskie, Kathleen. *Dekker and Heywood: Professional Dramatists.* London: St. Martin's, 1994.

——. "Feminist Deconstruction: The Example of Shakespeare's *Taming of the Shrew.*" *Red Letters: Communist Party Literature Journal* 12 (1982): 33–40.

——. *Renaissance Dramatists.* Atlantic Highlands, N.J.: Humanities Press International, 1989.

McManus, Barbara. "Whose Voice Is It Anyway? Teaching Early Women Writers." In *Crossing Boundaries: Attending to Early Modern Women,* edited by Jane Donawerth and Adele Seeff, 227–41. Newark: University of Delaware Press, 2000.

McPherson, David C. *Shakespeare, Jonson, and the Myth of Venice.* Newark: University of Delaware Press, 1990.

Mendelson, Sara, and Patricia Crawford. *Women in Early Modern England.* Oxford: Clarendon, 1998.

Merry, Sally Engle. "Rethinking Gossip and Scandal." In *Toward a General Theory of Social Control.* Vol. 1, *Fundamentals,* edited by D. Black. Orlando, Fla.: Academic, 1984.

Mikalachi, Jodi. "Women's Networks and the Female Vagrant." In *Maids and Mistresses, Cousins and Queens: Women's Alliances in Early Modern England,* edited by Susan Frye and Karen Robertson, 52–69. New York: Oxford University Press, 1999.

Mills, David. "Chester's Midsummer Show: Creation and Adaptation." In *Festive Drama,* edited by Meg Twycross, 132–54. Cambridge, U.K.: Brewer, 1996.

Montrose, Louis Adrian. "*A Midsummer Night's Dream* and the Shaping Fantasies of Elizabethan Culture: Gender, Power, Form." In Ferguson, Quilligan, and Vickers, 61–94.

Morgan, Paul. "Frances Wolfreston and 'Hor Bouks': A Seventeenth-Century Woman Book-Collector." *Library* 11, no. 3 (1989): 197–219.

Morgan-Russell, Simon. "'No Good Thing Ever Comes Out of It': Male Expectation and Female Alliance in Dekker and Webster's *Westward Ho.*" in Frye and Robertson, 70–84.

Morreall, John, ed. *The Philosophy of Laughter and Humor.* Albany, N.Y.: SUNY Press, 1987.

Morse, Charlotte. "The Exemplary Griselda." *Studies in the Age of Chaucer* 7 (1985): 51–87.

Morton, Frederick M. *Woman in Epigram: Flashes of Wit, Wisdom and Satire from the World's Literature.* Chicago: McClurg, 1899.

Moulton, Ian Frederick. *Before Pornography: Erotic Writing in Early Modern England.* New York: Oxford University Press, 2000.

Moxey, Keith. *Peasants, Warriors, and Wives: Popular Imagery in the Reformation.* Chicago: University of Chicago Press, 1989.

Muchembled, Robert. *Popular Culture and Elite Culture in France, 1400–1750.* Baton Rouge: Louisiana State University Press, 1985.

Mullaney, Steven. *The Place of the Stage: License, Play and Power in Renaissance England.* Chicago: University of Chicago Press, 1988.

Mullenix, Elizabeth Reitz. "Private Women/Public Acts: Petticoat Government and the Performance of Resistance." *The Drama Review* 46, no. 1 (Spring 2002): 104–117.

Nash, Jerry C. "The Male Butt of Comic Infidelity." In *Heroic Virtue, Comic Infidelity: Reassessing Marguerite de Navarre's "Heptaméron,"* edited by Dora E. Polachek, 152–73. Amherst, Mass.: Hestia, 1993.

Neuberg, Victor. *Popular Literature: A History and a Guide.* Harmondsworth, U.K.: Penguin, 1977.

Newcomb, Lori Humphrey. *Reading Popular Romance in Early Modern England.* New York: Columbia University Press, 2002.

——. "The Romance of Service: The Simple History of Pandosto's Servant Readers." In *Framing Elizabethan Fictions: Contemporary Approaches to Early Modern Prose,* edited by Constance C. Relihan, 117–40. Kent State University Press, 1996.

Newman, Karen. *Fashioning Femininity and English Renaissance Drama: Women in Culture and Society.* Chicago: University of Chicago Press, 1991.

Novy, Marianne. "'An You Smile Not, He's Gagged': Mutuality in Shakespearean Comedy." In *Love's Argument: Gender Relations in Shakespeare.* Chapel Hill: University of North Carolina Press, 1984.

Nussbaum, Felicity. *The Brink of All We Hate: English Satires on Women, 1660–1750.* Lexington: University Press of Kentucky, 1984.

O'Connell, Sheila. *The Popular Print in England.* London: British Museum, 1999.

O'Malley, Susan Gushee. *Custom Is an Idiot.* Urbana: University of Illinois Press. Forthcoming.

Oldham, James C. "On Pleading the Belly: A History of the Jury of Matrons." *Criminal Justice History* 6 (1985): 1–64.

Ong, Walter. *Orality and Literacy: The Technologizing of the Word.* London: Methuen, 1982.

——. "Oral Residue in Tudor Prose Style." *PMLA* 80, no. 3 (1968): 145–54.

Orgel, Stephen. *Impersonations: The Performance of Gender in Shakespeare's England.* Cambridge: Cambridge University Press, 1996.

——. "Nobody's Perfect: Or Why Did the English Stage Take Boys for Women?" *The South Atlantic Quarterly* 88, no. 1 (Winter 1989), 7–29.

Orlin, Lena Cowen. *Elizabethan Households: An Anthology*. Washington, D.C.: Folger Shakespeare Library, 1995.

——. *Private Matters and Public Culture in Post-Reformation England*. Ithaca, N.Y.: Cornell University Press, 1994.

——. "Women on the Threshold." *Shakespeare Studies* 25 (1997): 50–58.

Otto, Beatrice L. *Fools Are Everywhere: The Court Jester Around the World*. Chicago: University of Chicago, 2001.

Parker, Patricia. *Literary Fat Ladies: Rhetoric, Gender, Property*. London: Methuen, 1987.

Parten, Anne. "Falstaff's Horns: Masculine Inadequacy and Feminine Mirth in *The Merry Wives of Windsor*." *Studies in Philology* 82, no. 2 (1985): 184–99.

——. "Masculine Adultery and Female Rejoinders in Shakespeare, Dekker, and Sharpham." *Mosaic* 17 (1984): 9–18.

Paster, Gail Kern. *The Body Embarrassed: Drama and the Disciplines of Shame in Early Modern Drama*. Ithaca: Cornell University Press, 1993.

Patterson, Annabel. *Fables of Power: Aesopian Writing and Political History*. Durham: Duke University Press, 1991.

——. *Shakespeare and the Popular Voice*. Oxford: Blackwell, 1989.

Pechter, Edward. "*Patient Grissil* and the Trials of Marriage." In *Elizabethan Theatre IV*, edited by A. L. Magnusson and C. E. McGee. 83–108. Toronto: Meany, 1996.

Peterson del Mar, David. *"What Trouble I Have Seen": A History of Violence Against Wives*. Cambridge: Harvard University Press, 1996.

Polachek, Dora E., ed. *Heroic Virtue, Comic Infidelity: Reassessing Marguerite de Navarre's "Heptaméron."* Amherst, Mass.: Hestia, 1993.

Prescott, Anne Lake. "Crime and Carnival at Chelsea: Widow Edith and Thomas More's Household." In *Miscellanea Moreana: Essays for Germain Marc'hadour*, edited by Clara E. Murphy, Henri Gibaud, and Mario A. Di Cesare. 247–64. Binghamton, N.Y.: Medieval and Renaissance Texts and Studies, 1989.

Prior, Mary. "Women and the Urban Economy, 1500–1800." In *Women in English Society*, edited by Mary Prior, 93–117. London: Methuen, 1985.

Purdie, Susan. *Comedy: The Mastery of Discourse*. Toronto: University of Toronto Press, 1993.

Purkiss, Diane. "Material Girls: The Seventeenth-Century Woman Debate." In *Women, Texts and Histories, 1575–1760*, by Clare Brant and Diane Purkiss, 69–101. London: Routledge, 1992.

——. *Troublesome Things: A History of Fairies and Fairy Stories*. London: Allen Lane, 2000.

Quaife, G. R. *Wanton Wenches and Wayward Wyves: Peasants and Illicit Sex in Early Seventeenth Century England.* New Brunswick, N.J.: Rutgers University Press, 1979.

Rackin, Phyllis. "Foreign Country: The Place of Women and Sexuality in Shakespeare's Historical World." In Burt and Archer, 68–95.

———. "Misogyny Is Everywhere." In Callaghan (2000), 42–58.

Randolph, Mary Clare. "Female Satirists of Ancient Ireland." *Southern Folklore Quarterly* 6 (1942): 75–87.

Rappaport, Stephen. *Worlds Within Worlds: Structures of Life in Sixteenth-Century London.* Cambridge: Cambridge University Press, 1989.

Reay, Barry, ed. *Popular Culture in Seventeenth Century England.* London: Croom Helm, 1985.

———. *Popular Cultures in England, 1550–1750.* London: Longman, 1998.

Relihan, Constance C., ed. *Framing Elizabethan Fictions: Contemporary Approaches to Early Modern Prose.* Kent, Ohio: Kent State University Press, 1996.

Richlin, Amy. *The Garden of Priapus: Aggression in Roman Humor.* New York: Oxford University Press, 1992.

Riddle, James, and Stanley Stewart. *Jonson's Spenser: Evidence and Historical Criticism.* Pittsburgh: Duquesne University Press, 1995.

Riggs, David. *Ben Jonson: A Life.* Cambridge: Harvard University Press, 1989.

Roberts, Sasha. "Women Reading Shakespeare in the Seventeenth Century." Unpublished essay, 2002.

Rogers, Katharine. *The Troublesome Helpmate: A History of Misogyny in Literature.* Seattle: University of Washington Press, 1966.

Rollins, Hyder Edward. "An Analytical Index to Ballad Entries in the Registers of the Company of the Stationers of London, 1557–1709." *Studies in Philology* 21, no. 1 (1924).

———. "The Black-Letter Broadside Ballad," *PMLA* 27 (1919): 258–339.

Rollinson, David. *The Local Origins of Modern Society: Gloucestershire, 1500–1800.* London: Routledge, 1992.

Roper, Lyndal. *Oedipus and the Devil: Witchcraft, Sexuality and Religion in Early Modern Europe.* London: Routledge, 1994.

Rosenfeld, Sybil. *Strolling Players and Drama in the Provinces, 1660–1675.* Cambridge: Cambridge University Press, 1939.

Rubin, Gayle. "The Traffic in Women: Notes on the 'Political Economy' of Sex." In *Toward an Anthropology of Women,* edited by Rayna Reiter, 157–210. New York: Monthly Review, 1975.

Russell, H. Diane. *Eve/Ave: Woman in Renaissance and Baroque Prints.* New York: National Gallery of Art/Feminist Press, 1990.

Russo, Mary. *The Female Grotesque: Risk, Excess, and Modernity.* New York: Routledge, 1995.

Salingar, Leo. *Shakespeare and the Traditions of Comedy.* Cambridge: Cambridge University Press, 1974.

Sanders, Barry. *Sudden Glory: Laughter as Subversive History*. Boston: Beacon, 1995.

Sanders, Eve Rachele. *Gender and Literacy on Stage in Early Modern England*. Cambridge: Cambridge University Press, 1998.

Schechner, Richard. *Performance Theory*. Rev. ed. London: Routledge, 1994.

Schenck, Mary Jane Stearns. *The Fabliaux: Tales of Wit and Deception*. Amsterdam: Benjamins, 1987.

Scott, James C. *Domination and the Arts of Resistance: Hidden Transcripts*. New Haven: Yale University Press, 1990.

———. *Weapons of the Weak: Everyday Forms of Peasant Resistance*. New Haven: Yale University Press, 1985.

Scribner, Robert. *For the Sake of Simple Folk: Popular Propaganda for the German Reformation*. Cambridge: Cambridge University Press, 1981.

———. "Is a History of Popular Culture Possible?" *History of European Ideas* 10, no. 2 (1980): 175–91.

Sedgwick, Eve Kosofsky. *Between Men: English Literature and Male Homosexual Desire*. New York: Columbia University Press, 1985.

Seidel, Michael. "Crisis Rhetoric and Satiric Power." *New Literary History* 20, no. 1 (1988): 165–86.

Sharp, Buchanon. *In Contempt of All Authority: Rural Artisans and Riot in the West of England, 1586–1660*. Berkeley: University of California Press, 1980.

Sharpe, J. A. *Defamation and Sexual Slander in Early Modern England: The Church Courts at York*. Borthwick Papers, no. 38. York, U.K.: University of York, 1980.

———. "The People and the Law." In Reay (1985), 247–57.

———. "Plebeian Marriage in Stuart England: Some Evidence from Popular Literature" *Transactions of the Royal Historical Society*, 5th ser., no. 36 1986): 69–90.

———. "Such Disagreement betwyx Neighbors." In *Disputes and Settlements: Law and Human Relations in the West*, edited by John Bossy, 167–87. Cambridge: Cambridge University Press, 1983.

———. "Women, Witchcraft and the Legal Process" In Kermode and Walker 106–24.

Shepard, Leslie. *The Broadside Ballad: A Study in Origins and Meaning*. London: Jenkins, 1962.

———. *The History of Street Literature*. Newton Abbott, U.K.: David and Charles, 1972.

Shepherd, Simon. *Amazons and Warrior Women*. Brighton, U.K.: Harvester, 1981.

Shershow, Scott Cutler. "New Life: Cultural Studies and the Problem of 'The Popular.'" *Textual Practice* 12, no. 1 (1998): 23–47.

———. *Puppets and "Popular" Culture*. Ithaca: Cornell University Press, 1995.

Shevelow, Kathryn. *Women and Print Culture: The Construction of Femininity in the Early Periodical.* London: Routledge, 1989.

Simpson, C. M. *The British Broadside Ballad and Its Music.* New Brunswick: Rutgers University Press, 1966.

Smallwood, R. L. "'Here, in the friars': Immediacy and Theatricality in *The Alchemist.*" *Review of English Studies* 32, no. 126 (1980): 142–60.

Smith, Bruce R. *The Acoustic World of Early Modern England: Attending to the O-Factor.* Chicago: University of Chicago Press, 1999.

Smith, Molly. *Breaking Boundaries: Politics and Play in the Drama of Shakespeare and His Contemporaries.* Aldershot, U.K.: Ashgate, 1998.

Spacks, Patricia Meyer. *Gossip.* New York: Knopf, 1985.

Spargo, John. *Virgil the Necromancer: Studies in Virgilian Legends.* Cambridge: Harvard University Press, 1934.

Spivack, Charlotte. "Woman on the Jacobean Stage: Type and Anti-type." In *Traditions and Innovations: Essays on British Literature of the Middle Ages and the Renaissance,* edited by Robert A. White and David G. Allen, 177–86. Newark: University of Delaware Press, 1990.

Spufford, Margaret. "First Steps in Literacy: The Reading and Writing Experiences of the Humblest Seventeenth-Century Autobiographers." *Social History* 4 (1979): 407–35.

———. *Small Books and Pleasant Histories: Popular Fiction and Its Readership in Seventeenth-Century England.* Athens: University of Georgia Press, 1982.

Stallybrass, Peter. "Patriarchal Territories: The Body Enclosed." In Ferguson, Quilligan, and Vickers, 123–44.

Stallybrass, Peter, and Allon White. *The Politics and Poetics of Transgression.* Ithaca: Cornell University Press, 1987.

Stanton, Domna C. "Recuperating Women and the Man behind the Screen." In Turner 247–66.

Stavreva, Kirilka. "Fighting Words: Witchspeak in Late Elizabethan Docu-Fiction." *Journal of Medieval and Renaissance Studies* 30, no. 2 (2000): 309–38.

Stevenson, Burton. *The Home Book of Proverbs, Maxims, and Familiar Phrases.* New York: Macmillan, 1948.

Stevenson, Laura Caroline. *Praise and Paradox: Merchants and Craftsmen in Elizabethan Popular Literature.* Cambridge: Cambridge University Press, 1984.

Stokes, James. "Women and Mimesis in Medieval and Renaissance Somerset (and Beyond)." *Comparative Drama* 27, no. 2 (1993): 186–96.

Stone, Laurence. *The Family, Sex, and Marriage in England, 1500–1800.* New York: Harper and Row, 1977.

Storm, Melvin. "*Uxor* and Alison: Noah's Wife in the Flood Plays and Chaucer's Wife of Bath." *Modern Language Quarterly* 48, no. 4 (1987): 303–19.

Streip, Katharine. "Just a *Cérèbrale:* Jean Rhys, Women's Humor, and *Ressentiment." Representations* 45 (1994): 117–44.

Stretton, Timothy. *Women Waging Law in Elizabethan England.* Cambridge: Cambridge University Press, 1998.

Strong, Roy. *The Cult of Elizabeth: Elizabethan Portraiture and Pageantry.* London: Thomas and Hudson, 1977.

Sullivan, Garrett, and Linda Woodbridge. "Popular Culture in Print." In *The Cambridge Companion to English Literature, 1500-1600,* edited by Arthur Kinney. Cambridge, U.K.: Cambridge University Press, 2000.

Suzuki, Mihoko. "Margaret Cavendish and the Female Satirist." *Studies in English Literature* 37 (1997): 483–500.

Taylor, Gary. *Castration: An Abbreviated History of Western Manhood.* New York: Routledge, 2000.

Teague, Frances, ed. *Acting Funny: Comic Theory and Practice in Shakespeare's Plays.* Rutherford, N.J.: Fairleigh Dickinson University Press, 1994.

Tebbutt, Melanie. *Women's Talk? A Social History of "Gossip" in Working-Class Neighbourhoods, 1880–1960.* Aldershot, U.K.: Scolar, 1995.

Thomas, Keith. "The Double Standard." *Journal of the History of Ideas* 20 (1959): 195–216.

———. "The Meaning of Literacy in Early Modern England." In *The Written Word: Literacy in Transition,* edited by Gerd Baumann. 97–131. Oxford: Clarendon, 1986,

———. "The Place of Laughter in Tudor and Stuart England." *Times Literary Supplement,* January 21, 1977, pp. 77–81.

———. *Religion and the Decline of Magic.* 1971; reprint, Harmondsworth, U.K.: Penguin, 1978.

Thompson, E. P. *Customs in Common: Studies in Traditional Popular Culture.* New York: New Press, 1993.

Thompson, Janet A. *Wives, Widows, Witches and Bitches: Women in Seventeenth Century Devon.* New York: Lang, 1993.

Thompson, Roger. "Popular Reading and Humour in Restoration England." *Journal of Popular Culture* 9, no. 3 (1975): 653–71.

———. *Unfit for Modest Ears.* London: Macmillan, 1979.

Thompson, Stith. *Motif-Index of Folk Literature.* 6 vols. Bloomington: Indiana University Press, 1955–56.

Tilley, Morris Palmer. *A Dictionary of Proverbs in England in the Sixteenth and Seventeenth Centuries.* Ann Arbor: University of Michigan Press, 1950.

———. *Elizabethan Proverb Lore in Lyly's "Euphues" and Pettit's "Petite Palace,"* with *Parallels from Shakespeare.* New York: Macmillan, 1926.

Tilly, Louise, and Joan Scott. *Women, Work, and Family.* New York: Holt, Rinehart, and Winston, 1978.

Traub, Valerie. *Desire and Anxiety: Circulations of Sexuality in Shake-spearean Drama*. London: Routledge, 1992.

Travitsky, Betty. "The Lady Doth Protest: Protest in the Popular Writings of Renaissance Englishwomen." *English Literary Renaissance* 14, no. 3 (1984): 255–83.

Travitsky, Betty, and Adele Seeff, eds. *Attending to Women in Early Modern England*. Newark: University of Delaware Press, 1994.

Turner, James Grantham, ed. *Sexuality and Gender in Early Modern Europe: Institutions, Texts, Images*. Cambridge: Cambridge University Press, 1993.

Turner, Victor. *The Anthropology of Performance*. New York: PAJ Publications, 1988.

———. *From Ritual to Theatre: The Human Seriousness of Play*. New York: PAJ Publications, 1982.

Twycross, Meg. "Transvestism in the Mystery Plays." *Medieval English Theatre* 5, no. 2 (1983): 123–80.

Tyson, Gerald P., and Sylvia S. Wagonheim, eds. *Print and Culture in the Renaissance: Essays on the Advent of Printing in Europe*. Newark: University of Delaware Press, 1986.

Underdown, David. "The Taming of the Scold: The Enforcement of Patriarchal Authority in Early Modern England." In *Order and Disorder in Early Modern England*, edited by A.J. Fletcher and John Stevenson. Cambridge: Cambridge University Press, 1985.

Utley, Francis. *The Crooked Rib: An Analytical Index to the Argument about Women in English and Scots Literature to the End of the Year 1568*. New York: Octagon, 1970.

Verberckmoes, Johan. *Laughter, Jestbooks and Society in the Spanish Netherlands*. London: Macmillan, 1999.

Waage, Frederick O. "Meg and Moll: Two Renaissance London Heroines." *Journal of Popular Culture* 20, no. 1 (1986): 106–17.

———. "Social Themes in Urban Broadsides of Renaissance England." *Journal of Popular Culture* 11, no. 3 (1977): 734–35.

Wack, Mary. "Women, Work, and Plays in an English Medieval Town." In Frye and Robertson, 33–51.

Waller, Gary. *Edmund Spenser: The Construction of a Literary Life*. London: Macmillan, 1994.

Watt, Tessa. *Cheap Print and Popular Piety, 1550–1640*. Cambridge: Cambridge University Press, 1991.

Wayne, Valerie. "The Dearth of the Author: Anonymity's Allies and *Swetname the Woman-Hater*." In Frye and Robertson, 221–40.

———. "Refashioning the Shrew." *Shakespeare Studies* 17 (1985): 159–87.

Weber, Samuel. "The Divaricator: Remarks on Freud's *Witz*." *Glyph* 1 (1977): 25–26.

Weimann, Robert. "Laughing with the Audience: *The Two Gentlemen of*

Verona and the Popular Tradition of Comedy." *Shakespeare Survey* 22 (1969): 35–42.

——. *Shakespeare and the Popular Tradition in the Theater: Studies in the Social Dimension of Dramatic Form and Function,* edited by Robert Schwartz. Baltimore: Johns Hopkins University Press, 1978.

——. "Toward a Literary Theory of Ideology: Mimesis, Representation, Authority." In Howard and O'Connor, 265–72.

Weiss, Harry B. *A Book About Chapbooks: The People's Literature of Bygone Times.* Trenton: n.p., 1942.

Welsford, Enid. *The Fool: His Social and Literary History.* London: Faber and Faber, 1935.

White, Allon. *Carnival, Hysteria, and Writing: Collected Essays and Autobiography.* Oxford: Oxford University Press, 1993.

Wilcox, Helen, ed. *Women and Literature in Britain, 1500–1700,* Cambridge: Cambridge University Press, 1996.

Willen, Diane. "Women in the Public Sphere in Early Modern England: The Case of the Urban Working Poor." *Sixteenth Century Journal* 19, no. 4 (1988): 559–76.

Williamson, Marilyn L. "Doubling, Women's Anger, and Genre." *Women's Studies* 9 (1982): 107–19.

Wilson, F. P. "English Jestbooks of the Sixteenth and Early Seventeenth Centuries." In *Shakespearean and Other Studies,* edited by Helen Gardner. Oxford: Clarendon, 1969.

——, ed. *The Oxford Dictionary of English Proverbs.* 3d ed. Oxford: Clarendon, 1984.

Wiltenburg, Joy. *Disorderly Women and Female Power in the Street Literature of Early Modern Germany and England.* Charlottesville: University of Virginia Press, 1992.

Wiseman, Susan. "'Adam, the Father of All Flesh': Porno-political Rhetoric and Political Theory in and after the English Civil War." In *Pamphlet Wars: Prose in the English Revolution,* edited by James Holstun, 134–157. London: Cass, 1992.

Womack, Peter. *Ben Jonson.* Oxford: Blackwell, 1986.

——. "Imagining Communities: Theatres and the English Nation in the Sixteenth Century." In *Culture and History, 1350–1600,* edited by David Aers, 108–9. Detroit: Wayne State University Press, 1992.

Woodbridge, Linda. "Patchwork: Piecing the Early Modern Mind in England's First Century of Print Culture." *English Literary Renaissance* 23 (Winter 1993): 4–45.

——. *Vagrancy, Homelessness, and English Renaissance Culture.* Urbana: University of Illinois Press, 2001.

——. *Women and the English Renaissance: Literature and the Nature of Womankind, 1540–1620.* Urbana: University of Illinois Press, 1984.

Wright, Louis. *Middle-Class Culture in Elizabethan England.* 1935; reprint, Ithaca: Cornell University Press, 1958.

Wrightson, Keith. "Alehouses, Order and Reformation in Rural England, 1590–1660." In Yeo and Yeo, 1–27.

——. *English Society, 1580–1680.* 6th ed. London: Unwin Hyman, 1990.

——. "The Politics of the Parish in Early Modern England." In Griffiths, Fox, and Hindle, 10–46.

Wurzbach, Natascha. *The Rise of the English Street Ballad, 1550–1650.* Cambridge: Cambridge University Press, 1990.

Yeo, Eileen, and Stephen Yeo, eds. *Popular Culture and Class Conflict, 1590–1914.* Brighton, U.K.: Harvester, 1981.

Zall, Paul M. *English Prose Jestbooks in the Huntington Library: A Chronological Checklist.* San Marino, Calif.: Huntington Library, 1983.

Index